Hospitality Cost Control
A Practical Approach

Asch, Allen B.
Hospitality cost control

Library of Congress Cataloging-in-Publication Data

Asch, Allen B.
  Hospitality cost control : a practical approach / Allen B. Asch.
    p. cm.
  ISBN 0–13–111600–2
  1. Hospitality industry—Cost control.   I. Title.
  TX911.3.C65A83 2005
  647.94'068—dc22

                                        2005019744

Director of Development: Vernon R. Anthony
Senior Editor: Eileen McClay
Production Editor: Bruce Hobart, Pine Tree Composition
Production Liaison: Jane Bonnell
Director of Manufacturing and Production: Bruce Johnson
Managing Editor: Mary Carnis
Manufacturing Manager: Ilene Sanford
Manufacturing Buyer: Cathleen Petersen
Creative Director: Cheryl Asherman
Cover Design Coordinator: Miguel Ortiz
Cover Designer: Linda Punskovsky
Cover Image: Art Montes De Oca, Getty Images/Photographer's Choice
Executive Marketing Manager: Ryan DeGrote
Senior Marketing Coordinator: Elizabeth Farrell
Marketing Assistant: Les Roberts
Interior Design and Composition: Pine Tree Composition
Printing and Binding: R. R. Donnelley & Sons Company

Pearson Education LTD.   Pearson Education Canada, Ltd.
Pearson Education Australia PTY, Limited Pearson Educación de Mexico, S.A. de C.V.
Pearson Education Singapore, Pte. Ltd.   Pearson Education—Japan
Pearson Education North Asia Ltd.   Pearson Education Malaysia, Pte. Ltd.

10 9 8 7 6
ISBN 0-13-111600-2

Contents

Preface

In the course of teaching cost control to my university students, I have found that most textbooks did not meet my need to easily explain the material to the student. Many students cannot wait to sell their textbook after the class has finished, and I wrote *Hospitality Cost Control* hoping that students will keep this book as a manual for running a hospitality operation. Unlike most cost control textbooks, which are written from an accounting point of view, this book is written from a hands-on practical approach. It would be an ideal aid for any person working in the food and beverage industry needing an overview of cost control procedures, including purchasing, storage, issuing, production and financial cost control matters.

The book is divided into five sections: The first section deals with overall operations lessons, formulas and facts. This includes a section on terminology used in cost control, as well as profit and loss calculations and formulas to determine whether an operation should make or outsource the production of certain products and services. This will help management decide whether it is cost effective to prepare something themselves rather than hiring another company to do it. Outsourcing is also explored for labor issues. The last part of this section deals with the formulas used in cost control, to show where money is distributed within an operation. Formulas will also be given to calculate the break-even point in dollar sales and the break-even point in unit sales. These formulas take into account the money that is needed to cover fixed costs, those paid before profitability can be reached.

The second section deals with food cost control and is set up to illustrate costs and savings that can be attained in a well run kitchen. These controls begin with the proper purchasing of products: Profitability is very hard to attain if you don't get the right product at the right price at the right time. This section also discusses the proper way to maintain inventory through correct storage procedures, both for maintaining quality and avoiding a loss of product—purchasing and storing food focuses on the perishable nature of the product. The last part of the section deals with controls that need to be in place during production of the food; these can make or break an operation's financial success.

The third section covers beverage cost control. Although beverages can generate big profits, they allow for misuse that can negatively affect profits in an operation. Beverage cost control will vary depending on whether there are alcoholic beverages served and what type of outlet is being established or analyzed. There are also many laws that are used in *each* different jurisdiction; it is crucial for managers to be aware of these regulations so they can be compliant with the laws wherever they work.

The fourth section involves labor cost control, which affects every aspect of an operation. Labor costs accumulate in all components of the hospitality industry and carry over to many other industries as well. These costs can be fixed or variable. Fixed costs, which are incurred whether sales are generated or not, are the same during every period. Variable labor costs, which change every period, need to be controlled through effective scheduling and management oversight. If fixed cost employees—those earning salaries—are idle during a slow period, they should be scheduled to replace variable cost—hourly—employees, which will help reduce overall labor cost.

The fifth section is about controls in other expenses and sales and marketing. Many of the expenses discussed are not exclusive to the hospitality industry, and involve concepts that can be used in any business operation. These expenses include the costs for business operations and facilities. The concept of increasing sales can be considered the most crucial part of an operation, as certain costs—those that are fixed—will occur independent of how much in sales is generated. An increase in sales will help pay those costs while generating additional revenue to go toward profits. The proper marketing of an operation will help increase and maintain customer counts and should also promote an increase in average guest checks. Through efficient marketing, management should have the ability to sell high profit margin items as well as additional items to the guest.

Every chapter consists of components to make this book more user friendly to the student than many books that are presently available. These components include:

Chapter Objectives
Key Terms
"Why This Is Important," which takes key concepts and explains the reason the student needs to take extra time learning a principle
Example Problems
Summary Bullets
Websites
Practice Problems

ACKNOWLEDGMENTS

Thanks go to Dr. John Stefanelli, University of Nevada/Las Vegas (UNLV); Dr. Donald Bell, UNLV; Mandi Phillips, UNLV; Karyn Asch, UNLV/ Clark County School District; Vicki Herman, Clark County School District;

Andy Feinstein, UNLV; Melissa Fielding, Caesar's Palace; Derrick Lanham; Faith Zozsky; Cathy Scruggs; Judy Feliz, UNLV; Valerie Nehmer, UNLV; Camille Shaver, Area Technical Trade Center; all my students in FAB 461 at UNLV, all of whom were a part of this project. Thanks also to the faculty and staff at the Area Technical Trade Center and to Vernon Anthony and everyone at Prentice Hall.

I would like to thank Jerrold K. Leong, Oklahoma State University; Chef Michael Nenes, The Art Institute of Houston; and Alice Spangler, Ball State University for reviewing my manuscript.

I hope you enjoy reading this text and learning about cost control and how it can help your managerial skills and create profitability anywhere you work.

Allen B. Asch

Photo Credits

About the Author

Allen B. Asch has been involved with the restaurant industry since he was 12 years old. Although accounting was his first career choice, the restaurant industry involved him at an early age. His entire career has been devoted to garnering new information about the culinary arts field. This book brings him back to the accounting roots that were developed in high school. A degree from the Culinary Institute of America helped him run a successful restaurant until the calling to become a teacher brought him to Johnson and Wales University, from which he graduated with high honors. He continued his education at Northern Arizona University, graduating Summa Cum Laude. Chef Asch is a member of both Phi Kappa Phi and Alpha Beta Kappa national honor societies, and is presently teaching culinary arts at a vocational high school in Las Vegas. He is an adjunct professor at the University of Nevada, Las Vegas. He continues to keep track of current trends and travels internationally, expanding his food and cultural knowledge about other countries. He has contributed to several culinary textbooks; this book is his first solo venture. Chef Asch is one of a limited number of current Certified Culinary Educators in the country, a prestigious certification bestowed by the American Culinary Federation.

1
Introduction

Chapter Objectives

After finishing this chapter the student will be able to:

Describe reasons restaurants fail

Differentiate among statistical data in the hospitality industry

Relate management's role in cost control

Define the control process

Distinguish between basic cost control terminologies

Differentiate between fixed costs and variable costs

Differentiate between controllable costs and non-controllable costs

Examine the concept of total sales

Calculate sales mix

Differentiate between basic cost control formulas

Introduction

This chapter will give an overview of the cost control function, including basic terminology needed throughout the book and food cost formulas that are essential to cost control. These food formulas can be interchanged with beverage and labor costs by changing the wording of the problem, but keeping the formulas the same. This chapter will outline for students and potential future managers the steps to cost control from management's perspective. With the basic procedures outlined in this chapter, managers can control certain costs, even if food and beverage is not their strength.

PURPOSE OF COST CONTROL

This textbook is written about the control of costs, from the hands-on perspective of a chef. Although the formulas used are the same as in any other text, this version will look at how and why to use each formula in an actual situation from the hospitality industry. Food and beverage, and hospitality as a whole, are different from every other industry in that the main item sold is a service. Customers can stay at many hotel brands; the difference will lie in how comfortable the guest feels. Additionally, the customer can order a hamburger at many different restaurants and the taste will be similar in many of them; the difference will lie in the environment and service given the guest. The main difference is that this industry has quantity performance highs and lows that are not distinguishable in other industries. In other industries, for example manufacturing, there are quantity standards that need to be met every day for an extended period of time. But hospitality is based on the immediate needs of the guests. Additionally, unlike most other industries, the products that are sold are perishable, adding a new element of control. In this industry, the "rush" comes and goes; there will be many customers at one time and an empty facility a short time before or after that (imagine the front desk of a hotel at check-in time or a restaurant in the evening). Costs cannot be controlled the same way those of other industries can.

The purpose of cost control is to manage labor and inventory to ensure profitability for an organization. Without controls in place there are very limited opportunities for a business to make a profit. Due to the nature of this industry, labor costs can be increased or decreased for a variety of reasons, and raw costs can be managed through purchasing and production control. For this text, costs can be defined as the expenses associated with the production of food and beverage. When using this definition, the assumption of costs must include all financial outlay, whether sales are produced or not. This will include food that has spoiled or been overproduced, and beverages that are spilled or given as complimentary drinks. The other cost associated with restaurant sales is the cost of labor. Labor costs are accrued whether sales are made or not. If employees are idle, they are still earning pay, even though they are not generating sales. For optimum labor cost control, either the number of employees should be lessened, or employee's time on the job must be made more efficient.

What does the fast food industry do which is different from many other segments of this industry? Fast food operations, due to their cookie cutter image and consistent product from market to market, have a very strong market research department that knows how to accurately calculate expected sales per store. Within the fast food segment, the check average can be calculated very accurately. However, within other segments of the industry, check average may vary depending on exact sales mix or varied menu prices. Fast food companies know who their customers are, how often they will visit a store, and how many cars that drive by will stop in for a visit. With the corporate sales volume as high as it is for most fast food chains, they can afford to study an area and determine if they can be successful. Many independent operations do not have the financial resources to analyze location and the target audience as well as large chains can.

More than two-thirds of foodservice operations that close in the first three years do so in the first year. The reasoning for this is the industry only affords an average profit margin of 3–7% profit. Certain segments have larger profit margins (see Figure 1.1), but overall the industry does not generate large percentages of earnings. The two main roles that management must fulfill to ensure profitability are controlling costs and increasing sales. Both components are needed for a successful operation.

FIGURE 1.1   Statement of Income and Expenses

Check Average	Under $15.00		$15.01 to $24.99		Over $25.00	
Sales Volume	Below 500,000	500,000–1,000,000	Below 500,000	500,000–1,000,000	Below 2,000,000	Above 2,000,000
Sales						
Food	86.2	81.9	81.2	78.6	74.8	71.2
Beverage	13.8	18.1	18.8	21.4	25.2	28.2
Total sales	100.0	100.0	100.0	100.0	100.0	100.0
Cost of sales						
Food	38.6	35.5	37.3	36.2	33.0	33.8
Beverage	31.7	30.0	33.0	33.9	32.5	29.3
Total cost of sales	34.4	33.3	37.2	35.8	33.4	32.7
Gross profit	65.6	66.7	62.8	64.2	66.6	67.3
Operating expenses						
Salaries and wages	31.2	32.6	32.0	32.0	30.9	27.0
Employee benefits	2.8	3.1	3.8	4.1	5.3	4.9
Direct operating expenses	5.5	5.0	4.7	5.3	5.6	5.1
Music and entertainment	0.1	0.1	0.0	0.2	0.1	0.2
Marketing	1.5	1.7	0.9	1.6	2.3	2.4
Utility services	3.4	3.3	3.0	3.0	2.1	1.6
Restaurant occupancy costs	7.6	4.9	7.0	4.6	4.8	5.3
Repairs and maintenance	1.5	1.4	1.6	1.7	1.6	1.6
Depreciation	1.5	1.4	1.4	2.0	1.3	1.6
General and administrative expenses	2.3	0.7	3.3	4.3	6.3	4.5
Corporate overhead	N/A	N/A	N/A	0.5	1.0	1.3
Total Operating Costs	61.3	60.6	56.7	62.8	62.6	57.1
Interest expenses	0.2	0.3	0.1	0.7	0.3	0.7
Income {loss} before income tax	1.2	3.9	6.1	1.4	1.3	6.2

Source: National Restaurant Association.

WHY THIS IS IMPORTANT

Many people think the restaurant industry is very lucrative and affords an opportunity to make money. In reality most businesses do not succeed, and those that do usually do so on a very small profit margin. All expenses need to be carefully observed and controlled.
∎

WHY RESTAURANTS SUCCEED

There are many successful foodservice operations throughout this country, and generally speaking, most are successful because they follow the basic principles outlined in this book. The major reason for profitability is the ability to retain money after all expenses have been met. This may seem like an easy task, but the challenges are so sizeable that more restaurants fail than succeed. The ability to preserve money comes from the knowledge of where the money comes into an establishment and where the money goes. To ensure profit after paying expenses, a restaurateur needs to control costs, control revenue and maximize sales. Successful operators either have the ability to control each of these elements, or hire people to augment their abilities. This book will discuss various techniques to control each of these three elements. As seen in Figure 1.1, the expenses in the hospitality industry are vast and varied. With controls in place within each of these elements, profit can be maintained. However, even if an operation is profitable, as seen in the chart, profits can be a very small percentage of sales.

MANAGEMENT'S ROLE

Management's role in the control process is paramount due to the large number of employees involved in the production of food and beverage. Management's role begins during the hiring process. Without a high quality, knowledgeable staff, the control process would be impossible to manage (this will be discussed further in Chapter 11). After management has hired a qualified staff, their four jobs requirements include:

- Planning
- Organizing
- Directing
- Controlling

Management's job is to plan each aspect of the operation to ensure profitability for the hospitality operation. Within planning, management needs first and foremost to determine the clientele for the hospitality operation. When calculating clientele, management needs to decide which type of customers will fulfill the goals of the operation. The goals may not necessarily be to make a lot of money; however, without profit, an operation's life expectancy is short. One goal, other than money, may include the need to serve food in a high-end hotel even though it will never generate a profit; it may be needed to support the room portion of a hotel. In this situation, planning to support customer service would be much different than the need to make a profit.

After the initial planning is done, there is a continual need to plan for the present and future. The interesting aspect of this industry is that no two days are the same. Some of the planning is done on a daily, weekly, quarterly, yearly and multi-year basis. Planning may include scheduling, design changes, future projects, menu plans and purveyor selection, to name just a few. Depending on the operation, planning can be the sole job of a manager or just one aspect of that person's responsibilities.

Another responsibility of management is organization. Within a department or property, there are many projects that need to be organized. The largest organizational task for management is that of labor. The proper scheduling of employees will allow an operation to make money, but if management does not have organization when preparing a work schedule, making a profit becomes much more difficult. Management also has to organize workflow to allow for efficient use of employees. If management does not organize the warehouse, the kitchen, or back of the house in a hotel, the employee's ability to work efficiently will be hampered. If an employee needs continually to take extra steps to fulfill a task, then profitability can be lost.

Once management has planned and organized within an operation, the next big task is directing employees to do the jobs outlined in the manner established. Directing employees is one of the most time consuming jobs of management. In many cases, management has multiple employees doing multiple tasks, and the directing of each can become overwhelming. Having different management levels allows for distribution of tasks, but as management levels increase, the number of people being directed decreases. This in turn means the overall responsibility and liability increases. One of management's goals is to hire competent personnel that do not need constant direction. If managers need constantly to direct staff, they may be forced to relinquish some of the other duties and tasks associated with the job. This may result in lost profits.

The fourth responsibility of management is control within the operation. Controls need to be in place throughout the entire operation. This control takes place from the planning, purchasing, production and sales within an operation. Once sales are generated, control also needs to be in place for the revenue generated. These controls will be discussed throughout the book.

The control process discussed in each of these chapters includes four steps for each control process. The first step that will be discussed is the development of standards, which are measurable for each of the financial components of the operation. After the standards are developed, the next step is to measure whether the standards in place are being met. If the standards are being met, this is the end of the control process; if the standards are not met, corrective action needs to be taken. The most important aspect of corrective action is to make sure that from that point on, there is work being done to make sure standards are being met. Corrective action may include discipline of employees that continually fail to meet the standard, but there are many procedures that can be done prior to discipline. If discipline is mandated, there are many degrees of discipline management can take from verbal warnings to dismissal of an employee, and many in between. After corrective action is taken the scenario is re-evaluated and additional changes may occur. If a standard cannot be met, management needs to decide if the standard is too difficult, or if additional training needs to be given to allow the standards to be accomplished.

Additional resources for management are the use of professional organizations and trade publications. The hospitality industry is very well represented with organizations which help management either as a resource, or as a guiding principle for employees. One great resource of many organizations is the basic ethics code governing each. Although membership does not guarantee ethics, members of organizations have been instructed in common ethical practices used and expected among peers. Other indispensable resources for management are trade publications that discuss current trends in the industry. Many industry and trade publications explain detailed techniques that are beneficial in training of new or current employees. Trade publications also discuss new and innovative technology, which may be implemented and may create a money saving environment.

WHY THIS IS IMPORTANT

As future managers the role you play in an operation will differ from the role you will play as a non-manager employee.

■

COST CONTROL COMPONENTS

Prior to learning a new concept or a new field one should learn the vocabulary used within the industry. This next section will cover certain terminology and formulas useful in the cost control segment of the hospitality industry. Although the general direction of this textbook is food and beverage cost control, the text also covers labor, which is used in every segment of the industry and most other industries as well. Much of the terminology and many formulas can be transferred to other segments of the hospitality industry and, to an extent, costs can be inserted which are associated with rooms and conventions into the formulas used for food. The main difference that needs to be kept in mind is many foods are perishable and need to be used within a certain timeframe.

Cost terms include **fixed costs,** costs that do not fluctuate with the rise and fall in business volume. As business volume increases or decreases, fixed costs will stay the same, except with very large fluctuations. Examples of fixed costs are rent, insurance, certain labor costs including salaried employees, taxes, and depreciation. Fixed costs can be looked at as a portion of each sale, or cover, registered by a restaurant. If a restaurant has fixed costs of $1000 a month, and they average 1000 costumers a month, $1 of each patron's sale will be going to cover fixed costs. If customer counts can be increased, then there will be a lower contribution each patron makes toward fixed costs.

WHY THIS IS IMPORTANT

Fixed costs are the costs that are constant, whether there is business or not.

■

Variable costs include costs that will change with the increase or decrease in the volume of business. These costs include food and beverage costs and labor costs, not including salaried employees. This makes labor cost a **semi-variable** expense. Variable expenses will fluctuate according to the change of business. Using the previous example, the fixed costs are unchanged at $1,000, but the cost of food will increase if 1500 customers are now served. The fixed cost will go down to $0.67 per customer, but overall food cost will go up because the cost of food for an additional 500 customers has been added. The cost per plate will actually go down, but overall costs will increase.

WHY THIS IS IMPORTANT

Variable costs are the costs that can be manipulated, based on the volume of business.

■

Controllable costs are the expenses that can be increased or decreased within the short term. These controllable costs are usually the variable costs. Changing the quantity or the quality standard associated with a particular menu item can control food or beverage costs. Labor cost is controllable for non-salaried employees by either adding or removing shifts or hours within a shift.

Non-controllable costs are those that are associated with fixed costs and are unchangeable in the short term. The amount of money owed on taxes or the government allowance for a deduction of depreciation, which does not change without catastrophic changes in the volume of business.

Forecasted costs are what management expects the costs to be in the future. This is attained by having controls, like recipe cards and standardized recipes, in place. **Actual costs** are the true costs associated with the preparation and distribution of the food product, whether standards have been followed or not. Actual cost should be the same as forecasted costs; without controls in place this will not happen.

Average costs are calculated within many different categories. In the hospitality industry the calculation will always include the *total divided by the category quantity.* The categories will vary depending on the needs of comparison. Management may want to compare average cost per entrée or average costs per cover or per shift. To find average cost per cover, divide total costs by number of items prepared. If total costs are $500 and 100 customers are served, 500/100 = $5.00 cost per cover. If looking for average cost per entrée, divide total entrée costs by the number of entrées prepared.

Overhead costs are costs that are associated with all costs other than food, beverage and labor. Overhead costs refer to the costs associated with operating the business, such as utilities, franchise fees, landscaping, etc.

SALES COMPONENTS

As with cost terms, there is a need to identify and to explain certain sales terms. As explained in the average costs definition, these terms cover many different control areas, just by changing the category being used. These sales terms can be expressed in dollar figures or in units. **Total sales** are considered all sales that contribute to a particular category; this can include total sales per shift, per server, or per year. **Sales by category** are expressed as total numbers of sales within whatever category is being assessed, for example how many appetizers or desserts are being sold.

The term **average sales** is used in conjunction with an additional term, which will be used to describe what the average relates to. **Average sale per customer,** or **average sales per check,** is an important barometer when assessing profitability of a restaurant. Average check is used to compare among multiple periods, whether by season or by day of the week. Average check is also used to compare promotional ability of servers. If management were to compare average checks between servers and find a large difference, it may be questioned why one has the ability to generate more sales than the other, whether total sales, or sales by category.

Sales mix, also called **menu mix,** is considered the percentage of sales for any item within a certain category. To calculate sales mix, divide sales of each item by total sales. This can be done within a menu category such as entrées. To calculate the sales mix of steaks, divide the number of steaks sold, 10, by the total number of entrées sold, 100; 10/100 = 10%. The sales mix formula can also be used to calculate how many customers order an appetizer. If 20 customers out of 100 customers order an appetizer, 20/100 = 20%; 20% have ordered the additional course.

IMPORTANT FORMULA

Sales of a particular item/total sales

EXAMPLE PROBLEM

Number sold	Sales mix
Item A — 23	Item A — 23/292 = 7.88
Item B — 45	Item B — 45/292 = 15.41
Item C — 56	Item C — 56/292 = 19.18
Item D — 78	Item D — 78/292 = 26.71
Item E — 90	Item E — 90/292 = 30.82
Total number sold — 292	Total—100 percent

WHY THIS IS IMPORTANT

This formula is an integral component of production forecasting.

■

At this point the topic of rounding needs to be addressed. Management will decide at what point percentages should be rounded. Depending on the operation, this figure could be rounded to whole number percentages or to any decimal management selects. Be aware that in high volume operations one one-hundredth of one percent can equal many thousands of dollars in miscalculations or incomplete calculations. As an example, food cost is calculated to the whole percentage number in many operations. But in an operation such as Taco Bell, many ingredients are included in the dishes in such small quantities that they may not be calculable if using whole percents. Percentage with a decimal must be used. In this book all numbers will be rounded to two numbers past the decimal, using the standard rounding of 1–4 down and 5–9 up to the next hundredth.

MATH CALCULATIONS

Basic math calculations that are imperative components of cost control include some essential yet versatile formulas that once learned can be manipulated, allowing them to be used for many different calculations. The basic formula follows:

IMPORTANT FORMULA

$$\underline{Food} \text{ sales} \times \underline{food} \text{ cost \%} = \underline{Food} \text{ cost}$$
$$\underline{Food} \text{ cost}/\underline{food} \text{ sales} = \underline{Food} \text{ cost \%}$$
$$\underline{Food} \text{ cost}/\underline{food} \text{ cost \%} = \underline{Food} \text{ sales}$$

All the formulas contain the same three components; they are just rearranged to calculate the values of each individual component. If one of these formulas is memorized, and the transformation calculations are performed correctly, every one of the formulas will be readily available. The reason that the word <u>food</u> is underlined is that this word is interchangeable with the word <u>beverage</u> to help calculate the cost percentages of that facet of the operation. In the examples below, all of the numbers are represented by whole numbers and whole percentages; this is not a realistic situation in the hospitality industry. Very rarely are the percentages calculated in whole percents. They will usually be at least two numbers past the decimal within a percent. Sales and costs will usually be numbers that will not calculate out evenly. These numbers are utilized here to demonstrate the relationship between the two numbers and to allow for easier comprehension of the formulas. More complex problems will be represented in the homework assignments. Labor cost can be calculated with the formulas above if this cost needs to be calculated within each department. In many situations, labor cost will be calculated for the entire facility, both food and beverage. In those situations the following formula will be used.

IMPORTANT FORMULA

Labor cost/total sales = labor cost %

EXAMPLE PROBLEM

If food cost percent was calculated at 25% and sales generated equaled $4,000.00, how much was the cost of food?

.25 × $4,000.00 = $1,000.00

If labor cost percent was calculated at 30% and sales generated equaled $12,000.00, how much was the cost of labor?

.30 × $12,000 = $3,600

If beverage cost percent was calculated at 20% and sales generated equaled $400.00, how much was the cost of beverages?

.20 × $400.00 = $80.00

If food sales were $1,500.00 and food cost was $300.00, how much was food cost percent?

300/$1,500 = 20%

If sales were $2,000.00 and labor cost was $500.00, how much was labor cost percent?

500/$2,000 = 25%

If beverage sales were $500.00 and beverage cost was $125.00, how much was beverage cost percent?

125/$500 = 25%

If food cost was 30% and cost of food was $10,000.00, how much was food sales?

$10,000/.30 = $33,333.33

If labor cost was 25% and cost of labor was $1,000.00, how much was sales?

$1,000/.25 = $4,000.00*

If beverage cost was 20% and cost of beverages was $2,000.00, how much was beverage sales?

$2,000/.20 = $10,000

*Since labor cost may not be created by separated sales (food/beverage) it can be a representation of total sales.

Calculation Standard

In these examples, the calculations yielded percents that worked out to an even number; this rarely happens in actual computations. It is management's responsibility to establish the standard of how many numbers past the decimal is used to complete the calculation. In this book for the homework assignments, the standard will be four numbers past the decimal and rounded according to the rounding standard of five and above it will be rounded up. This standard will be adhered to whenever a decimal is calculated, throughout an entire problem. This standard is lower than would be used in an industry situation, where computers calculate the problem to a more exact standard.

DEPRECIATION

Depreciation—wear and tear on a building and equipment—is a deductible allowance given to owners of commercial buildings. Owners can depreciate the building's original cost, plus the cost of subsequent building renovations and improvements, over a period of 15 years. If management takes advantage of the depreciation, it will lower the profits of an establishment, thus lowering taxes. Until 2004, this had been spread over $39\frac{1}{2}$ years. This is a better timeline within the hospitality industry, where the average operation updates facilities every six to eight years. This is because restaurants and hotels are high-volume businesses open every day, and for longer hours than the average commercial business.

SUMMARY

- Basic terminology used in cost control for the hospitality industry, especially foodservice, is presented.
- Calculations for sales mix and basic mathematical formulas for food cost, beverage cost, and labor cost percents are explained.

KEY TERMS

Fixed costs
Variable costs
Semi-variable costs
Controllable costs
Non-controllable costs
Forecasted costs
Actual costs
Average costs
Overhead costs

Total sales
Sales by category
Average sales
Average sale per customer
Average sales per check
Sales mix
Menu mix
Depreciation

WEBSITES

www.bplans.com
www.restaurant.org
www.acfchefs.org
www.nraef.org
www.ih-ra.com
www.ahma.com

www.e-hospitality.com/
    storefronts/ahma.html
www.bizstats.com
www.fsafood.com
www.beginnersinvest.about.com/

PROBLEMS

1. List three examples of fixed costs in the hospitality industry.
2. List three examples of variable costs in the hospitality industry.
3. What is the sales mix for the week for a restaurant with the following sales numbers?

    Item A — 321
    Item B — 434
    Item C — 98
    Item D — 123
    Item E — 235
    Item F — 344

All answers will be calculated two numbers past the decimal within a percent.

4. If beverage cost was 21.5% and cost of beverages was $1,534.90, how much was beverage sales?

5. If labor cost percent was calculated at 21.7% and sales generated equaled $76,453.33, how much was the cost of labor?

6. If beverage sales were $5,241.66 and beverage cost was $1460.01, how much was beverage cost percent?

7. If beverage cost percent was calculated at 17.5% and sales generated equaled $56,234.33, how much was the cost of beverages?

8. If food sales were $23,648.42 and food cost was $6,349.09, how much was food cost percent?

9. If food cost percent was calculated at 25.6% and sales generated equaled $21,234.87, how much was the cost of food?

10. If labor cost was 22.5% and cost of labor was $1,089.33, how much was sales?

11. If food sales were $933.45 and food cost was $223.56, how much was food cost percent?

12. If sales were $145,909 and labor cost was $35,640.22, how much was labor cost percent?

13. If labor cost percent was calculated at 28.1% and sales generated equaled $653.11, how much was the cost of labor?

14. If food cost percent was calculated at 31.3% and sales generated equaled $154.78, how much was the cost of food?

15. If labor cost was 35.3% and cost of food labor was $12,534.99, how much was food sales?

16. If food cost was 25.9% and cost of food was $476.78, how much was food sales?

17. If sales were $2,347.67 and labor cost was $445.78, how much was labor cost percent?

18. If food cost was 31.6% and cost of food was $23,672.89, how much was food sales?

19. If beverage sales were $334.21 and beverage cost was $87.50, how much was beverage cost percent?

20. If beverage cost was 18.7% and cost of beverages was $1,987.34, how much was beverage sales?

21. If sales for the shift were $1,456.09 and 264 customers were served, how much was the average check?

22. If beverage cost percent was calculated at 21.1% and sales generated equaled $1,656.02, how much was the cost of beverages?

23. If an operation had total sales of $348,902.00, food sales made up 80% of total sales, and food cost was 29.45%, beverage cost was 18.34% and variable labor cost was 19.32% how much were the variable expenses?

24. The sales record for the week at Joe's Diner was as follows:

    Item A – 37
    Item B – 42
    Item C – 61
    Item D – 66
    Item E – 108
    Item F – 35

    Calculate sales mix.

25. If a restaurant has food sales of $12,502, beverage sales of $1,938, and runs a food cost percent of 23.43%, a beverage cost percent of 18.67% and labor cost percent of 31.93%, how much money is left for overhead and profit?

26. If food cost percent is 31.65%, beverage cost percent is 20.9%, total sales are $197,561, and food cost is $45,681, how much is beverage cost?

27. What is depreciation?

28. How does depreciation affect profit?

2
An Overview of Cost Control

Chapter Objectives

After finishing this chapter the student will be able to:

Differentiate among the three standards used in food and beverage: quality, quantity, and cost

Calculate food cost using the basic formula for food cost

Differentiate between asset and debit calculations for food cost

Calculate food cost percent

Utilize an operating budget

Perform a make or buy analysis

Investigate outsourcing

Recognize techniques of revenue control

Discriminate among the various threats to profit due to theft

Introduction

This chapter will introduce the three most important standards in the hospitality industry. These standards can be used in many facets of the industry, both in food and beverage and in other aspects of the hospitality industry. This chapter brings in the food cost and food cost percent formulas that are the basis for many cost control calculations, and includes introductory lessons in the reading, use of, and creation of operating budgets and profit and loss statements. The chapter concludes with an introduction to the potential for loss, due to theft, that can occur in the food and beverage industry.

ESTABLISHING STANDARDS

The first job of any food and beverage management team is to develop the standards needed for the operation. The first of these is to decide the clientele of the operation. Once the customer base is established, the next step is to develop the standards needed to satisfy the customer. There are three standards that are always important when discussing food and beverage: quality, quantity, and cost. These standards will be discussed at length throughout the book.

WHY THIS IS IMPORTANT

Without establishing policies and standards that are based on the expectations of the forecasted customer base, management will not create the appropriate environment to maintain customer satisfaction and create repeat business.

First is the **quality standard.** The quality of food, tableware, equipment, décor and many other facets of the operation need to be established. Should prime grade beef be served, or is choice grade the standard? Should silver be the standard for silverware, or does stainless steel fit the client profile? Second is the **quantity standard** of food, labor and supplies. How much food should be served; should five shrimp or eight shrimp be the quantity standard? Should a 60-count or an 80-count potato be served with entrees? Should there be front and back waiters, or just one waiter per table? How much are the inventory par levels? Third is the **price/cost standard.** This is associated with the raw costs of items as well as the menu price. Should food cost percent be an overall 25% of menu price, or be closer to 27%? Should menu prices reflect the cost of raw goods, or be based on a perceived value for additional factors such as location or a differentiated product?

DEVELOPING STANDARDS

The development of standards will be established with input from many sources. The type of operation will dictate who, and what facts, will be involved in the establishing of these standards. Many multi-unit operations have a preset group of standards, **standard operating procedures,** outlined by a franchisor or corporate officer. If individual standards need to be established the first question to be answered is, Will the establishment have internal standards, created by owner/operators, end-users and buyers, or will an establishment create standards by comparing their operation to a comparable restaurant marketing to the same clientele?

Once these standards are established it is management's responsibility to make sure that employees are aware of them. Management's main job is training employees to follow the standards set forth. If employees are properly trained in the standards and execute them fully, the ability to make a profit in the establishment is greatly expanded.

There are three main expenditures for a restaurant, all expenses can be accounted for within these three categories. The first one is food/beverage cost, the second is labor cost, and the third is other expenses. All three of these expenses need to be controlled for efficiency in a restaurant. Later chapters in the book will include an explanation of the labor and other expenses categories.

CALCULATING FOOD COST

When calculating **food cost** there are many financial factors that need to be considered. The basic formula for food cost follows:

IMPORTANT FORMULA

> Opening inventory + Purchases = Value of food available
> — Ending inventory = Cost of food issued

Once the cost of goods issued is calculated, you need to make adjustments to calculate the actual cost of food. Just because the food is issued, it does not necessarily create sales. When calculating food cost, the only money that should be figured in is the money that was used to generate sales. For this reason we will add figures to, and subtract figures from, the cost of food issued. Cost of food issued only reflects the cost of foods that are no longer in the storeroom.

EXAMPLE PROBLEM

Given the following data, compute the food cost.

Last month's ending food inventory: $45,600
This month's ending food inventory: $47,000
Food purchases this month: $78,000

$$
\begin{array}{r}
45,600 \\
+\,78,000 \\
-\,\underline{47,000} \\
\$76,600
\end{array}
$$ Cost of food issued

Figure 2.1 shows how the cost of goods sold (COGS) is calculated. Cost of goods sold is calculated from the cost of food issued. Depending on the operation, cost of food issued may include inventory value that does not generate sales. If that is the case, the food was issued and accounted for, but it needs to be subtracted out when calculating how much was spent to generate sales. Additionally, certain other expenses will be added into the cost of food issued to calculate an accurate figure for the cost of goods sold.

IMPORTANT FORMULA

The rule of thumb in calculating cost of food sold is, if the item is used to generate sales it is added to the cost of food issued; if the line item does not generate sales it is deducted from food issued. Once cost of food sold is calculated, food cost percent can be calculated. Cost of food sold is divided by food sales to generate food cost percent.

FIGURE 2.1   Cost of Goods Sold (COGS)

	Opening inventory + Purchases = Value of food available − Ending inventory Cost of food issued

Transfers-in are the expenses associated with items received from another kitchen or restaurant outlet. An example of an outside transfer-in would be a sandwich shop that has multiple units, with one store making the rolls for other stores. An example of an inside transfer-in would be a can of beer transferred from the bar to be used to produce beer batter. **Transfers-out** are the costs associated with food or beverage that has been charged to a kitchen and then sent to another outlet. This might include food prepared in one kitchen but served in a different kitchen, food given away for free during happy hour, or lemons for the bar. The types of transfers will depend upon the operation. Many large facilities order separate food for the bar, or have commissary kitchens that prepare the soups and sauces for other kitchens.

+ Outside transfers-in
+ Inside transfers-in
− Transfers-out

If employee meals are offered in an establishment, those costs are associated with operating the facility, but they do not generate sales. They are accounted for elsewhere, not as part of food cost. There are many different ways to calculate employee meal costs, depending on the policies established by management. In many large operations employee meals are served out of a separate kitchen and the kitchen requisitions food from the warehouse like any other kitchen. This type of operation can deduct the exact costs associated with feeding the employees. Smaller operations may not have the facilities to feed the staff in a separate room, so staff is usually fed through an existing kitchen that is used to generate sales. The costs associated with feeding the staff need to be kept separate from all other expenses of the kitchen. This can be done by allocating a certain amount per meal period to be spent on food for the staff. This number may vary depending on the meal period and the day of the week. Another method is to write off a certain dollar amount for each employee to cover the costs of meals. This preset amount changes for breakfast, lunch and dinner. Another method is allowing employees to order off the menu and deduct the average food cost for each meal ordered. Menu price multiplied by food cost percent will equal the costs for the meal.

− Employee meals

Promotional expenses include costs associated with promoting a restaurant. This occurs after the food has been issued to a kitchen, and may include buying a dessert for a customer for a special occasion or to amend a mistake made by staff. It may also include meals given away in raffles. Write off expenses might include an order that was prepared wrong or a steak that fell on the floor.

− Promotional/write off expenses

Steward sales, although discouraged by larger companies, is when employees are allowed to buy products from the establishment at wholesale or slightly marked up prices. Many larger companies realize the potential for abuse and theft that can occur when steward sales allow staff to leave the property with product.	– Steward sales
Grease sales are generated when an establishment sells the by-product grease from either the deep fryer or from butchering of meat. Many companies utilize the fat for making cosmetics, soap and other products. When this exchange happens, money is given to the establishment and this value should be deducted from the food issued.	– Grease sales = Cost of food sold

WHY THIS IS IMPORTANT

If these adjustments are not made, true food cost cannot be calculated. Without accurate food cost figures, management will not be able to calculate expenses correctly and may not create profitability. Depending on the size and setup of an operation, these adjustments can make a considerable difference in overall percents.

IMPORTANT FORMULA

$$\frac{\text{Cost of food sold}}{\text{Food sales}} = \text{Food cost percent}$$

This figure represents the percentage of every dollar in sales that is used to pay for the food to generate that sale. If food cost is 25%, out of every dollar in sales, 25 cents is used to buy the food. Operations will run highly varied food cost percents, based on the type of business they are running and the type of product they are offering. Food cost can run from 18% and lower to 33% and higher. For an operation to stay in business, it needs to balance out the costs associated with running it. Generally speaking, establishments that run higher food cost percents, like fast food, will run lower labor cost percents. Likewise, establishments that run higher labor costs, such as classic French restaurants, will run lower food costs. This same formula can be used to calculate labor cost percent.

EXAMPLE PROBLEM

If the cost of food sold is $1,000 and sales dollars are $4,000, what was the food cost percent?

$$\frac{1,000}{4,000} = 25.00\%$$

CAUSES OF LOSS

The most common reason for a restaurant to lose money is the failure to control costs and revenue. If standards are not created and followed, it is very hard to maintain profitability. If an establishment does not properly purchase products at the most financially feasible price, whether prepared or in the raw state, and control the food product through the flow of the operation it creates more difficulty in making a profit, in an industry that already has many challenges to profitability. The second reason is failure to control revenue. This is just as much of a reason for loss of profitability. When sales are made and revenue generated, if it gets lost in the flow and does not end up being used to pay the expenses, the restaurant will have a hard time generating profits.

Theft is a major concern in the hospitality industry. Theft, internal and external, is very costly. According to the United States Chamber of Commerce, 30% of all business failures are caused by employee theft and employee dishonesty. This costs businesses 1–2% of gross sales. It is estimated that revenue in the hospitality industry would increase by 3–7% if theft were eliminated. Although elimination of theft is unrealistic, through implementation of some major and minor controls, theft can be reduced. Some of these tools will be discussed further in the book, but they include a Point of Sale (POS) machine, security cameras, mystery shoppers, and employee background checks. By implementing some of these techniques, the reduction of theft will result in increased cash flow and profitability.

OPERATING BUDGET

One of the most important aspects in running any business is to prepare an **operating budget.** An operating budget is prepared prior to the start of the period for which it is written. When writing an operating budget, management needs to take into account all forecasts for sales and expenses for the upcoming period.

The operating budget is then compared to the **profit and loss statement.** A profit and loss statement (P & L) for a hospitality operation includes the actual food and beverage sales, food and beverage costs, as well as operating expenses.

Once sales are forecasted, expenses need to be predicted. This operating budget should be made with the flexibility to adjust any of the figures as needed, as additional information becomes available. After sales, the first figures to calculate are food cost and beverage costs. These costs can be calculated by multiplying forecasted sales by the forecasted food and beverage percentages. Management needs to estimate what the expected cost percentages are going to be. Although food cost percent and beverage cost percent will vary within each category of the menu, overall food cost percentage should be calculated and adhered to.

The next expenses to be calculated are labor costs and operating expenses, including rent, utilities, depreciation, and taxes. All of these expenses are subtracted from total sales and the remaining number is either profit or loss. Once all the figures are included, management can evaluate if all the forecasts are realistic and operational. If the figures do not work on paper, adjustments can be made. Once the figures are acceptable they must be implemented in the operation. Often the numbers do not come out exactly as forecast, so adjustments can be made throughout the period. Certain numbers can be accurately forecast a year ahead, like rent, but others like sales and cost percentages can easily deviate from a figure calculated earlier.

To calculate sales management, forecast average check and turnover, and multiply that figure by the number of seats and the operating periods.

IMPORTANT FORMULA

Average check $\times$ turnover $\times$ # of seats $\times$ days of operation = Total sales

This formula can be used for both food and beverage. It can be utilized for operations that have different turnover periods and days of operation for lunch and dinner or weekdays and weekends. Many operations will include Friday evening as a weekend, due to a shift in customer spending and time spent at a restaurant.

EXAMPLE PROBLEM

A proposed restaurant concept will have 210 seats. It will be open for lunch and dinner Monday through Saturday, and for dinner only on Sunday. Seat turnover for lunch is estimated to be 1.3, with dinner and Sunday turnover at 1.4 each. The average food check for lunch is expected to be $6.20, with a dinner average food check of $9.75 and a Sunday dinner average food check of $12.00. In addition, the restaurant will have a small catering area where an estimated 1000 guests per month will generate an average food check of $10.00.

Beverage revenue is estimated at 20% of lunch food sales, plus 25% of dinner food sales, plus 30% of catering food sales. Food cost is expected to be 33% of total food revenue, and beverage cost is expected to be 20% of total beverage revenue. Salaried employee wages are estimated at 14% of total sales, with wages for all other employees forecast to be 13% of total sales. Benefits are expected to be an additional 20% of total salaries and wages. Other controllable expenses are estimated at 6% of total sales. Depreciation is expected to be $18,000 per year, with occupancy costs and interest charges of $33,000 and $16,500 per year, respectively.

Prepare a financial operating budget for one year.

Meal period	No. of seats	Turnover	Average check	No. of days	Weeks	Beverage %
Mon.–Sat. Lunch	210 ×	1.3 ×	6.20 ×	6 ×	52 = 528,091.20	× .20 = 105,618.24
Mon.–Sat. Dinner	210 ×	1.4 ×	9.75 ×	6 ×	52 = 894,348.00	× .25 = 223,587.00
Sunday Dinner	210 ×	1.4 ×	12 ×	1 ×	52 = 183,456.00	× .25 = 45,864.00
Catering			1,000 × $10 × 1 × 12 = 120,000.00			× .30 = 36,000.00

Total food sales 1,725,895.20	Beverage sales 411,069.24

SALES

Food	1,725,895.20	
Beverages	411,069.24	
Total sales		2,136,964.44

COST OF SALES

Food	569,545.41	
Beverages	82,213.85	
Total cost of sales		651,759.26

GROSS PROFIT   1,485,205.18

CONTROLLABLE EXPENSES

Fixed payroll	299,175.02
Variable payroll	277,805.38
Total payroll	576,980.40
Employee benefits	115,396.08
Other controllable expenses	128,217.87
Total controllable expenses	820,594.35

INCOME BEFORE OCCUPANCY COSTS, INTEREST, DEPRECIATION, AND INCOME TAXES   664,610.83

Occupancy costs   33,000

INCOME BEFORE INTEREST, DEPRECIATION, AND INCOME TAXES   631,610.83

Interest	16,500
Depreciation	18,000
Restaurant Profit/(Loss)	$ 597,110.83

The advantage of calculating this within a computer program is that when changes need to be made, each line item does not need to be recalculated. You need to change only the one line that needs adjustment; the computer will recalculate the rest. If recalculating by hand, each line would need to be changed by hand.

EXAMPLE PROBLEM

In the example above, if sales cannot be generated as forecast, all sales figures would need adjusting. This would cause the recalculation of food—everything except for occupancy costs, interest, and depreciation. Other figures that may need correction include salaries and other controllable expenses that may have been estimated incorrectly. If food cost percent increases to 34% and fixed labor costs go up to 15%, and other controllable costs go down to 5.5%, we would need to recalculate almost every figure because they are all interconnected.

Mon.–Sat. Lunch	$210 \times 1.3 \times 6.20 \times 6 \times 52 = \$528,091.20$	$\times .20 = \$105,618.24$
Mon.–Sat. Dinner	$210 \times 1.4 \times 9.75 \times 6 \times 52 = 894,348.00$	$\times .25 = 223,587.00$
Sunday Dinner	$210 \times 1.4 \times 12 \times 1 \times 52 = 183,456.00$	$\times .25 = 445,864.00$
Catering	$1,000 \times \$10 \times 1 \times 12 = \underline{120,000.00}$	$\times .30 = \underline{36,000.00}$
	Total food sales 1,725,895.20	Beverage sales 411,069.24

SALES		
Food	1,725,895.20	
Beverages	411,069.24	
Total sales	2,136,964.44	
COST OF SALES		
Food	569,545.41	586,804.37
Beverages	82,213.85	82,213.85
Total cost of sales	651,759.26	669,018.22
GROSS PROFIT	1,485,205.18	1,467,946.22
CONTROLLABLE EXPENSES		
Fixed payroll	299,175.02	320,544.67
Var. payroll	277,805.38	277,805.38
Total payroll	576,980.40	598,350.05
Employee benefits	115,396.08	119,670.01
Other cont. expenses	128,218.87	117,533.04
Total controllable expenses	820,595.35	835,553.10
INCOME BEFORE OCCUPANCY COSTS, INTEREST, DEPRECIATION, AND INCOME TAXES	664,609.83	632,393.12
Occupancy costs	33,000	33,000
INCOME BEFORE INTEREST, DEPRECIATION, AND INCOME TAXES	631,609.83	599,393.12
Interest	16,500	16,500
Depreciation	18,000	18,000
Restaurant Profit/(Loss)	$ 597,109.83	$ 564,893.12

The categories represented here might not be the same figures on every profit and loss statement. A more detailed version of other controllable expense might include specific expenses such as linen, music, landscaping, or any of the many expenses associated with the hospitality industry. What line items are included in the profit and loss statement will be based on management requirements, accounting requirements, and the specific needs of those receiving the sheets.

WHY THIS IS IMPORTANT

Without the ability to anticipate and schedule around forecasted business, an operation may over/under-purchase or over/under-staff an operation. Some components of the operating budget will be static and can be permanently calculated; others may be adjusted to maintain accuracy as actual costs are incurred and sales made.

■

MAKE OR BUY ANALYSIS

One tool often used in the industry is the **make or buy analysis.** When deciding whether it is cost effective to make something yourself or use a convenience pre-prepared product, the most important criterion to keep in mind is the quality of the product purchased. If a product can be purchased that meets or surpasses the quality standard established by management, a decision as to whether to make it yourself or whether to buy the product needs to be made. If the quality is acceptable, the most common criterion used to make the decision is the cost. To be able to calculate the cost of making a product, one needs to calculate all of the costs associated with producing it. This includes food costs as well as labor costs and, possibly, energy costs. At times the labor cost may not need to be added, if there is an employee with the time to prepare the product without taking time away from other duties. Energy costs may not need to be added if there are no added energy costs due to the ovens being on and the operation being open. The main costs that are associated with the analysis will be the cost of the ingredients.

The first step in the make or buy analysis is the calculation of how much product is needed to prepare one serving of an item. If the recipe is for multiple servings, the total cost of making the larger quantity can be calculated, and then the total costs are divided by the number of servings prepared

When services are discussed in the hospitality industry, the main financial decision is whether or not to perform the task at hand or to **outsource** the job to another company. Outsourcing has become a very popular option for the hospitality industry (as well as many other industries) due to the potential savings that can be obtained. When outsourcing an operation or task, the first step is to perform a **cost-benefit analysis.** When completing the analysis, management calculates the costs associated with performing the task. These costs will include employee labor and benefits as well as insurance, supplies and any other expenses associated with the task. These expenses will vary depending on the type of task being performed. Once the costs are compiled, they are evaluated against the price quotes given by companies that are interested in performing the task.

These tasks can include maintenance or cleaning of equipment, and can be as complex as running food and beverage operations within a hotel property. While doing a cost-benefit analysis evaluation, one of the major factors in the decision is that the quality of the services matches the same quality standards that management has set for the entire operation. If management is comparing quotes for services with the assessed in-house costs, the quality and quantity standards need to be identical. Outsourcing has become commonplace in hospitality operations that are located in cities with strong union representation. The major advantage of outsourcing is when the price of labor becomes cost prohibitive; many times an outsourced labor force becomes less expensive.

When entire segments of a property are outsourced, it is done for many reasons. One reason that management would want to outsource is to bring in a company with brand recognition that will draw additional customers into an operation, or to help keep customers happy with a brand that they are familiar with. The second reason that an entire food and beverage department would be outsourced is that management does not have the expertise to run the operation keeping to the standards that are set. In these situations, companies are retained by management on the basis of their ability to run the outlets to management's standards.

EXAMPLE PROBLEM

If a restaurant can buy a gallon of cream of broccoli soup for $5.50, is it more cost effective to make the soup or buy it, assuming the quality is either the same or close enough that the quality standard will still be met? The first step in making this decision is to cost out the homemade soup. If the recipe is:

1# broccoli
8 oz butter
8 oz flour
1 gal chicken stock
12 oz cream
Salt and pepper to taste

If the cost of:

Broccoli is $.69 per pound
Butter is $2.29 per pound

Flour is $1.99 for 5 pounds
Chicken stock is $1.25 per gallon
Cream is $4.49 per quart
Salt and pepper is calculated at $.03 per gallon

How much does it cost to make the soup?

Broccoli	$1\# \times .69$	=	.69
Butter	$\frac{1}{2}\# * 2.29$	=	1.15, or Butter 8 oz $\times$ 14.3 cents = 1.144
Flour	$\frac{1}{2} * .40$	=	.20
Chicken stock	1×1.25	=	1.25
Cream	$12 \times .14$	=	1.68
Salt and pepper			.03
Total cost			$5.00

We can conclude that it is more costly to purchase the soup than it is to make it on the property. However, this does not include the labor cost associated with making the soup. If additional labor needs to be paid to make this soup, it may be is more cost effective to buy it rather than make it. On the other hand, if labor is already being paid and has the ability to add on the extra task, it would be less expensive to make the soup rather than buy it. This scenario is taking into account that the quality of the purchased soup meets the standards established if the soup were to be prepared on property.

WHY THIS IS IMPORTANT

Very few operations make everything from scratch. Each establishment needs to decide if they can, or want to, make items themselves or purchase them. Some restaurants make their own ketchup, while most buy it. The decision may be based on quality, but it also may be decided by cost factors.

■

SUMMARY

- ■ The controls of money are introduced, allowing the student to see how money is generated and the many places that assets are spent before the profit line can be realized.
- ■ The chapter also introduced some strategies that will allow future management to save money, while keeping the three industry standards in place.

KEY TERMS

Quality standard   Price/cost standard
Quantity standard   Standard operating procedures

Food cost
Transfers-in
Transfers-out
Operating budget

Profit and loss statement
Make or buy analysis
Outsource
Cost-benefit analysis

PROBLEMS

1. Explain the quality standard.

2. Explain the quantity standard.

3. Explain the cost standard.

4. A restaurant will have 120 seats. It will be open for lunch and dinner Monday through Friday, and for dinner only on Saturday and Sunday. Seat turnover for lunch is estimated to be 1.7, with weekday and Sunday dinner at 2.0 and weekend (Friday and Saturday) turnover at 2.4. The average food check for weekday lunch is expected to be $4.43, with a weekday dinner average food check of $8.31. The weekend dinner average check will be $11.56 and Sunday dinner average food check, $10.00. Beverage revenue is estimated at 15% of lunch food sales, plus 20% of dinner food sales. Food cost is expected to be 28% of total food sales, and beverage cost is expected to be 18% of total beverage sales. Salaried employee wages are estimated at 10% of total sales, with wages for all other employees forecast to be 20% of total sales. Benefits are expected to be an additional 18% of total salaries and wages. Other controllable expenses are estimated at 5% of total revenue. Depreciation is expected to be $10,000 per year, with occupancy costs and interest charges of $27,345 and $9,453 per year, respectively. Create a yearly operating budget.

5. In the above example, if food cost percent changes to 30%, beverage costs change to 20%, fixed labor costs go up to 11% and other controllable costs go down to 4.5%, recalculate the profit and loss statement.

6. If a restaurant can buy a loaf of French bread for $0.39 each, is it more cost effective to make the bread or buy it? The recipe for 10 loaves is:

Item	Cost
4# water	Free
3 oz yeast	$3.99 per pound
7# bread flour	$8.00 for 25 pounds
2 oz salt	$1.19 per pound
$\frac{1}{2}$ oz malt syrup	$1.99 per pint
2 oz sugar	$11.50 per 50 pounds
2 oz shortening	$2.99 for 5 pounds

7. Given the following data, compute the cost of food issued.

Last month's ending food inventory: $ 22,345
This month's ending food inventory: $ 27,651
Food purchases this month: $34,509

8. If the cost of food sold is $21,499 and sales dollars are $78,454, what is the food cost percent?

9. If labor cost is $4,554 and sales are $23, 678, how much is labor cost percent?

10. Given the following figures from the financial record of a unit in a small restaurant, determine the cost of food sold.

Closing inventory	$11,475
Grease sales	$34
Purchases	$42,155
Opening inventory	$9,475
Transfers from other units	$816
Cooking liquor	$140
Gratis to bar	$280
Food to bar	$751
Transfers to other units	$267

Employees' meals: $4,621 sales value; recent average food cost percent: 27.7%

11. A purveyor has offered to sell you fudge cakes for $5.75 each. You try to determine whether you can make the cakes cheaper. Assuming you will need to pay an additional employee $9.25 per hour plus $1.45 per hour for benefits, and further assuming that this employee can make 20 cakes per hour, which alternative should you select? Would you make or buy the cakes? Why (cost for each)?

The recipe for one cake is:	The AP price is:
8 oz shortening	$0.45 per pound
1/2# sugar	$11.75 for 25 pounds
1 oz vanilla	$6.00 per pint
3 eggs	$1.20 per dozen
10 oz cocoa	$1.99 per pound
27 oz cake flour	$11.50 per 25 pounds
$1\frac{1}{2}$ pint buttermilk	$8.50 per gallon

12. A financial forecast is needed for a proposed new restaurant concept that will have 210 seats. It will be open for lunch and dinner Monday through Saturday, and for dinner only on Sunday. Seat turnover for lunch is estimated to be 1.3, with weekday dinner and Sunday turnover at 1.4 each. Weekend (Friday and Saturday) dinner turnover is forecast at 1.8. The average food check for weekday lunch is expected to be

$6.20; weekend lunch will be $7.00, with a weekday dinner average food check of $9.75, Sunday average check of 10.54, and weekend dinner average food check of $12.00.

Beverage sales are estimated at 12% of lunch food sales and 19% of dinner food sales. Food cost is expected to be 33% of total food sales, and beverage cost is expected to be 20% of total beverage sales. Salaried employee wages are estimated at 14% of total sales, with wages for all other employees forecast to be 13% of total sales. Benefits are expected to be 20% of total salaries and 10% of wages. Other controllable expenses are estimated at 6% of total sales. Deprecation is expected to be $58,000 per year, with occupancy costs and interest charges of $83,000 and $16,500 per year, respectively.

Prepare a financial operating budget for one year.

13. Reevaluate the operating budget in Problem 12 if the numbers are actually as follows:

> Food cost goes down 1%
> Weekday lunch check is actually $5.50
> Salaries are actually 13% of total sales
> Other controllable costs rise to 7%

3

Controlling Costs and Improving Revenue Control with Technology

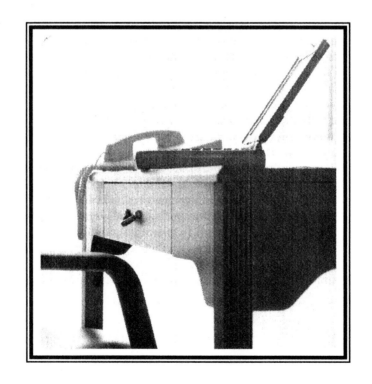

Chapter Objectives

After finishing this chapter the student will be able to:

Analyze why technology is created

Analyze technology for the hospitality industry

Evaluate technology available for the guest

Evaluate computer technology used for purchasing and warehousing

Evaluate technology in the processes of production, sales increases, and revenue control

Examine advances in product packaging

Evaluate the value of Point of Sale equipment

Evaluate negative responses to technology

Introduction

Technology changes on a daily basis, but the commonality of it is that it makes work more efficient and usually prepares a higher quality, more accurate end product. Technology upgrades in the hospitality industry began in the 1960s, when mainframe-based systems were installed in large hotels properties; property management systems were introduced into smaller properties in the 1970s. In the 1980s the microcomputer was the major upgrade, and the 1990s started the networking of computers between departments and multiple outlets. The technology available to assist in the control of costs and increase efficiency is expanding in every facet of the industry. This chapter will divide the technology into three categories: the first is technology, which can help all aspects of the industry; the second, technology, affects hotel operations and the third is geared toward restaurant advances.

WHAT DRIVES NEW TECHNOLOGY

Technological advances have been made both for the comfort of the guest and to create opportunities for a business in the hospitality industry to realize financial savings. These savings can be generated from efficiency created through advanced computers and software, energy savings from ecologically designed equipment and/or labor cost savings from efficient and effective equipment design principles.

With four main goals in mind, hotels and restaurants are constantly updating their technology. The first goal is guest driven. In this case, the main objective is the implementation of technology for the comfort and enjoyment of guests. Often this technology results in cost savings for the establishment by lowering operating expenses. An example of this might be the installation of a temperature control system in hotel guests' rooms.

The second technological goal for the hospitality industry is implemented to control costs. Computer hardware and software programs are available for every department within the hospitality industry. The efficiency created by the proper programming and use of these products can generate a financial savings for any size operation. An example of a program that can be implemented by any property is an inventory control system. The system will account for all products that are received and distributed by the operation. Although this can be done manually, with a computer system in place, larger operations can keep track of their entire inventory, lower the "shrinkage," and ensure that the correct departments are charged the specified price for each item issued.

The third goal for implementing technological advancement in an operation is to generate increased sales and control revenue. New cooking equipment available for the kitchen enables employees to work more quickly and efficiently, which speeds up plating of food and increases accuracy of the orders. This will allow restaurant tables to turn more quickly, which can create an increase in covers served. Once the sale is made, a **Point of Sale** system can help increase security and accountability in control of revenue.

Last is labor cost savings. This can be realized by every department and hospitality operation that implements technology, even less current technology. Technology has the ability to decrease the number of employees, which in addition to lowering payroll can protect a business against low workforce availability. New technology may also allow an operation to hire less experienced and lower waged employees. With improvements in the process of making and packaging convenience foods and the increase in commissary style production for multi-unit properties, kitchen employees using the end product do not need as much training, experience or pay. This compares to employees in properties that utilize items made from scratch.

TECHNOLOGY FOR THE HOSPITALITY INDUSTRY

Much of the technology available can be used in every aspect of the industry. Due to the frequent interaction between departments, which is a cornerstone for the profitable hospitality operation, the use of technology is essential for success. A widely adopted use of technology in the industry is in the accounting department. At minimum, an accounting department consists of accounts payable and accounts receivable. Depending on the operation and the scope of the department, accounting may also include computing of payroll, compiling monthly income statements, generating liquor sales reports for state monitors, and accumulating operating data. With the new software and Point of Sale hardware available, the tasks of the department can be streamlined through effective interfacing of the operation.

Current use of technology in the retail industry has given the ability to data mine information for marketing purposes. **Data mining,** an information extraction process to discover hidden facts contained in databases, gives operators information about consumers. Using a combination of machine learning, analysis of statistics, and modeling, data mining will find patterns and subtle relationships in the stored information, which will allow the prediction of future results. Data mining can be done with in-house information, as well as information available through other databases. If customer likes and dislikes and purchasing history are stored, guest preferences for future reservations will be available when the customer returns.

Technology is available to all companies; however, due to the costs, larger companies lead in its use. The costs of installing of new products and training can be astronomical due to the many locations large companies operate. As the prices decrease, smaller operations are beginning to pick up the newest technology. However, technology is only as good as the way it is implemented. Finding a balance in the very costly investment in technology is a critical issue among hospitality operations. Given the importance to improve the guest's experience through faster and more efficient services and the ability to lessen operating costs, the owner/operator needs to prioritize what technology to implement.

More than most industries, hospitality operations are reliant on all types of information, including customer information, product information and availability information, due to the human nature element of the business. The success or failure of a hospitality business can be related directly to the accuracy of the historical data contained in databases and the speed with which it is retrieved. Technological advances used in the industry will set increasingly higher standards for guest services and operations. As a result, investments in technologies and effective application of them will become one of the most decisive factors in the creation of a successful organization. At the pace that technology changes, an asset to any purchase is the ability to upgrade the hardware and software as new ideas and products emerge.

WHY THIS IS IMPORTANT

To be competitive, hospitality operations need as much information about the potential guest that they can get.

■

TECHNOLOGY FOR THE HOTEL

Whether a client is at a hotel for business or pleasure, there are many opportunities to utilize basic and advanced technology during their stay. Usually the first step in a hotel stay starts with researching of the appropriate hotel, either for price, amenities or location. The booking of a hotel room has evolved over a relatively short period of time, from the travel agent (more on this later) to the Internet. Besides individual hotel websites, there are myriad search engines that hunt through multiple websites and databases to locate the room that meets the standard established by the user. After the room is booked, the reservations process can be automated, allowing the hotel to reduce the chance of human error while increasing productivity and functionality of employees. Although the myriad websites available has the potential to discount room rates and lower dollar sales per room, in many cases either a different clientele may be introduced to the property, or a room may be booked, generating cash flow rather than being empty.

When the guest arrives at the hotel, current technology allows for checking in and checking out of the hotel either through a kiosk in the lobby or through the networked television in the guest's room. Either method speeds and simplifies the process for the guest. By eliminating the need to stand in line for a transaction, employee numbers and labor costs can be decreased, while increasing guest satisfaction and customer service created by using the same labor cost standard. The technology that allows a guest with a reservation the ability to check in is used in many hotels, and is currently being used at airports to allow flyers to check in using a credit card. After the guest has checked into the hotel, the next step is getting into the room. Most hotel properties have moved the technology away from the room key and have installed magnetic key card entry systems. The next phase of the technology is either to establish a fingerprint or retina scan of the guest, so that only that guest will be allowed entry, enhancing the security of the room, thereby eliminating the costs and negative publicity of theft.

Smart cards, which contain an integrated circuit, can allow a guest access to the hotel room or other services in the hotel. They have the potential to increase peripheral sales at hotel properties due to the fact that they can be programmed and coded for use in charging retail items, meals, minibar use, or other purchases. Advantages for properties that implement smart card technology include the decrease in costs associated with processing sales that are charged to a smart card, as compared to either cash sales or charge card sales. Cash sales create costs associated with counting and depositing money, and credit cards cost more to process than smart cards because smart cards are processed off line. Additionally, there is less fraud with smart cards because most of them have picture identification and built-in pin codes. Advanced uses of smart cards will decrease travel expenses and increase efficiency while traveling, as they can be programmed with an entire itinerary for a trip, including segments of the trip that utilize product, rooms and airfare, purchased from a multitude of companies.

According to a study by Dr. Frederick DeMicco (see reference 1), the ten most important technology amenities and services sought by business travelers are in-room temperature controls, easily accessible electrical outlets, alarm clocks, remote control TV, a phone on a desk, an additional data line accessible to the desk, electronic key cards, high-speed Internet access, voice-mail, and express check-in/check out. The same study identified technology amenities business travelers consider least important when choosing a hotel: smart card read capability, in-room electronic safety boxes, wireless Internet access, wireless access to the hotel website (Palm), in-room personal computer, printer, and fax machine, video-conferencing capabilities, pay per view TV, and Web TV.

Although most hotel operations offer updated amenities and a great deal of technology, specific products may be the deciding factor in whether a guest stays at a certain property or not. Many consumers have a personal priority when selecting which hotel to stay in, such as wireless Internet capability or the ability to have any hometown or business newspaper printed on property and delivered directly to the guest. Properties that offer the largest selection of potential guests needs will market themselves to the largest audience, thus, in theory, creating increased sales.

WHY THIS IS IMPORTANT

Guest satisfaction will generate repeat business and positive word of mouth advertising.

■

TECHNOLOGY FOR THE RESTAURANT

The restaurant industry is not known for investing in technology. Many restaurants did not used to see the value of investing in technology because they thought technology was best used as an aid to compiling data and for making reports, not an aid in production. This mindset is changing as chefs are becoming aware of the need to update equipment due to higher consumer awareness about food safety, labor costs, space constraints and the intensifying competition across all segments of the industry (see Figure 3.1). Another factor that is fostering this new thinking, and increasing the usage of technology in the kitchen, is the data protocol that was recently created by the North American Association of Food Equipment Manufacturers (NAFEM). The protocol creates a common code that enables different pieces of equipment to interact with one another and can give the operator information pertaining to food safety, inventory, energy consumption, and labor and asset management. Prior to this protocol all manufacturers created equipment that was proprietary and could not integrate with other pieces of equipment. This hindered companies from purchasing certain equipment if they were currently using other manufacturers' brands.

FIGURE 3.1   Technology in Use

McDonald's is experimenting with three technological ideas to increase customer service by allowing employees to take care of the guest rather than performing certain functions. The company is testing an automated grill, a robotic fryer and a touch-screen self-service order kiosk. The devices were created to increase the speed of service and to deliver products that will be more consistent and hotter. The automated grill will season the beef after cooking rather than having a cook do that. The deep fryer is designed to prepare, salt and bag both French fries and hash browns. The order kiosks allow the guests to order themselves, and are similar to ATM terminals.

Source: Reference 2.

FROM THE FARM TO THE TABLE

The use of technology has played an integral part in the early steps of the flow of food to an operation. Through the growth and processing cycle, whether the product is farmed or raised, technology plays a key role in the growth and protection of almost all food products. The exceptions are products that are grown organically. Many farm animals are given growth hormones to enhance the growth process, which allows the animals to eat less, come to market younger, and ultimately be less expensive. Many are also given antibiotics to help keep them healthy. Technologies in the agricultural industry have created new, and sometimes better, products by genetically modifying foods. This is accomplished by combining qualities of two or more varieties of vegetables or fruit to create a unique or more durable product that can withstand high or low temperatures or other factors. Genetically modified food may also take characteristics from other species to create a new product. Technology used in the breeding of animals has created breeds that produce larger muscles in certain parts of the body that are more in demand and higher priced, and produce either less or more fat, depending on what the market is looking for.

Technology has also changed the industry by allowing manufacturers and processors to prepare frozen and canned foods quickly after harvest. This helps maintain quality and nutritional value of foods. With the addition of preservatives, the shelf life of many products can be extended. Added to that is increasing use of irradiation for fresh products to increase shelf life and maintain quality. The technologies that increase shelf life allow for lower food costs due to less product spoilage, as well as money saved by decreasing the frequency with which product needs to be purchased and received.

SUPPLY CHAIN MANAGEMENT

Supply chain management is the overseeing of supplies, information, and monies as they move from supplier to manufacturer to wholesaler to restaurant. Supply chain management involves establishing and integrating systems and procedures with suppliers, as well as in house. The ultimate goal of any supply chain management system is to reduce inventory, and the investment of money, so that the products will be available when needed. This is accomplished by sharing of data between suppliers and a hospitality operation, which allows all companies involved to better manage current resources and plan for future needs.

COMPUTERS IN PURCHASING AND WAREHOUSE OPERATIONS

Technology is continually advancing, making the purchasing job a much more manageable component of an operation. Purchasing, a fundamental element of cost control, has become a major financial component of any successful operation. Some basic, older technological advances such as the fax, e-mail, product specifications available on CD-ROM, and computers with spreadsheets, have created a situation that speeds the purchasing function while making it more accurate. Technological advances have also allowed for multi-unit properties to create corporate purchasing departments that perform centralized bidding of products, and then allow the individual properties to purchase the product. Smaller operations also have vast opportunities with computer applications within the purchasing department. Inventory programs that can be integrated with purchasing programs and Point of Sale equipment have become very useful in generating reports that highlight items that need to be purchased, reports that track pricing trends for commodity items, and reports that show the most and least frequently purchased items. Many systems have the capacity to produce orders and send them to distributors based on predetermined par stock levels. As the technology has advanced, the use of Point of Sale equipment and online purchasing allows operations the ability to find suppliers that can service the operation, as needed. If the purchasing department can bring in the right product at the right price, a business has a much higher chance of generating a profit.

The technology available to warehouse operations, as well as to distribution centers, helps to maintain the quality of the products and maintain par levels. Most warehouse operations rely on computers to keep track of inventory using a perpetual inventory method. This is done using computers, which delete items when they are issued and adds items when they are received. There are management overrides that can be implemented for adjustments due to product spoilage or breakage, but these should be kept to a minimum. This type of software is programmable to alert management if a product has been in stock for an extended period of time, which could lead to spoilage, or to indicate that the inventory value is too high. Warehouse software can also be programmed to generate reports of the most frequently used items and the most requested products. With these reports warehouse managers can arrange the warehouse with the frequently used products in the most accessible locations. Buyers can be made aware of the products they purchase that sell and do not sell. With this information they may be able to arrange for a different purchasing method to generate lower prices for high volume items.

Although a physical inventory, hand counting and valuing of items, should be performed at least once a month, with computer inventory controls in place, an inventory value can be generated immediately. This information is useful to ensure that an operation remains profitable. Many modern warehouses utilize either manufacturers' bar codes or create their own. Using scanners to pick inventory and issue products allows for a more accurate distribution of product. Technology available allows for accurate storage temperatures and conditions to be maintained.

Purchasing in every aspect of the industry has been greatly affected by advances in technology. Besides the ability to streamline the purchasing function, manufacturers and distributors can create virtual tradeshow websites, allowing for a greater customer base. This results in greater awareness about the products available, as well as allowing for cheaper prices due to the lower expenses needed to show their wares on line, rather than having to move the equipment to a regional industry show.

USE OF TECHNOLOGY IN PRODUCTION

A critical part of an operation that should use advanced technology, but usually does not, is in the production of food. The newest ovens that are available use a combination of dry heat and moist heat to cook, which allows for less shrinkage of product generating a higher yield percent and more products to sell. Another advantage of these ovens is that the computer inside allows for programming to cook certain items. This frees up the cook's time, as well as generates a standard product and the ability to maintain data showing the compliance to Hazard Analysis Critical Control Point (HACCP) cooking principles (see Figure 3.2).

Technology available is also used to convert recipes to the appropriate quantities needed for production. Nutritional analysis by computers is becoming much more frequent with the change in the eating habits and the

FIGURE 3.2 Value of the Combination Oven

Some manufacturers claim that their product will cook prime rib with less than 3 percent shrinkage, as compared to 10–15 percent that might be realized in a standard oven. If those numbers are accurate, when a 20-pound prime rib is cooked using both methods, the one in the conventional oven would yield 17 pounds while the one in the combination oven would yield almost 19.5 pounds. If an operation sells 8-ounce portions, it would yield five additional servings. Due to the efficiency of the oven, it cooks quicker than a conventional oven and does this while saving money on energy costs.

large percentage of the population dieting. Recent technology has allowed the federal government to re-examine the temperature danger zone—the temperature at which foodborne bacteria grow—allowing them to lower the temperature to 135°F. This was due to new technology that allowed advanced research and tests that revealed that the reproduction of bacteria is not significant between 135° and 140°F.

With a computer and menu-making software on property, many operations can create daily menus. When creating a daily menu an operation can take advantage of discounts or deals available when purchasing foods, and can also give the restaurant the ability to create menu items that utilize products that are losing quality. Computer software will also allow an operation to calculate preparation costs of menu items and then calculate selling prices for the menu items.

PACKAGING

Technology is in widespread use in the packaging of either convenience food, itself a result of technology, or other products that can be purchased in large quantity and repackaged into smaller units while maintaining quality.

Many operations prepare food in a commissary system and send the product to end users. These operations save labor costs by preparing products in large batches using trained chefs. End users need only to reheat food, using less trained and lower waged employees. Cooking in large quantities, cooling the

FIGURE 3.3   Types of Packaging

Sous Vide
French for "under vacuum," sous vide is a food-packaging technique pioneered in Europe. Fresh ingredients are combined into various dishes and then vacuum packed in individual portions. The food is then cooked under a vacuum and chilled. Sous vide food is used most often by hotels, restaurants and caterers, but it is becoming more available in supermarkets. (*Source:* Reference 3.)

Modified Atmosphere Packing
MAP packaging is a process when a combination of carbon dioxide, nitrogen, and oxygen replaces the ordinary air in the food package. This creates a low-oxygen environment, where many foodborne pathogens cannot thrive. The low-oxygen environment also inhibits spoilage by preventing growth of molds and yeasts. The ratio of gases and the packaging material will vary depending on the product packaged. (*Source:* Reference 4.)

Ultra-High Temperature Pasteurization
These products, popular for many years in Europe and increasingly popular in the United States, are heated and pressurized to above the boiling point, 245°–255°F for a very short period of time. After UHP the product is sealed in a sterilized container creating a product that does not need to be refrigerated. A negative aspect of UHP packaging is that some products develop a cooked flavor from the high heat.

food in a blast chiller, and packaging it can save money for large operations (see Figure 3.3).

SALES INCREASE AND REVENUE CONTROL APPLICATIONS

Technology is also a component in the sales end of the restaurant business. Sales volume has the potential to increase if a restaurant utilizes the technology that is available. Restaurants that have web pages to promote the operation have created an economical but effective method of marketing their establishment. If a web design is attractive and eye catching, it can help patrons decide whether or not to dine at the restaurant. A growing resource restaurants are utilizing is the outsourcing of on-line reservation sites, which usually market the restaurant to a different clientele than do other marketing efforts. Reservation systems can be computerized to help maintain data about clients while speeding up the reservation time.

Fast food restaurants have been the most aggressive segment of the industry to create and utilize technology for increasing sales volume. One example of this technology being used in many operations is the implementation of self-ordering kiosks, as described in Figure 3.1. This technology is not new, but due to wider consumer acceptance of technology it is being re-implemented in restaurants. Self-ordering kiosks improve speed of ordering, allow for a new marketing tool, allow operators the ability to re-direct or eliminate labor costs and allows for more accurate ordering and preparation. This lowers food cost generated when items need to be re-made.

Companies that have take-out or delivery and have multiple outlets in a condensed area can utilize a centralized ordering system by installing a single phone number or location for customers placing orders. Once the orders are taken, they are entered into a computer that will distribute them to the closest branch. With this technology, labor cost will be lowered due to not having an employee at each outlet with the job of answering the phone.

Once the sale is generated, the Point of Sale equipment can be an integral part of management of the money by allowing charges to be posted to the correct ledger. In the case of a room charge in a hotel, it can be posted to the correct room, when the systems are interfaced. The POS system can also generate reports detailing how much money self-cashiering servers have to submit, as well as how much money should be in a cash draw at any time during a shift.

WHY THIS IS IMPORTANT

With consolidation of all aspects of the industry, from distributors to retail outlets, all money and time savings are needed to be competitive.

■

NEGATIVE ASPECTS CREATED BY TECHNOLOGY

Technology that helps an operation run efficiently can also create some negative repercussions. One negative consequence of advanced technology is the reduction of many entry-level jobs that are being replaced by new equipment that is more efficient, or fulfilling the jobs previously done by these employees. Although this creates a savings in labor costs, the jobs lost can create higher unemployment, and might inhibit potential employees, who may have excelled in the hospitality industry, from ever pursuing a career.

One component of the industry that has been hit hard by technology is the travel agency industry. With airline websites, as well as other search engines allowing people to search for flights and book them for themselves, the loss in revenue has hurt the industry, eliminating many jobs.

Many small business wholesalers have been forced to make business adjustments due to the expanded ability to procure items through a bidding process on the Internet. Smaller distributors that do not have the buying and pricing ability of larger companies have had to lower their prices to compete. Although this scenario will get the purchaser the lowest price for a product, it takes away any supplier services that may be offered from the distributor.

PBX, one department that in the past has been a generator of income for most hotels, has continually created less profit in recent years due to the increase in cell phone usage and the fees charged by many hotels for local and long distance calls. Additionally, many phone companies offer a virtual PBX, which allow the calls to be sent to the phone company base before being assigned a particular phone line. This allows smaller manpowered operations to work with a system without having to make an investment in equipment and labor.

PBX, which stands for private branch exchange, is a switching station within a hospitality operation that allows the property to maintain many internal phone extensions while switching them between a small number of external phone lines. In the past PBX has been a department that has been a generator of income for most hotels, which has continually created less profit in recent years due to the increase in cell phone usage and the fees charged by many hotels for local and long distance calls.

THE FUTURE OF TECHNOLOGY

As technology advances, increases in use of technology include the use of fingerprint identification technology being created by many software companies. Fingerprint technology can help minimize employee "buddy punching," when one employee punches in or out for another employee. This can also minimize employee mistakes in entering orders into a POS system and speed up ordering when employees do not have to enter their POS number or slide the identification card. The negative aspects of this system include a possible employee distrust of the system and the problems that could occur if an employee has a cut or bandage on the finger.

SUMMARY

- The reasons why new technology is created and implemented
- The roadblocks to implementing the new technology
- The advantages of implementing new technology
- A variety of technology across the industry already in use
- Technology in the flow of food into and through an operation
- Negative reactions to new technology
- A variety of websites listed for future research

WEBSITES

www.htmagazine.com
www.hotel-online.com
www.nrn.com
www.techtarget.com

http://www.hotel-technology.com
http://www.hotelinteractive.com
http://www.restaurant.org

KEY TERMS

Point of Sale
Data mining

Smart cards
Supply chain management

PROBLEMS

1. What are the four leading factors in the industry push for the creation of new technology?
2. What are the major causes in the delay of implementation of new technology?
3. What are the negative repercussions of advanced technology in the hospitality industry? List some positions that are negatively affected by technology.
4. What major development has lead to an increase in the implementation of kitchen technology?
5. How can technology improve sales in all aspects of hospitality?
6. What technology is available to help ensure quality and maintain safety in packaged foods?

7. With regard to the flow of food through an operation, how can point of sale equipment be used to eliminate labor and make an operation more efficient?

8. Discuss one item that is technological and is not discussed in this chapter.

9. Explain the concept of data mining.

10. Explain how smart cards can increase sales.

11. What will drive the next level of technology?

12. List some of the technology mentioned in the book and add any additional technology you are aware of. Categorize it as to implementation for customer satisfaction, decrease in labor, or efficiency of operations.

13. Do you think that the main drive for technology is customer satisfaction, the decrease of labor costs, or efficiency? Why?

14. Should the hospitality industry embrace genetically modified foods? Why?

REFERENCES

1. Frederick J. DeMicco, Ph.D., "White Paper: High-tech and high-touch hospitality," http://www.htmagazine.com/zone/8-02_isolutions.html, August 5, 2002.

2. Amy Garber, "McDonald's unveils technology upgrades to improve service," http://www.nrn.com/story.cfm?ID=503960485&SEC=Technology.

3. http://allrecipes.iwon.com/encyc/terms/S/8632.asp From *The New Food Lover's Companions,* 3rd ed. by Sharon Tyler Herbst. Copyright © 2001 by Barron's Educational Series, Inc. Prior editions copyright © 1995, 1990 by Barron's Educational Series, Inc. Reprinted by arrangement.

4. http://www.dmaonline.org/fppublic/connect38.html. Adapted from "MAP Packaging: It's in the Air" *Dietary Manager* magazine, published by Dietary Managers Association, May 2003. Reprinted by permission.

4
Cost–Volume–Profit Relationships

Chapter Objectives

After finishing this chapter the student will be able to:

Explain variable costs
Describe the variable rate
Describe the components of the contribution margin
Describe the contribution margin

Calculate the variable cost and rate, contribution margin and rate, and calculate the break-even point in sales dollars and sales units
Determine which formula to use for various calculations

Introduction

To understand how to make a profit in the food and beverage industry, as well as other segments of the hospitality industry, the knowledge of certain terminology is imperative. Terminology will clarify the complexity and interrelation between different factors in cost control and the management of money. An in-depth understanding of how money, generated in sales, is spent will allow management to distribute or re-distribute revenue. There is a direct relationship between sales volume and profit.

COMPONENTS OF SALES

These terms are divided into dollar terms and percentage terms. Each term has a direct relationship with total sales. Each can be used for total sales and sales per unit, depending on what analysis or comparison is needed.

Variable Costs and the Contribution Margin

The first terms are dollar terms, and the first is variable costs. As defined in Chapter 1, this represents costs that will change with the increase or decrease in the volume of business. These costs usually include food and beverage costs, supplies, wages and benefits costs, which do not include salaried employees. Variable costs are a dollar figure that is the actual cost of the product and service that is for sale.

Next is the **contribution margin.** The contribution margin is defined as the fixed costs and the profit generated by sales. As with the variable costs, the contribution margin can be used as a figure for an individual item or for total sales. It is *essential* to understand that sales are made of these two components, variable cost and contribution margin.

Understanding this formula is an important step in working toward profitability. As with many formulas, this formula can be manipulated depending on what data is available and what data is needed.

IMPORTANT FORMULA

Sales (S) = Variable costs (VC) + contribution margin (CM)

This can also be represented by the formula:

Sales (S) = Variable costs (VC) + fixed cost (FC) + profit (P)

Therefore:

Contribution margin (CM) = Fixed cost (FC) + profit (P)

IMPORTANT FORMULA

Variable costs (VC) = Sales (S) − contribution margin (CM)

This can also be represented by the formula:

Variable costs (VC) = Sales (S) − fixed cost (FC) − profit (P)

IMPORTANT FORMULA

Contribution margin (CM) = Sales (S) − variable costs (VC)

Knowing that the contribution margin is equivalent to fixed cost plus profit, this formula can then be changed to the following two formulas.

IMPORTANT FORMULA

Profit (P) = Sales (S) − variable costs (VC) − fixed cost (FC) or
Fixed cost (FC) = Sales (S) − variable costs (VC) − profit (P)

EXAMPLE PROBLEM

If sales are $200,000 and variable costs are $50,000, how much is the contribution margin?

$200,000 − $50,000 = $150,000 (s − vc = cm)

This figure represents what is left over to cover the fixed costs and the profit. If fixed costs are greater than $150,000 the establishment loses money, and if they are less than that amount the establishment earns that amount as profit. This is the most common use of this formula, but the formula can also be used to calculate other data.

EXAMPLE PROBLEM

If the contribution margin is $150,000 and the variable costs are $50,000 calculate the sales.

$150,000 + $50,000 = $200,000 (cm + vc = s)

This formula will be used to create an operating budget or to forecast for the future, as well as to analyze whether an establishment will be profitable during certain scenarios.

EXAMPLE PROBLEM

If the fixed costs are $125,000 and profit is $25,000 and the variable costs are $50,000, calculate the sales.

$125,000 + $25,000 + $50,000 = $200,000 (fc + p + vc = s)

This formula can also be used to calculate the break-even point, when profit equals zero.

EXAMPLE PROBLEM

If sales are $200,000 and the contribution margin is $150,000 calculate the variable costs.

$200,000 − $150,000 = $50,000 (s − cm = vc)

Since variable costs are usually known, this is the least used formula and is used for forecasting an operating budget. If sales are forecast and fixed cost and profit are anticipated, this formula will allow management to ascertain how much money they can spend on controllable or variable expenses.

EXAMPLE PROBLEM

If sales are $200,000 and the fixed costs are $125,000 and the variable costs are $50,000, calculate profit.

$200,000 − $125,000 − $50,000 = $25,000 (s − fc − vc = p)

This formula is used to calculate profit after sales and costs have been established.

EXAMPLE PROBLEM

If sales are $200,000, the profit is $25,000 and the variable costs are $50,000, calculate fixed costs.

$200,000 − $25,000 − $50,000 = $125,000 (s − vc − p = fc)

This formula is not used very often in business, unless an establishment uses a backward method of accounting and takes profit out after expenses without calculating how the money was used.

WHY THIS IS IMPORTANT

Without understanding where sales revenue is spent, it is hard to control costs and create profitability. Since profitability is why most operations are in business, formulas to calculate profit are needed.

■

Variable Rate and Contribution Rate

The next term to be discussed is the **variable rate.** The variable rate is the percentage of sales that goes toward the variable costs. The second term used for percentages is **contribution rate.** The contribution rate is the percentage of sales that goes toward paying for the fixed costs and generating profit. These terms are used to make comparisons and to forecast future profitability and expenses based on anticipated sales. It is important to understand that sales are made of two components, variable rate and contribution rate.

IMPORTANT FORMULA

$$\frac{\text{Variable cost (VC)}}{\text{Sale (S)}} = \text{Variable rate (VR)}$$

This formula can be used for total variable rate for all sales as well as the variable rate for a particular dish or a segment of the menu such as appetizers or desserts.

IMPORTANT FORMULA

$$\frac{\text{Contribution margin (CM)}}{\text{Sale (S)}} = \text{Contribution rate (CR)}$$

This formula can be used for total contribution rate for all sales as well as the contribution rate for a particular dish or a segment of the menu such as appetizers or desserts.

EXAMPLE PROBLEM

Using the same numbers as above, if sales are $200,000 and variable costs are $50,000, how much is the variable rate?

$50,000/$200,000 = 25% (vc/s = vr)

This figure represents that 25 percent of every sales dollar (an average when not calculating for a single dish) will go toward the variable costs associated with preparing the dish or dishes. This figure represents the portion of sales that is controllable. If this figure is too high to generate a profit, management has two options. The first option available is to raise the selling prices. If the prices are increased and sales volume remains the same, this will lower the variable rate and raise the contribution rate. The second option is to lower the variable costs. Management's changing one of the standards that has been established will lower the variable costs. If management changes the quantity standard, the quality standard, or the cost standard, it can effectively lower the variable rate, thus raising the contribution rate. The main assumption with either of these methods is that business volume will not decrease. Smart consumers may be aware of price increases or food and service changes such as amount of food and quality of food and service, and may stop patronizing an establishment.

EXAMPLE PROBLEM

Using the figures above, if sales are $200,000 and contribution margin is $150,000, how much is the contribution rate?

$150,000/$200,000 = 75% (cm/s = cr)

This formula will be used to help calculate the break-even point.

It should be noted that since sales are made up of two factors—variable costs and contribution margin—which are used to calculate the contribution rate and the variable rate, another important factor is that the variable rate and the contribution rate must add up to one, representing total sales.

IMPORTANT FORMULA

$$1 - \text{Variable rate (VR)} = \text{Contribution rate (CR)}$$

This formula will be used when the calculation for the variable rate is possible with the information available, but the contribution rate is needed.

IMPORTANT FORMULA

$$1 - \text{Contribution rate (CR)} = \text{Variable rate (VR)}$$

This formula will be used when the calculation for the contribution rate is possible with the information available, but the variable rate is needed.

EXAMPLE PROBLEM

Using the figures above, if sales are $200,000 and contribution margin is $150,000, how much is the variable rate?

$150,000/$200,000 = 75% (cm/s = cr)

1 − .75 = .25 (1 − cr = vr)

EXAMPLE PROBLEM

Using the figures above, if sales are $200,000 and variable cost is $50,000, how much is the contribution rate?

$50,000/$200,000 = 25% (vc/s = vr)

1 − .25 = .75 (1 − vr = cr)

WHY THIS IS IMPORTANT

The percentage of each dollar in sales that goes towards different expenses is needed in forecasting, planning and analysis of financial data.

■

BREAK-EVEN POINT

One of the most important calculations to be performed is to determine the **break-even point** in business. This formula is used in every industry to calculate either the dollar sales or unit sales needed to break even in business or to generate a certain amount of profit. At the break-even point, the business is self-sufficient and pays all of the bills, but does not create additional revenue that can be invested in the business, split among stockholders or taken out by an owner.

IMPORTANT FORMULA

$$\text{Sales in dollars (S)} = \frac{\text{Fixed cost (FC)} + \text{profit (P)}}{\text{Contribution rate (CR)}}$$

This formula is used to calculate how much sales dollars need to be generated to break even (BE), or if a desired profit level is inserted, sales volume needed to generate that profit will be calculated.

EXAMPLE PROBLEM

If fixed costs are $125,000 and the contribution rate is 75%, how much sales need to be generated to break even?

$$\frac{\$125,000 + 0}{.75} = \$166,666.67 \qquad \frac{fc + p}{cr} = s \,(be)$$

This figure is different than any of the others we have been using because it does not use the profits that are generated in the chapter example.

EXAMPLE PROBLEM

If fixed costs are $125,000, the contribution rate is 75%, and management has decided that it wants to generate a profit of $25,000, how much in sales will be needed?

$$\frac{\$125,000 + \$25,000}{.75} = \$200,000 \qquad \frac{fc + p}{cr} = s$$

This formula works because 75 percent of sales need to generate enough revenue to cover fixed costs and profit. The other 25 percent is used to pay for the variable costs associated with the sale.

Through making a minor change in the formula, we can calculate the number of units needed to be sold to break even or to generate a profit. When using this formula, we need to calculate the average contribution margin of each unit sold. If the contribution margin is the same for every item sold, or averaged out, this number will be an exact number of units needed. More frequently, we need to calculate the average contribution margin based on the number of items sold and the total contribution margin.

IMPORTANT FORMULA

$$\text{Sales in units (S)} = \frac{\text{Fixed cost (FC)} + \text{profit (P)}}{\text{Average contribution margin (ACM)}} \qquad \text{or}$$

$$\text{Sales in units (S)} = \frac{\text{Fixed cost (FC)} + \text{profit (P)}}{\text{Average check (AC)} - \text{Average variable cost (AVC)}}$$

This formula is used to calculate how many sales units need to be generated to break even (BE), or if a desired profit level is inserted, sales volume, in units, needed to generate that profit will be calculated.

EXAMPLE PROBLEM

If fixed costs are $125,000 and the average contribution margin is $10 per unit, how much sales need to be generated for the establishment to break even?

$$\frac{\$125,000 + 0}{\$10} = 12,500 \text{ units} \qquad \frac{fc + p}{cm} = su \text{ (be)}$$

EXAMPLE PROBLEM

If fixed costs are $125,000 the average contribution margin is $10 per unit and profit desired is $25,000, how much in sales need to be generated?

$$\frac{\$125,000 + \$25,000}{\$10} = 15,000 \text{ units} \qquad \frac{fc + p}{cm} = su \text{ (be)}$$

WHY THIS IS IMPORTANT

Understanding how many products or how much in sales dollars are needed to break-even will allow management to set sales goals that will create profits.

∎

AVERAGE VARIABLE COSTS

The variable cost and contribution margin can be calculated for individual dishes, or a weighted average can be calculated for any meal or any period of time period. In some instances the contribution margin is calculated on each individual item sold (contribution margin per dish divided by selling price per dish), but in many instances the contribution margin is calculated as a weighted average of all items sold. This takes into account the different quantities of each item sold and the different variable costs of each dish.

EXAMPLE PROBLEM

Item	# Sales	Menu Price	Variable Cost	Contribution Margin	Total Sales Dollars	Total Variable Cost
Item A	40	5.00	1.00	4.00	200.00	40.00
Item B	30	6.00	2.00	4.00	180.00	60.00
Item C	20	7.00	3.00	4.00	140.00	60.00
Item D	10	8.00	4.00	4.00	80.00	40.00
Total	100				600.00	200.00

Average check: 600/100 = $6.00
Average variable rate: 200/600 = .3333
Average contribution rate: 1 − .3333 = .6667
Average contribution margin = .6667 × $6.00 = $4.00

In this example, the quantity of each item sold is taken into account as well as the variable costs associated with preparing the each dish. If the sales mix remains stable, the weighted average of the variable rate or contribution rate will assist in forecasting future financial trends. Forty Item As were sold at a menu price of $5.00, which created total dollar sales of the item at $200.00. Each item's variable cost was $1.00, so the total variable costs for that item were $40.00. With these numbers one can calculate the variable rate or contribution rate of each dish. When each item's total sales dollars and variable cost is calculated, and the individual items' variable costs are totaled, the average variable rate can be calculated by dividing total variable costs by total sales. The average check can be calculated with this data by dividing the total sales by the total number of items sold. This information can be used to calculate the average contribution margin as well, by multiplying the average contribution rate by the average check.

WHY THIS IS IMPORTANT

Average contribution margins take into account the number of sales of each item as well as the contribution margin of each item. This information is used to compare one item to another and to analyze overall financial data.

■

CHANGING THE BREAK-EVEN POINT

After calculating the break-even point, management may need to reevaluate its standards to ensure profitability. There are three chief methods to change the break-even point; each method has pros and cons associated with it. The methods directly relate to the three standards that have been established for the operation.

- The first method is to raise prices. If management raises prices it may generate more revenue, but the negative is that this may cause customer dissatisfaction and ultimately lower sales by alienating customers. This may, in turn, create a situation where the customer purchases an entrée, but does not order an appetizer.
- The second method is to lower the quality of the product being served. This can include service as well as food, or any aspect of the hospitality industry. If quality is lowered, the costs associated with the sale, either fixed or variable, will decrease. This will lead to a higher contribution margin for each unit sold. If the quality is lowered, management may create lower costs, but the negative is that this may cause customer dissatisfaction and ultimately lower sales by creating non-repeat business.
- The third method is to lower the quantity standard for the product or service. This too may lower the variable costs associated with the sale,

but again the negative in this situation is that this may cause customer dissatisfaction and ultimately lower sales by creating non-repeat business.

SUMMARY

■ The relationship between the financial components of the hospitality industry are compared and contrasted.

■ The various formulas to calculate the financial components are given.

■ The concept of the break-even point is established.

FORMULA SUMMARY

Sales − variable costs = Contribution margin (S − VC = CM)
Contribution margin + variable costs = Sales (CM + VC = S)
Fixed cost + profit = Contribution margin
Fixed cost + profit + variable cost = Sales (FC + P + VC = S)
Variable cost/variable rate = Sales (VC/VR = S)
Contribution margin/Contribution rate = Sales (CM/CR = S)
Sales − contribution margin = Variable costs (S − CM = VC)
Sales − fixed costs − Variable costs = Profit (S − FC − VC = P)
Sales − variable costs − profit = Fixed costs (S − VC − P = FC)
Variable cost/Sales = Variable rate (VC/S = VR)
Contribution margin/Sales = Contribution rate (CM/S = CR)
1 − Contribution rate = Variable rate (1 − CR = VR)
1 − Variable rate = Contribution rate (1 − VR = CR)
Fixed cost + Profit/Contribution rate = Break-even point in sales dollars

$$\frac{FC + P}{CR} = S\$ \text{ (BE)}$$

Fixed cost + Profit/Contribution margin = Break-even point in unit sales

$$\frac{FC + P}{CM} = SU \text{ (BE)}$$

KEY TERMS

Contribution margin	Contribution rate
Variable rate	Break-even point

PROBLEMS

When calculating the following problems different formulas may be used to calculate the correct answers.

1. Given the following information calculate variable costs.
   a. Sales $12,986, fixed costs, $5,673, profit $956
   b. Sales $129,458, variable rate .31
   c. Sales $12.67, contribution margin $8.14
   d. Sales $27,493, contribution rate .56
   e. Contribution margin $189,458, contribution rate .61

2. Given the following information calculate fixed costs.
   a. Sales $27,369, variable costs, $13,532, profit $4,693
   b. Sales $342,760, variable rate .36, loss $11,562
   c. Sales units 34,739, variable cost $156,389, profit $12,509, selling price per unit $10.00

3. Given the following information calculate contribution margin.
   a. Sales $18.90, variable costs $10.87
   b. Sales $122,577, variable rate .33
   c. Sales $565,890, contribution rate .59

4. Given the following information calculate dollar sales.
   a. Fixed cost $12,532, profit $9,871, variable costs $23,590
   b. Variable costs $9.89, variable rate .29
   c. Variable costs $45,567, contribution rate .72
   d. Fixed costs $45,888, profit $11,875, variable rate .36
   e. Contribution margin $12,509, variable costs $8,698
   f. Contribution margin $9.45, variable rate .35

5. Given the following information, find unit sales.
   a. Average contribution margin $4.67, fixed costs $34,988, profit $6,873
   b. Average sales price $23.56, variable rate .34; fixed cost $12,123, profit $990
   c. Average sales price $8.75, contribution rate .59; fixed cost $145,983, profit $23,678

6. Given the following information calculate variable rate.
   a. Sales $239,099, variable costs $87,934
   b. Sales $13.45, contribution margin $8.09
   c. Sales $434,646, fixed costs $189,809, profit $23,589

7. Given the following information calculate contribution rate.
   a. Sales $18.99, variable costs $8.08
   b. Sales $212,545, contribution margin $145,890
   c. Sales $478,890, fixed costs $234,678, profit $78,823

8. Given the following information calculate profit.
   a. Variable rate .39, sales $98,368, fixed costs $34,645

  b. Variable costs $12.45, sales $36.78, fixed costs $21.56
  c. Contribution rate .61, fixed costs $1,346, sales $4,234
9. Given the following information calculate break-even point in dollars.
  a. Fixed cost $46,498, contribution rate .55
  b. Fixed cost $178,045, variable rate .33
  c. Sales price per unit $15.78, fixed costs $45,789, contribution rate .61
10. Given the following information calculate break-even point in unit sales.
  a. Fixed cost $34,643, average contribution margin $4.67
  b. Average sales price $14.56, variable rate .39, fixed costs $45,727
  c. Average sales price $9.95, contribution rate .71, fixed costs $223,789
11. What are the three ways to change the break-even point in sales?
12. What is the contribution margin?
13. What does the variable rate represent?
14. What does the contribution rate represent?
15. Why is it important to calculate the break-even point?
16. Calculate average variable rate, average contribution margin and the average check for the following menu items.

Item	Cost	Number Sold	Selling Price
Steak	$7.75	15	$17.95
Chicken	$4.79	26	$13.95
Fish	$3.99	11	$12.95
Duck	$6.57	8	$16.95

17. Calculate average variable rate, average contribution margin and the average check for the following menu items.

Item	Cost	Number Sold	Selling Price
Hamburger	$1.99	65	$7.50
Salad	$1.23	48	$6.75
Pizza	$1.01	89	$3.95
Tuna sandwich	$1.87	67	$6.25

5
Controls
in Food Purchasing

Chapter Objectives

After finishing this chapter the student will be able to:

Define and utilize food purchasing terminology

Differentiate among the three purchasing standards

View forms associated with purchasing

Describe the different purchasing methods

Use formulas including:
   Periodic ordering amount
   Perpetual ordering amount
   As purchased (AP) calculations
   Edible portion (EP) for both food quantity and food cost

Introduction

This chapter is critical to understanding the proper flow, and control, of food through an operation. If an establishment does not purchase the food in a cost effective and streamlined manner, it is very hard to obtain profits. Proper food purchasing brings in the precise amount of the needed product at the proper price. If successful, through stringent operational management, it allows for the production of food in a cost efficient manner.

PROCUREMENT FUNCTION

The procurement function is one of the most important aspects in the control of costs. If the establishment does not order and receive the correct raw ingredients at the correct price, employees cannot create an end product consonant with the financial goals of the operation. Initially, the buying team has to establish the purchasing standards for the operation. The first step in establishing standards is to come up with a concept for the establishment. To come up with a concept, management needs to decide who the clientele are expected to be. Then they can begin the development of the purchasing standards, based on the expectations of the restaurant created. The three standards associated with purchasing are quality, quantity and price.

The first stage to developing the quality standard is to develop a **product specification** (see Figure 5.1) and a **purchase specification** (see Figure 5.2). A product specification is a listing of all the criteria for ingredients and supplies. This will comprise information about the product's grade, color, size and place of origin. A purchase specification includes all of the information about receiving the product into the establishment, including delivery instructions, compatibility requirements, and credit terms.

FIGURE 5.1   Product Specification, Fresh Produce

Intended use: _____

Exact name: _____

U. S. grade: _____

Brand name: _____

Product size: _____

Size of container: _____

Type of packaging material: _____

Minimum weight per case: _____

Product yield: _____

Point of origin: _____

Color: _____

Product form: _____

Degree of ripeness: _____

After the quality level is established, management needs to develop the quantity standard. Quantity standards are developed based on usage, delivery schedules and warehouse capabilities. When an establishment sets the quantity standard, it usually creates a **par stock or par level.** Foodservice establishments generally establish minimum par stocks; when the inventory reaches this level it triggers the purchase of additional product. Foodservice establishments will develop order quantities and maximum par stocks. Inventory quantity control is a major function of cost control and profitability of a restaurant.

FIGURE 5.2   Purchase Specification, Fresh Produce

Credit terms: _____

Delivery schedule: _____

Supplier services: _____

Guarantee of available product: _____

Intended use: _____

Exact name: _____

U. S. grade: _____

Brand name: _____

Product size: _____

Size of container: _____

Type of packaging material: _____

Minimum weight per case: _____

Product yield: _____

Point of origin: _____

Color: _____

Product form: _____

Degree of ripeness: _____

ORDERING METHODS

When purchasing food and beverages two ordering styles are used. The first one, the **periodic order method,** will be utilized depending upon the supplier, the proximity to that supplier, and the types of products that are purchased. In this method the order dates are set at consistent intervals, and order quantities change according to the amount needed at that preset order time. This method will be used for establishments that are not near distribution centers, and areas that have pre-scheduled truck routes. An example: Every Tuesday a delivery truck comes into the area, which means that every Monday the buyer will order whatever product is needed to bring the inventory up to the maximum par level, or enough to last until the next delivery date. In the many markets where deliveries can be scheduled on a daily basis, this buying method will not be used. The calculation used to create the correct order quantity will be the same no matter how frequently deliveries are scheduled. In either buying method, buyers may include a **safety stock,** an additional amount to cover any emergency, such as unexpected increased sales or a delivery delay for the upcoming period. This may be called a safety stock, or may be referred to as a desired ending inventory. Many operations that have multiple suppliers or can obtain daily deliveries will not have a need for a safety stock, but operations without a guaranteed ability to obtain product will need to build the safety stock into their purchasing operation.

IMPORTANT FORMULA

Amount required for upcoming period
+ Desired ending inventory (safety stock)
<u>− Amount on hand</u>
= Amount to order (This number may need to be adjusted to the case amount.)

EXAMPLE PROBLEM

Periodic method
A restaurant has 33 cans of green beans in inventory and uses an average of 12 cans a day. If the desired ending inventory is one day's supply, how many cans should be purchased?

$12 \times 7 = 84 + 12$ desired ending inventory = 96 (amount needed)
<u>− 33 on hand</u>
= 63 order amount (If cans only come in cases of 6, 11 cases would need to be ordered.)

If the purchasing policy includes a safety stock, that amount would be added at this point. The safety stock may be a percentage of the order, a set amount, or the usage for a certain period of time. The method implemented will be selected after management has taken into account all the factors involved. These factors may include ability to obtain product elsewhere, or weather conditions in the area. If management decides that it needs one day's safety stock for the next period, it would then add 12 cans to the purchase quantity and order 75 cans or 7 cases.

$12 \times 7 = 84 + 12$ used before the next delivery day = 96 (amount needed)
$+ 1 \times 12 = 12$ (safety stock)
$- $ 33 on hand
= 75 order amount (if cans only come in cases of 6, 12 cases would need to be ordered)

The second method used is the **perpetual ordering method.** This is usually implemented for perishable items and items that a supplier might sell only in larger quantities. In this method, the quantity of product that can be ordered remains the same and the order dates change, fluctuating around the needs of the buyer. An example is if an establishment needs to purchase oranges by the case. When the inventory gets to a predetermined **ordering point,** the buyer orders the case for next day delivery, whatever day of the week it falls on. The ordering point is the amount of inventory needed to cover the usage of the product from the moment that the order is created, to the time the order is delivered. When using the perpetual ordering method the safety stock is added into the order point. If usage is 3 cans per day and it takes two days to deliver, the order point is 6. If a 50% safety stock is added, the order point will be 9.

IMPORTANT FORMULA

Maximum storage par stock
$- $ Ordering point
= Amount needed
+ Amount used until delivery arrives
= Amount to order (this number may need to be adjusted to the case amount)

It is very important to include the delivery timeline when preparing orders. In the periodic ordering method, this is accounted for in the formula where the inventory needed until the next delivery is calculated in. In the perpetual ordering method, the ordering point is calculated to include the usage until the delivery arrives.

EXAMPLE PROBLEM

Perpetual method

A restaurant has set a maximum par stock on #10 cans of peaches at 36. If 4 cans are used every day and it takes 1 day to receive an order, the ordering point, to ensure consistent inventory, is calculated by 4 cans per day × 1 day = 4. This is the point at which the safety stock is added. If management sets the stock at 50%, because deliveries are never more than a half-day late, 2 cans would be added, so the ordering point is set at 6.

36 Maximum par stock
− 6 Ordering point
= 30 Amount to order

At this point you need to add back in the 4 cans that will be used before the delivery comes.

30 Amount to order
+ 4 Amount that will be used before the delivery
34 Cans amount to order (Since #10 cans come 6 to a case, 6 cases would be ordered.)

WHY THIS IS IMPORTANT

When ordering food and beverage, it is essential to order the correct amount. If too little is ordered, an establishment could run out of inventory or need to increase order costs and receiving costs. If too much inventory is ordered, storage and inventory investment costs will increase and the potential for spoilage will also increase.

■

INVENTORY LEVELS

It is important in either method to know how much product is on hand. To order the correct amount of product, one must know how much product is in inventory and how much is needed. As mentioned earlier, par stock is a minimum and a maximum amount to be kept on hand; after par stock is established the buyer needs to check the forecasts for upcoming business to make any adjustment in the maximum amount on hand for the buying period. The additional products might include banquets or a change in business expectations. The two most common ways to account for inventory are the **perpetual inventory method** and a physical inventory method. In the perpetual inventory method the product is counted as an on-going, theoretical count of what should be in inventory. This could be done in the computer, where every transaction is accounted for: The warehouse started with 4 each of product A and 10 more product A were purchased and received, 8 were issued, so the warehouse ends up with 6 at the end of the period. This can also be done manually with a **bin**

card, (see Figure 5.3) which allows the warehouse receivers and issuers to write down the transactions on the card that is attached at the inventory location.

The second method is more exacting and should also be included in operations that utilize the perpetual inventory. In the **physical inventory method,** all of the products are physically counted and valued. A physical inventory should be conducted monthly and compared to the perpetual inventory. The perpetual inventory needs to be adjusted, as needed, and any discrepancies should be investigated. Many large operations conduct physical inventories on a daily or weekly basis, systematically counting one section at a time. In situations like this, the section of warehouse that is physically inventoried will not be recounted until the end of a predetermined time-frame, usually monthly.

WHY THIS IS IMPORTANT

It is imperative that every operation knows how much inventory is in stock to create orders correctly. A physical inventory is ideal, but it can be impractical in many operations to keep an accurate physical count of all inventories. Ongoing inventories will allow an operation to estimate accurately what is in stock, if security and storage standards are maintained.

■

The last standard is the cost (price) standard. This is developed using menu price and food cost principles, while keeping the clientele base and restaurant expectations in mind. Establishing a cost standard can be done in many different ways, depending on which buying plan is being utilized. Foodservice operations usually use a combination of buying plans, depending on the products they are purchasing.

First, there is a need to discuss the importance of vendor selection. There are many factors to be addressed prior to sending out bids or orders. Vendor selection is based on many factors; the chief criterion has to be the needs of the buyer and the operation. Some of the factors included in the selection process are minimum order size, delivery schedule, full or broken cases, one-stop shopping, plant visitations, references and other supplier services.

FIGURE 5.3   Bin Card, Canned Whole Peeled Tomatoes

Date		Amount	Balance
1/1	Opening inventory	6	6
1/5	Purchase	12	18
1/7	Issue	9	9
1/12	Purchase	6	15
1/16	Issue	4	11

Depending on the size of the operation, minimum orders may be a factor in which supplier is chosen to purchase from. Certain distributors have minimum orders, anywhere from $100.00 to $250.00. Smaller operations may need to limit the number of distributors they purchase from due to these minimums. Another factor for smaller operations is whether the supplier is willing to break a case or if the buyer must buy a full case of a product. This may not be a factor for a hotel or larger property, but a bed and breakfast or small café might not be able to use the whole case.

Delivery schedules are another factor. If one supplier could guarantee Monday morning delivery, the buyer might choose to buy from them, even if they are more expensive than another company that makes the buyer wait for the product. One-stop shopping is another factor in deciding from whom to purchase. If the establishment is in a small community or has limited receiving capabilities, finding a supplier for different commodities might not be practical. Many distributors carry all of the products needed, thereby lessening the amount of deliveries. Using one-stop shopping has the advantages of limiting the costs associated with ordering and receiving and its convenience, but sometimes this leads to higher prices for certain products. When choosing a qualified supplier, ask for references from other clients that use the supplier and ask them about their relationship in working with that company. Supplier selection can be clarified by a visit to the plant. A tour of the distribution facility should show the cleanliness and organization of the plant, which affects getting a quality and sanitary product into the restaurant.

Supplier services may include many intangible assets as well as measurable qualities that could be essential to supplier selection. Supplier services might include having a salesperson hand deliver a product to the restaurant if it runs out, training staff on how to use new merchandise, and helping with menu pairings or menu design. This may also include giving the property promotional material, helping supply equipment, or repairing and maintaining equipment.

BUYING METHODS

Open bid. Open bid purchasing, one of the most commonly used methods, is when an establishment sends out its specification to a variety of companies that supply the items needed. Any of the companies can put a bid on the items and send it back to the buyer. The buyer can buy all, or part, of the order from whomever solicits the lowest bid. The process is open and the buyer can then tell one company the lowest bid offered and see if they will lower their bid. In the open bid process the buyer fills out a **Stewards Market Quotation Sheet.** This sheet (see Figure 5.4) includes a list of all the products used by the establishment and a place to take inventory of what is on hand. The sheet has a column that includes the required amount of the

FIGURE 5.4   Stewards Market Quotation Sheet, Chez Nous Restaurant

Item	On Hand	Amount Needed	Amount to Purchase	Bid 1	Bid 2	Bid 3
Iceberg lettuce	4 head	28 head	24 head	22.67	23.00	22.88
5 by 6 tomatoes	5 #	10 #	5 #	4.44	4.56	4.67
Cucumbers	6 ea	18	12	3.00	2.89	3.13
Carrots	2 #	5 #	3 #	.99	1.01	1.01
Yellow squash	1 #	8 #	7 #	4.56	4.66	4.34

product for the upcoming period and a place to put the bids of at least three suppliers. After the suppliers have sent in the bids, the buyer compares the prices from the suppliers and chooses which supplier to purchase from. Many times price is not the sole determination in selecting from whom to buy.

Advantage
Can obtain the lowest cost

Disadvantage
Time consuming

Sealed bid.   A **sealed bid** is where a specification is sent out to suppliers and they send back a bid that no one else is aware of. The buyer then examines every bid and chooses one over the others due to price or other factors like timeliness or reputation. Sealed bids can be re-sent out after the first round and re-bid on by the suppliers. This method is not used much in food and beverage, but is used often in purchasing furniture, fixtures and equipment.

Cost plus.   This is a very common buying plan used in the industry in which the buyer and the supplier agree upon a set mark-up for the product. This mark-up could be an agreed upon price per case or an agreed upon percentage mark-up. This is most commonly used in produce purchasing and has pros and cons associated with both sides of the negotiation. The biggest factor with **cost plus** purchasing is developing a trusting relationship between the buyer and the supplier.

Advantage
Generally lower prices per dollar volume
Do not have to get quotes

Disadvantage
Who determines the costs?
Only one relationship with supplier

This method of purchasing usually creates a win-win situation with a distributor and buyer. Many distributors who engage in cost plus purchasing will then be able to negotiate with their growers, manufacturers and processors to lower their costs due to increased and consistent business. With the increased business, the distributor may also be able to negotiate for higher quality supplies, due to increased volume of business.

Co-operative (co-op).   A common type of purchasing for small operations and foodservice establishments located in small communities is the **co-op** purchasing method. In co-op purchasing small buyers combine their purchasing needs with those of others in the co-op. The co-op then purchases the items in a larger quantity, with higher purchasing power, usually receiving a volume discount. When the products are delivered, the co-op manager splits the order among the many buyers.

One-stop shopping.   In this style of purchasing, the buyer purchases everything from one company that can supply all of its needs. There are few companies in the industry that can supply everything that an establishment needs, but in major markets it is common. Some of the national companies that supply **one-stop shopping** include U.S. Foodservice and Sysco. This type of purchasing plan is used very frequently in major national chains since they can usually supply the product, according to their specification, to any establishment throughout the country. Major chains usually establish corporate recipes and national distribution plans that give a consistent product when purchased anywhere in the country. For this to happen, the raw products need to be the same throughout the country. This is done with national distribution chains that supply everything that a restaurant or franchise would need.

Advantage	**Disadvantage**
Convenience	Less control of quality
Lower prices	Higher prices
	Ties you to one vendor

Contract.   Corporate chains, as well as some independent restaurants, also purchase products after negotiating a **contract** with a supplier. A contract is for a set period, and guarantees price and product availability to the buyer. Contracts are usually written for perishable items that have price fluctuations. Negotiations for prices on contracts can help make an establishment profitable and if written correctly for the buyer should not hurt the restaurant.

Advantage	**Disadvantage**
If market price rises, good for business	If it drops, bad for business
Set price for a certain period	

Warehouse buying.   This form of purchasing is used by smaller operations and is the least convenient for the foodservice operation. **Warehouse buying** usually includes the need to shop and carry back the product oneself.

Advantage	Disadvantage
Good for small quantities	Need to pick up

Standing/standard order. This form of purchasing is used when the restaurant has an order with a distributor that is the same for every delivery period. The order may be 10 dozen rolls every Monday and Wednesday, or 10 dozen on Monday and 15 dozen on every Wednesday. The product is delivered at a set time and date each week. Another form of **standing order** is when the distributor brings the quantity of inventory to a predetermined amount on a regular basis. An example of this is if the spice distributor comes into the storeroom every other week and takes the inventory of what is in stock. If the inventory level does not have enough of any of the products used they leave the additional amount, bringing the storeroom up to par.

Advantage	Disadvantage
Salesperson does the order	Does not take into account special orders

Centralized purchasing.   **Centralized purchasing** is done with multiple properties and franchises, where the corporate office develops the product specification and the purchasing contracts. The local establishment and the local buyer contact the suppliers or company distribution centers to obtain the product.

Advantage	Disadvantage
Minimum work	Lack of ability to purchase locally
Consistent product in any location	No local distributor

On-line purchasing.   The fastest growing segment of all of the buying plans mentioned is **on-line purchasing** plans like Purchase Pro. This type of buying allows the buyer to send out the specification to anyone connected to the system; they can bid on the item in real time and within the parameters set up by the buyer. This allows the buyer to pick and choose which products they buy from the list of suppliers that have submitted bids.

Advantage	Disadvantage
Low price	Lack of personal contact

WHY THIS IS IMPORTANT

Many buying plans are available. The selection of the correct one for an establishment will be based on the type of product being purchased, the amount of product being purchased, and the variety of suppliers available that sell the specific merchandise.

■

HOW MUCH PRODUCT IS NEEDED?

Purchasing food in the correct amount is paramount in the success of an operation and its ability to make money. To order the proper amount of food one must have a basic understanding of some of the terms and formulas needed in the kitchen. Two very important terms used with food are **edible portion (EP)** and **as purchased (AP).** These two terms take into account the **yield percent** of food products, or how much product is lost during processing. There are two ways that these terms are used: with the weight of a product, and with the cost of the product. When purchasing food, in order to procure the appropriate amount, the buyer needs to calculate how much to buy to prepare a recipe. This will depend upon how the recipe reads.

If a recipe reads:

10 Pounds of carrots, peeled and sliced
the chef needs 10 pounds of carrots and then they are peeled and sliced.

If the recipe reads:

10 Pounds of peeled and sliced carrots
enough carrots need to be purchased so that after they are peeled
and sliced there are 10 pounds.

The question in this example is, how much needs to be purchased to have 10 pounds of edible product? To correctly calculate how much to purchase (AP), the following formula is used.

IMPORTANT FORMULA

AP = EP/Yield percent

When using this formula, for the second recipe above, it is known that 10 pounds of edible product are needed and the unknown is the yield percent for carrots. The yield percent can be either calculated or looked up. Many trade publications and websites list yield percents of different products, or the chef can calculate yield by buying some of the product and trimming it, then weighing the edible product. The chef would then divide the usable product by the amount purchased to come up with the yield percent.

If 10 pounds of carrots were purchased and after being peeled and trimmed the end result is 8 pounds of edible carrots:

8 Pounds/10 Pounds = 80% Yield

If the chef needed 10 pounds of peeled and sliced carrots, what quantity needs to be purchased? Using the figure in the above yield percent example and the formula listed above:

EXAMPLE PROBLEM

AP = 10 Pounds/ .80 yield percent
AP = 12.5 Pounds

Using the same information the chef can calculate how many pounds of peeled and sliced carrots will be available, knowing the quantity of raw carrots started with. To correctly calculate how much edible product (EP) will be left, use the following formula.

IMPORTANT FORMULA

$$EP = AP \times \text{Yield percent}$$

If the chef had 10 pounds of raw carrots, how much peeled and sliced carrots will be produced? Using the figure in the above yield example, and the formula listed above:

EXAMPLE PROBLEM

EP = 10 Pounds $\times$ .80
EP = 8 Pounds

These formulas, along with the butcher's yield and cooking loss test (which will be discussed in Chapter 7), are paramount in knowing the proper amount of product to order. Without these formulas, the buyer would not be able to order the correct amount of product and would either spend extra money buying product that was not needed, or not buying enough product and running out of an item.

When purchasing a product, as in the carrots in the above example, one of the decisions to be made is whether to buy the product in its AP or EP form. Using the same formulas described above, calculation of true costs associated with buying products in their AP or EP state can be made. If the carrots used in the previous example cost $1.00 per pound in the raw unpeeled and untrimmed state (AP), how much will the product cost, after trimming, in the ready to use (EP) state? In the example above, 10 pounds of carrots were purchased at $1.00 per pound for a total of $10.00. When done with preparation there are 8 pounds left. The 8 pounds of edible carrots actually cost $10.00 to obtain.

EXAMPLE PROBLEM

EP cost = AP cost/yield
EP cost = $10/8 Pounds
EP cost = $1.25 per Pound

When deciding how to buy the product, whether in the EP or AP form the chef, buyer and owner would have to make the decision based on actual price per pound calculated using this formula. Management would also have to take into account the quality of the product and the savings associated with a decrease in the labor associated with the prepared product.

HOW MUCH TO PURCHASE

When purchasing goods or creating a requisition list, it is imperative to take into account that there may be a loss when preparing these foods for production. The correct edible yield, or loss percent, needs to be a component in creating purchase orders. Yield percent figures are available in many places, including product identification websites, purchasing manuals or through a product cutting or a hands-on yield analysis. When calculating how much product to purchase, a simple formula is enlisted to ensure that the correct amount of product is purchased so that after the trimming, the yield will be the amount needed to complete the recipe successfully. To purchase accurately the correct amount, one needs to assume that the yield percent would be similar among the entire product being processed. No matter where the yield percent figure comes from, it is assumed that all of the product will be very close to this figure in actual yield. The best way to ensure this is to purchase from responsible distributors and to always use a specification when purchasing. Once the average yield percent is established, the following formula can be utilized to purchase the correct amount.

The first calculation needed is how many pounds of processed product are needed to serve the number of customers forecasted. After this is established, you need to calculate how much raw product needs to be purchased so that after processing, the desired quantity is obtained.

EXAMPLE PROBLEM

As an example, if a banquet menu serving 100 people had mashed potatoes as an accompaniment item, the serving size is 4 oz. and the industry average yield percent of potatoes is 75%, the calculation of how much product to purchase is as follows:

100 × 4 oz. = 400 oz.
400 oz. /. 75 = 533.33 oz.
533.33 oz. / 16 (ounces per pound) = 33.33 pounds, or 33 pounds and 5⅓ ounces

---

This illustrates that to obtain 25 pounds of edible product (EP), 33⅓ pounds of raw product would need to be purchased. Without this calculation, the buyer might purchase too much or too little of a product to successfully fulfill the banquet's needs. If too much product is purchased, the establishment will not make money, and if too little product is purchased, the customers will not be satisfied.

This formula can be utilized with any product that has a loss during preparation or production:

Number of servings × weight per serving = Total ounces needed

Total ounces needed divided by yield percent = Total ounces to purchase

Total ounces purchased divided by unit of purchase (16 ounces in a pound, 8 ounces in a cup, 16 ounces in a pint, 32 ounces in a quart, 128 ounces in a gallon) = amount to purchase.

WHY THIS IS IMPORTANT

Without taking into account the edible yield percent of foods, it is very likely that a buyer will either purchase too much or too little of a product. Exact calculation for purchasing is a very important component of profitability, due to little waste and the potential to run out of menu items, creating fewer sales or customer dissatisfaction.

■

SUMMARY

■ The methods of purchasing are discussed and the differences between the different methods are discussed. There are many pros and cons to using any of the methods discussed, and the correct decision on which system to use is dependent upon each individual operation. The important discussion differentiating between the edible portion and the as-purchased portion are key terms and factors in successful food and beverage cost control.

KEY TERMS

Product specification

Purchase specification

Par stock/par level

Periodic order method

Safety stock

Perpetual ordering method

Ordering point

Perpetual inventory method

Bin card

Physical inventory method

Open bid

Steward's Market Quotation Sheet

Sealed bid   Standing/standard order
Cost plus   Centralized purchasing
Co-operative (co-op)   On-line purchasing
One-stop shopping   Edible portion (EP)
Contract   As purchased (AP)
Warehouse buying   Yield percent

WEBSITES

http://www.life.ca/nl/63/food.html   www.usfoodservice.com
www.purchasepro.com   www.foodsupplier.com/
www.sysco.com

PROBLEMS

1. What is the difference between a product specification and a purchase specification?
2. Why is yield percent a key factor when purchasing food?
3. What are the advantages and disadvantages of cost plus purchasing?
4. Why is edible portion important when purchasing food?
5. Why is the "as purchased" amount a critical figure when purchasing?
6. Explain at least three methods of finding edible yield percent.
7. How much product should be purchased if a banquet is booked for 200 people and every guest will have a 4-ounce serving of broccoli with a 60% yield?
8. In the above example, what is the EP cost of the broccoli if the AP cost is $0.75 per pound?
9. How much product should be purchased if a banquet is booked for 100 people and every guest will have a 6-ounce serving of soup with a 95% yield factor?
10. In the above example, if the soup cost $14.00 per gallon to purchase, how much is the cost per serving?
11. If carrots cost $0.40 per pound and they have a 75% edible yield, what is the edible portion cost?
12. If you are serving a banquet to 171 people, how much product do you need to purchase, and how much should the selling price be if the meal has a 17.5% food cost?

Item	Serving Size	Edible Yield	Price per Pound
Steak	10 oz.	85%	5.78
Mashed potatoes	4 oz.	75%	.29
Green beans	4 oz.	81%	.89

13. Why is a product specification important in food purchasing?

14. Describe five of the purchasing methods discussed in the chapter.

15. How is a Steward's Market Quotation Sheet used in bid purchasing?

16. Explain the difference between the periodic and the perpetual ordering methods.

17. Explain the difference between the physical inventory and the perpetual inventory.

18. Calculate the order amount for the following scenario using the periodic order method.

   Daily usage: 4 cans
   Open every day
   Eight cans in stock
   Delivery every 2 weeks
   Safety stock: 3 days

19. If using the periodic ordering method, determine the proper ordering amount using the following information.

   Placing orders every 2 weeks
   Open 7 days a week
   Normal daily usage 3 pounds
   Inventory on hand: 5 pounds
   Order quantity: 6-pound packages
   Safety stock: 2 days

20. If using the perpetual ordering method, determine the ordering point and ordering amount using the following information.

   Daily usage: 4 cans
   Delivery time: 2 days
   Maximum par stock: 43
   Safety stock: 25%

21. If using the perpetual ordering method determine the ordering point and the ordering amount using the following information.

   Maximum storage amount: 100 pounds
   Normal daily usage: 3 pounds
   Delivery time: 2 days
   Order quantity: 4-pound units
   Safety stock: 6 pounds

22. If using the periodic ordering method, determine the proper ordering amount using the following information.

    Desired ending inventory: 6 cans
    Delivery once a week
    Open 6 days
    Next day delivery
    Usage: 4 cans per day
    Inventory on hand is 10

23. If using the perpetual ordering method, determine the ordering point and the proper ordering amount of chicken breasts using the following information.

    Maximum inventory: 200 pieces
    Daily use: 21 pieces
    Delivery time: 1 day
    One-day safety stock
    24 chicken breast in one case

6
Controls in Food Receiving, Storage, and Issuing

Chapter Objectives

After finishing this chapter the student will be able to:

Understand product terminology connected with the flow of food

Differentiate among the three receiving standards

Understand receiving techniques

Understand storage principle

Differentiate between directs and stores

Understand issuing practices

Calculate the value of inventory via different methods, including:
   FIFO
   LIFO
   Weighted average
   Last purchase price
   Actual price

Use formulas including: Average inventory and inventory turnover

Introduction

This chapter follows the flow of food through an operation. We examine the controls put in place for obtaining and maintaining the quality and quantity of the products used in a foodservice operation. It is essential for profitability that the quality and quantity of the product does not decrease throughout the flow of the food within any operation.

RECEIVING

After the purchase of a product, the next step in the flow of food and money through an operation is to the receiving department. Many establishments do not stay in business due to improper receiving, or improper receiving standards. For effective receiving, management needs to establish standards for the receiving department. This will ensure that the correct supplies are being properly received.

The receiving department has three standards they are accountable for. These three standards go along with the purchasing standards set up in the previous chapter: quality, quantity, and cost (price). In the receiving department, the job of the receivers is to ensure that these standards are met.

Receivers need to verify that the *quality* of the product is the same quality that was ordered. For the receivers to do their job effectively, they must have information to comply with the company standards. The information needed for the receiver to ensure that the quality delivered and received is the same as that ordered is a copy of the specification written for each product.

With the specification on hand, the receiver can check the quality of the product and compare it to the company standard.

The second standard that needs to be met is the *quantity* standard. For this standard to be verified, the receivers need a copy of the purchase order. The receiver cross-references the delivery invoice with the purchase order to ensure that the quantity of the product received is the same that was ordered.

The third standard is the *cost* standard. The receivers will also cross-reference the delivery invoice with the purchase order that will include the prices for the product ordered. Some of the equipment that the receivers need to do their job are a scale, thermometer, calculator and a knife, to inspect the inside and taste certain products, most notably fruit.

WHY THIS IS IMPORTANT

If the right product is not received at the right price, it is very hard to make money in a hospitality operation.

■

In larger operations, one of the most important aspects of the receiving job is to fill out the **receiving sheet,** which includes a list of all of the delivery invoices for the day. The sheet is a checks and balances system for the receiving and accounts payable departments. At the end of the shift, the receiving clerk forwards all of the delivery invoices and the receiving sheet to accounts payable so that all of the paperwork can be processed and all of the orders are accounted for (see Figure 6.1).

Receiving Sheet	**Karyn's Hotel and Health Spa**	September 8, 2005
Invoice Number	Company Name	Invoice amount
Total		

FIGURE 6.1 Receiving Sheet

STORING

After the product is received, the next step is storage. One of the main principles in storage is the practice of FIFO, first in first out. This principle is a basic tenet of storage. The rotation of stock allows for older products to be used first, before time lessens the quality of the product. While practicing FIFO, storage personnel have other standards to be maintained. Storage standards include the protection of the product's quality, protection from theft, and accessibility of the product.

For storage personnel to maintain the quality of products in the warehouse, they must have sufficient and appropriate equipment and supplies. Although the National Restaurant Association advocates food storage as below 41°F, lower temperatures will maintain quality and shelf life of many products. Proper storage facilities include temperature and humidity controls that differ with every product. Some generally accepted temperatures:

Item	Temperature
Beef	34–38°F
Poultry	28–32°F
Fish	32–36°F
Live shellfish	30–40°F
Eggs	40–45°F
Dairy	35–41°F
Fruits and vegetables	34–50°F
Freezer	0°F
Dry storage	70°F

Humidity levels for fruits and vegetables are very high (85–95%) while humidity levels for dry storage need to be around 70%. Ideal storage for each of these products is in individual refrigerators so that the temperature and humidity can be controlled according to each product's need.

The second storage standard is to prevent the product from theft and pilferage. Although it is hard to design an establishment such as a restaurant against theft, there are many ways of preventing against pilferage. Although theft and pilferage are similar, pilferage is considered to be taking smaller items, theft larger items.

The first basic means of controlling inventory from pilferage is to have checks and balances in distribution. If the restaurant has the same person running purchasing and receiving, storing and/or issuing there is the potential for dishonesty. Many operations cannot afford to hire different people for each of these positions, or have the need for them; in facilities that cannot hire multiple employees, it is imperative to have someone trustworthy in these positions. One way to have a higher expectation of honesty is to hire people for these positions that belong to professional organizations that endorse a code of ethics. Although this does not guarantee honesty, it at least allows some ease of mind in knowing that the employees have been made aware of the ethics needed to be successful in the industry.

After hiring the right employees, management still needs to take other steps to ensure the security of the products. One easy precaution to take in a warehouse to prevent pilferage is to limit access to the facilities. If there are few controls in place on who is allowed to enter the facility, the potential for stealing is greater. By limiting access during regular working hours in the warehouse to only those directly involved in the distribution of the food, and limiting access during other hours to only one person, the possibility of pilferage is greatly reduced. The location of the warehouse with regard to the rest of the facility is also paramount in protecting the product. Warehouses should not be located near parking garages or other places where product could be hidden for later pickup.

WHY THIS IS IMPORTANT

Due to the perishable nature of the product, if inventory quality and quantity is not maintained, food cost will rise and profitability will decrease.

■

An additional step in securing the product is to develop a system that prevents the wrong product from leaving the facility: developing a **warehouse requisition form** that departments fill out before taking product out of storage. These forms are then used to pull the inventory and to charge the appropriate department for the materials taken out of storage (see Figure 6.2).

The third goal of storage is to ensure accessibility to the products. This depends on the hours of operation of the warehouse. If the warehouse is open 24 hours a day, accessibility is not necessarily an issue. Most warehouses usually are not open 24/7; policy needs to be set in regard to afterhours requisi-

FIGURE 6.2 Warehouse Requisition Form

Derricks Hotel

Storeroom Requisition

Department _____

Quantity	Item Number	Item Description	Price per Unit	Total Price
2 Each	12345	Iceberg lettuce	12.00	24.00
1 Case	23456	5 × 6 tomato	18.75	18.75
			Total cost	42.75

tions. In some businesses there is no way to get product after the warehouse is closed, so in these situations requisitions need to have a safety stock added to them. Generally speaking, the hospitality industry is not a standardized industry with the same number of customers every shift, so an added amount of product to ensure not running out of items may be necessary. Another option is controlled accessibility after hours, with someone having responsibility to allow others in to remove and account for product.

Within accessibility of the product, the internal layout of the warehouse is also essential. When designing the warehouse, products should be laid out effectively and efficiently to allow easy access. Products should be located with similar products, such as condiments together and baking goods together. For liquor storage, all of the vodkas should be stored together and all of the bourbons together.

Products that come into a receiving area can be grouped within many different categories. Storage standards will be different for many of these categories. Management can keep track of inventory by broad category of items such as meats, dairy, produce, dry goods, beer, and liquor. By categorizing the products like this, management can keep track of how the money is being spent and how much value each set of products has in the storage facility. Another way to differentiate products is to classify them as **directs** and **stores.** Directs are products that go directly to the department that utilizes them, and bypass the storeroom both physically and for accounting purposes. A charge for directs will get added to the department's costs immediately upon receiving them. Directs might include products that are used only by one outlet in a facility, or they may be products that are delivered and replaced on a daily basis. Directs might also include expensive items that the warehouse is not able to store safely. Stores get put into the warehouse and the products are distributed as needed. At the later date, when the products are requested and delivered, the charges are transferred to the department requesting them.

Another way to differentiate product is by perishable and non-perishable categories. Perishable products are products that decay or spoil in a short period of time or without a proper storage environment. Throughout the process of receiving and storing of products, employees must take special care of products that are perishable. When inventory spoils, the loss in value is a direct negative line item on the profitability of a restaurant. Non-perishable foods still need care taken while flowing through an operation, but the risk of losing product due to mishandling is greatly reduced.

As mentioned in the previous chapter, warehouses need to complete a physical inventory at least monthly, to compare to the perpetual inventories that are done in an on-going manner. Many operations, including some high volume restaurants, do a daily or weekly inventory. The advantage of more frequent inventories is the ability to notice any discrepancies before they become larger issues. If weekly inventories are completed and something is amiss—a new employee unaware of a standard operating procedure, or someone pilfering—the immediacy of catching the mistake can be worth the costs associated with taking inventory.

INVENTORY VALUATION

When taking the physical inventory, besides counting the quantity of the items in storage, a value is given to every item. This figure is essential when calculating food cost and food cost percent. There are many ways to calculate inventory value. The results from the different methods will give different totals. When calculating values of inventory, it is imperative that management consistently use the same method from period to period to ensure accuracy. Different methods give varied final values, and costs of food, if the prices fluctuate during the period between inventories. The five most common types of **inventory valuation** are FIFO, LIFO, weighted average, actual price, and last price methods.

The FIFO method of valuing inventory is done using the first in first out method of putting a value on products in inventory. At the end of the period the remaining products are valued at the latest purchase prices. As an example: If a restaurant were purchasing cases of oranges and wanted to have a value at the end of the period, management would need to know how much product the restaurant started with, what the purchase price of the product was, the documents showing what was purchased and at what price throughout the period. In this example, it is assumed that the restaurant had 4 cases of oranges at the beginning of the period and the cost was $29.00 per case. The restaurant then purchased 6 cases of oranges at $30.00 per case, 4 cases at $30.50 per case, and 6 cases at $31.00 per case. At the end of the period there were 9 cases remaining in the establishment, and they need to be valued. This value will then be used to calculate cost of food issued.

EXAMPLE PROBLEM

In this example the total outlay of money is

4 Cases $\times$ $29.00 = $116.00

6 Cases $\times$ $30.00 = $180.00

4 Cases $\times$ $30.50 = $122.00

6 Cases $\times$ $31.00 = $186.00

Total $604.00

For a perpetual inventory, when using a bin card for the inventory count you will have to calculate the remaining cases by adding purchases to opening inventory and subtracting out the issues.

EXAMPLE PROBLEM

Using the same figures as above, you can calculate that there are 9 cases left and the total value is the same $604.00.

1/1	Opening inventory 4 cases valued at $29.00 each
1/3	Purchased 6 cases at $30.00
1/7	Issued 5 cases
1/10	Purchased 4 cases at $30.50
1/11	Issued 6 cases
1/13	Purchased 6 cases at $31.00

Using the **First In First Out (FIFO) method,** there would be 6 cases left that cost $31.00 each and 3 cases that cost $30.50 per case, for a total of $277.50 in inventory left at the end of the period. This equates to a food cost of $326.50. If FIFO practices are strictly enforced this method will give a very accurate accounting of the value of the inventory and how much was spent to purchase the inventory.

The **Last In First Out (LIFO) method** is used when a particular accounting result is wanted that other methods may not bring about. When using the Last In First Out method of valuation, storeroom personnel continue to use FIFO in the storeroom for distribution of product, but after the physical inventory is completed the first prices paid for the products are used to figure out the value. In the example above there would be 4 cases that cost $29.00 each and 5 cases that cost $30.00 each, for a inventory value of $266.00 and a total food cost of $338.00.

The **weighted average price method** takes the average of all the cases purchased and gives that value to the remaining cases. In this example 20 cases were purchased for $604.00, giving each case an average purchase price of $30.20. In the example used there are 9 cases remaining, with a value of $271.80 and a food cost of $332.20. This method will give the most varied results during financially fluctuating times, but for items that are not commodities this method works well.

When using the **actual price method,** only the cases that are actually labeled with a price can be calculated. Without the actual price on each item left in storage there is no way to say with accuracy what the cost of each product is. This method is not used in large operations due to the labor involved in marking each item and physically reading the label during inventory. This type of inventory may be done in a small operation without a formal storeroom structure.

The **last price method** is the most accurate method of valuing inventory at that moment. The last purchase price method is the replacement cost associated with the product. In the example given, if the 9 cases needed replacement it would cost $31.00 per case, for a total value of $279.00 and a total food cost of $327.00.

The key element of placing a value on the cost of food issued is to remember that total expenditures for each of the five examples are $604.00. Each of the ending inventories is subtracted from the expenditure to find the cost of the food. To compare the differences between these methods the chart below shows the different methods, the inventory values, and food costs associated with these accounting principles. This is for only one product out of many that a restaurant would use.

Method	Ending Inventory Value	Food Cost
FIFO	$277.50	$326.50
LIFO	$266.00	$338.00
Weighted Average Price	$271.80	$332.20
Actual Price	Can not calculate in this example	Can not calculate in this example
Last Price	$279.00	$327.00

Once inventory calculations are done on individual items they are compared to the perpetual inventory bin cards, and the perpetual inventory is reconciled to agree with the physical inventory. The total book (perpetual) value is then compared to the total actual (physical) value. Once the totals are compared, any discrepancies should be investigated. The advantage of frequent physical inventories is that if there are discrepancies, they can be investigated and corrected in shorter timeframes.

WHY THIS IS IMPORTANT

Establishments need to perform a physical inventory at least once a month. The value system chosen will usually remain the same within an operation, but each operation chooses the method to create a total inventory value of merchandise in stock. Operations are required to use the same method when reporting taxes and informing shareholders.

■

INVENTORY TURNOVER

One of the many internal methods of checking the quality of work for the purchasing staff is evaluating **inventory turnover.** Inventory turnover is the average number of times that the value of inventory is replaced in the storeroom. Inventory turnover varies within the industry, depending on what type of restaurant is being operated. When using inventory turnover as a check on the purchasing department, management needs to investigate if the inventory turnover is higher or lower than industry standards or the standards set by the operation. Most full service restaurants run an **average inventory** turnover of between 20 and 25 times a year, while fast food runs 150 times a year. For full service restaurants this equates to the inventory value turning every other week, while in fast food the inventory will turn 3 times a week. Liquor inventory turns less frequently, averaging between 7 and 12 times a year or once a month. There are many restaurants within the industry that do not follow this standard and have many daily deliveries of goods, and a turnover rate much higher than this.

If inventory turnover is higher than expected, it means that the operation is spending extra money on the costs associated with purchasing. Differences of opinions exist concerning the dollar value of the ordering costs. Depending on the size and scope of the operation, many estimate that it costs $20 to $30 for each order, while others may set the cost as low as $3 and as high as $130. If an establishment has high inventory turnover there is the potential of running out of an item, which has additional negative effects on business, besides the direct costs associated with the purchase.

If inventory turnover is lower than what has been established as the standard, then the purchasing staff has tied up money that could be used elsewhere in the establishment. When money is tied up, management needs to evaluate where the money could be used more efficiently. Money can be used to pay other bills or sit in the bank earning interest. Besides the cost associated with tying up the money, there are additional expenses with excess product in storage. Although many operations have tried to calculate storage costs there are no concrete industry standards. Annual estimates run between 10 and 25 percent of the value of inventory, meaning that for every one hundred dollars that is tied up on the shelf, an expected storage cost will be somewhere between 10 and 25 dollars per year.[*]

To calculate inventory turnover, use the following formula.

IMPORTANT FORMULA

$$\frac{\text{Opening inventory} + \text{closing inventory}}{2} = \text{Average inventory}$$

$$\frac{\text{Cost of goods sold (issues)}}{\text{Average inventory}} = \text{Inventory turnover}$$

[*]Feinstein and Stefanelli, *Purchasing Selection and Procurement for the Hospitality Industry*, 5th edition, John Wiley & Sons, Inc., 2002.

EXAMPLE PROBLEM

If a restaurant has a monthly opening inventory (last month's closing inventory) of $15,000 and a closing inventory of $12,000 and yearly purchases of $321,000:

$15,000 + $321,000 − $12,000 = $324,000 (Cost of goods sold)

$$\frac{\$15,000 + \$12,000}{2} = \$13,500 \text{ Average inventory}$$

$$\frac{\$324,000}{\$13,500} = 24 \text{ (Inventory turnover)}$$

This figure shows that two times a month (24 times a year divided by 12 months) the inventory is rotated through the warehouse. This does not mean that every single thing in the warehouse is rotated; only the value of inventory is rotated. Industry standards will vary among the many varieties of food service establishments, with full service restaurants averaging around two times a month and fast food averaging close to three times a week, or 150 times a year. These figures can and will vary greatly depending on the operation, its location, storage facilities, the cash flow, and management's philosophy. Often management will use inventory turnover to assess personnel and establish job performance standards. If a purchaser runs high figures a bonus may not be earned, and employment may not be retained.

WHY THIS IS IMPORTANT

If too much money is invested in inventory, besides the risk of product spoiling, an operation may also create a negative cash flow scenario. If too little money is invested in inventory, besides the chance for running out of a menu item, expenses might increase in purchasing and receiving expenses.

■

ISSUING

The main function of the issuing department is to ensure that no product is ever to be taken out of the warehouse without a requisition sheet correctly filled out and/or a charge slip filled out. By accounting for all of the products that are in inventory, accurate cost control can take place. Additionally, prior to leaving the storage area, requisitions should go through a **checkpoint** to make sure all of the products are accounted for. This is similar to the employee checking the shopping basket when leaving a warehouse buying club. The checkpoint actually is useful for the entire operation, as the department that is getting the product will get a double check to make sure everything ordered is delivered and charged correctly. This will save labor in re-requisitioning something or questioning charges for items not delivered. It will also protect the warehouse employees for honest mistakes.

WHY THIS IS IMPORTANT

If inventory is allowed to leave a storage area without being charged to a particular department, effective cost control can never be realized.

■

SUMMARY

- The methods of receiving, storing and issuing were discussed and the need to have strict control over these departments for financial control were related within each operation.
- The important methods of valuing inventory through the industry-accepted methods of equating a value to the storeroom inventory and the connection to cost control in an operation were discussed.
- How to calculate average inventory and how to utilize this formula to calculate inventory turnover was described.
- Why inventory average and inventory average figures are important was discussed.

KEY TERMS

Receiving sheet   Weighted average price method
Warehouse requisition form   Actual price method
Directs   Last price method
Stores   Average inventory
Inventory valuation   Inventory turnover
FIFO method   Checkpoint
LIFO method

PROBLEMS

1. Why is a receiving sheet important in a large operation?
2. What are the differences between a direct and a store?
3. List three principles of proper storage.
4. What is the difference between FIFO storage practices and FIFO inventory control?

5. Using the following data, calculate closing inventory, calculate the value of the closing inventory and the cost of food issued, using the five methods given in the chapter (FIFO, LIFO, actual, latest purchase price, and weighted price):

1/1	Opening inventory 6 cans valued at $1.39 each
1/3	Purchased 12 cans at $1.46
1/7	Issued 8 cans
1/10	Purchased 6 cans at $1.35
1/11	Issued 6 cans
1/13	Purchased 12 cans at $1.41

6. Why would you utilize the different methods of inventory value calculations?

7. If opening inventory is valued at $34,362 and closing inventory is valued at $25,435, with food purchases at $69,745 and food sales at $181,456, what is the average inventory turnover for this establishment?

8. Give an example of when you would not utilize the industry standards when calculating inventory turnover.

9. Calculate the ending inventory value and the cost of food issued for each of the five inventory methods assuming there are 12 cans at the end of the month. (FIFO, LIFO, actual, latest purchase price, and weighted price)

   Purchases
   9 cans @ $8.25
   6 cans @ $8.44
   12 cans @ $8.65
   18 cans @ $8.78
   6 cans @ $8.50

10. Calculate inventory turnover given the following:

Opening inventory	$11,254
Closing inventory	$13,789
Food cost	$259,500

11. Explain how food cost can be affected in three points in the flow of food through an operation.

12. Although health code states that food should be held under 40°F, why would you have more specific temperatures for certain items?

13. Calculate the ending inventory, ending inventory value, and the cost of food issued for each of the five inventory methods, assuming there are 30 # beef at the end of the month. (FIFO, LIFO, actual, latest purchase price, and weighted price)

Purchases

25# @ $1.59
20# @ $1.69
30# @ $1.61
20# @ $1.52

14. What is the food and beverage inventory turnover average for a full service restaurant?

15. What is the inventory average for a fast food restaurant?

7
Controls in Food Production

Chapter Objectives

After finishing this chapter the student will be able to:

Understand the need and usage of a production schedule

Understand the need and usage of a standardized recipe

Understand the need and usage of a standard portion size including:
  Volume
  Count
  Weight

Calculate standard portion cost

Understand the concept of yield factor/percent

Complete a butcher's yield and a cooking loss test

Evaluate causes of over/under-production

Calculate daily and to date food costs

Understand the concept of potential savings

Introduction

This chapter follows the flow of food through an operation. Although this terminology can be used in many contexts, we are examining the control of both quality and quantity of product through the many facets of the property that interact with the product. It is a very important to keep the quality of the product through an operation. If the quality of the food is not maintained, it is very hard to obtain profits.

THE ROLE OF MANAGEMENT

The food and beverage management's role in the cost control during production begins with the establishment of the standards of production. Once standards have been established, management must train employees to adhere to the standards that have been created. If the cost, menu price and selling standards are all adhered to, the establishment should make a profit. If the cost standard is not followed, either due to a higher purchase or production cost, profitability will be questionable. Once a food cost is established, the continuity of the costs needs to be maintained.

During reconciliation of the production and sales data if the costs are not what they should be, management needs to investigate the variance between the **real portion cost** and the **planned portion cost.** These terms are also called **standard costs** and **actual costs.** Standard or planned portion costs are what is calculated by management and are the established standard. Every dish that leaves the restaurant should cost the standard amount. This calculation is created by one of the following methods; if the procedures are adhered to, they should be accurate. If through observation or an investigation differences are observed and the true costs are higher or lower, management needs to correct the actions that lead to the discrepancies.

FOOD PRODUCTION SCHEDULE

One of the most fundamental components of food cost control is the implementation of the **production schedule** (see Figure 7.1). The production schedule is a list of items that need to be prepared for the upcoming shift to ensure that the employees have the **mise en place,** known as the prepared product, to sell the anticipated covers. Anticipated individual sales figures are calculated by multiplying the **popularity index,** the menu mix percent, by the total sales forecast for the timeframe. This information is then transferred to the production schedule to assure that the correct amount of product is prepared. After the preparation par stocks are inserted into the list, an inventory of what is already prepared is taken. This number is subtracted from the par stock and the resulting number is the amount that should be prepared.

Fundamental to the effective use of the production schedule is that the production and distribution standards be continually met. These standards will include the standard recipe formulas as well as the standard portion size quantity. If both of these standards are being met, this helps ensure that the standard portion costs are also being met.

FIGURE 7.1   Production Schedule

Quantity On Hand	Quantity Needed	Quantity To Make	Item
6	11	5	Hamburgers
4	22	18	12 oz N. Y. steak
12	27	15	Breaded chicken breast

WHY THIS IS IMPORTANT

Preparing the correct amount of food is essential due to how perishable many food products are.

■

THE STANDARDIZED RECIPE

The **standardized recipe** is a recipe that is created specifically for an establishment and is written in a form that should be easily read by anyone preparing the dish. The recipe uses standard terms, measuring techniques, and equipment. By using industry standards to create the recipe, anyone who is familiar with the standards should be able to follow the recipe. This ensures that the product always tastes the same, as well as facilitates the calculations of the standard costs associated with the dish. If the standardized recipe is followed, the dish should cost the same every time it is prepared. If the price

FIGURE 7.2   Standardized Recipe

Product Name: Poached chicken breast Princesse Portion Size: 1 Chicken breast Cooking Time: 30 min.			Yield: 12 servings Pan Size: 2″ hotel pan Temperature: 325°F
Ingredients	**Quantity**		**Procedure**
	Wt	**Vl**	
Chicken breast, boneless, skinless Salt White pepper Lemon juice Chicken stock, cold Butter	12 ea. tt tt As needed	 2 tbsp 3c	Butter inside of pan. Season chicken. Add lemon juice and stock. Cover with parchment paper (buttered) or wax paper. Bring to simmer on stove and finish in oven at 325°F, 5–10 min. Remove chicken and keep warm.
Butter, softened Flour Heavy cream, hot Salt	1½ oz 1½ oz	 1¼ c tt	Reduce poaching liquid by half. Knead butter and flour together. Add to liquid with wire whip and cook 1 min to thicken. Add hot cream and season.
Asparagus tips	36 ea.		Serve each breast with 2 oz of sauce and 3 asparagus tips.

of an ingredient changes, the new standard cost can easily be calculated by inserting the new raw product cost figure into the formula.

STANDARD PORTION SIZE

The **standard portion size,** which should be established by management, is the amount of product to be served to the customer. This size, if adhered to, will assist in the calculations for the production schedule, as well as the costs and cost control associated with the dish. There are main methods used to establish standard portion size in the food service industry. Each method is used for a different type of product; once the standard is established, management needs to ensure that it is adhered to. The three standards are:

- Volume: Volume is used when calculating the amount of space that is dispersed by the product. This is for items measured with a scoop or a ladle, and may include soup or ice cream.
- Count: Count is used when the cost of the individual item is calculated by dividing total cost by the number of items purchased. This may include eggs, purchased by the dozen and the individual egg cost calculated. This can also be used for items such as shrimp or potatoes, which are purchased by the case, with the count standardized

• Weight: Weight is used for items that are put onto a scale and measured. This may include steaks or hamburgers.

STANDARD PORTION COST

Once the standard portion size is determined, **standard portion cost** can be calculated. This calculation can be performed using different methods, depending on how the product is prepared. One of the most common methods of calculating portion cost, used mostly when calculating dishes measured by volume, is the **recipe costing sheet.** This sheet is used when a standard recipe is followed. It details the cost of all of the ingredients in the recipe. With this form, multiply the ingredient quantity times the ingredient cost. It is important to ensure that you are multiplying like items, ounces times the cost per ounce and pounds times the per pound price. Once the entire recipe cost is calculated, the total cost of the recipe is divided by the total number of servings prepared. This calculation will yield the cost per serving (see Figure 7.3).

The standard portion cost for items that are counted is calculated by dividing the total cost of the item by the number of portions. This formula is as follows:

$$\text{Standard portion cost} = \frac{\text{Purchase price per unit}}{\text{No. of units}}$$

FIGURE 7.3   Recipe Costing Sheet

Crêpes Recipe, Yield: 12 crêpes				
Quantity	**Unit**	**Item**	**Cost per Unit**	**Total cost**
1	Pound	Butter	$2.39	$2.39
8	Ounces	Flour	$0.03	$0.24
2	Each	Eggs	$0.15	$0.30
			Total cost	$2.93
			No. of crêpes	12
			Cost per crêpe	$0.245

EXAMPLE PROBLEM

If eggs are $1.20 per dozen, standard portion cost is:

$$\frac{\$1.20}{12} = \$0.10 \text{ each}$$

If 2 are used, the cost per dish is $0.10 × 2 = $0.20.

EXAMPLE PROBLEM

If an 80-count potato is used for baking, and a case costs $24.00, standard portion cost is:

$$\frac{\$24.00}{80} = \$0.30 \text{ per potato}$$

EXAMPLE PROBLEM

If U10 shrimp are ordered and they cost $15.00 per pound, standard portion cost is:

$$\frac{\$15.00}{10} = \$1.50 \text{ per shrimp}$$

This method can be used for any item that is priced individually or sold by the unit. Other examples include shrimp or produce that is purchased by the count rather than weight.

WHY THIS IS IMPORTANT

Standard portion cost needs to be calculated, and adhered to, to control variable costs.

■

RECONCILIATION AND CORRECTION

After the shift has ended the production schedule needs to be reconciled with the sales slips to ensure the accuracy of the forecast. Any adjustments should be noted, and the forecast process or the menu mix might need to be re-evaluated for future periods. If sales are lower than forecast, an analysis of why sales did not meet expectations needs to be completed. If a production schedule has created over-production of any item, management needs to evaluate the quality of the foods to ensure that they are usable during the next shift, or to see if they can be saved for another use. If the over-production of food creates an unusable item, that item should be removed from service, and the cost added to the food cost percent for that shift.

If the sales for the shift are larger than forecast, an investigation into how the additional quantities were prepared should take place. Some of the causes and results of under-production include pilferage, spoilage, inadequate portion size or failure to follow the recipe. If the product is being stolen, systems need to be implemented to control the inventory. Some methods that can be implemented include management controlling the issuing of high-ticket items on an as-ordered basis, installation of cameras, or better, overseeing by management.

Spoilage is a major factor affecting the profitability of a restaurant. Spoilage is a controllable variable that creates bottom line losses in operations that allow it to exist. If an operation practices FIFO, first in first out, spoilage should and could be minimized. Additionally, management should be aware that product quality is deteriorating and create situations to promote the sales of these items. In the previous examples, inadequate portion size or failure to follow the recipe, it is important to determine if more portions of a product are sold than what were prepared on the production chart. If more portions are sold than prepared an investigation into how the additional portions were made should occur. Some of the unacceptable options include the chef having to stop production to do preparation, or the chef changing the portion size to allow more servings.

An additional cause of an inadequate production schedule can be poor product purchasing. When products are purchased for a restaurant, one of the chief factors to be taken into account is the yield percent. Yield percent is a factor in almost every food that is purchased. When buying canned products, such as canned fruit cocktail, the description on the can includes the term drained weight. When using the product, one needs to take into account how much edible product is actually in the can. This goes back to the purchasing specification to ensure a consistency in how much product is purchased. Prior to selecting a product for purchase, management personnel need to compare the many varieties of brands and styles of any product they are purchasing. This process is called a cutting and often it is done as a blind cutting. This allows tasters to analyze each product and compare them to others without the ability to be biased toward one brand. One of the differences that will be noticed among canned products is the amount and thickness of the syrup. When canned products are packed without any additional liquid it is called solid pack; if a small amount of liquid is added it is called heavy pack. The more liquid that is added, the fewer edible products in the package. If an incorrect product is purchased, staff may not be able to prepare all the products on the production schedule.

As shown in Chapter 5, yield factor is calculated by dividing the edible yield by the total amount purchased. In the example above, if purchasing bought a canned fruit that was heavy packed, but the specification was for a product that was solid packed, when portioning out sides of fruit cocktails there may not be enough product to complete the production schedule.

WHY THIS IS IMPORTANT

Management needs to ensure that any loss of product is investigated and controls are in place to avoid future losses.

■

BUTCHER'S YIELD

Yield percent is very important when working with meats. The main reason for this is that most restaurants spend proportionally more on meats than on any other product. When an establishment starts to develop standards and write specifications, one decision to be made is how much preparation is going to be done in house and how much prepared product is going to be purchased in its ready to use state. When deciding what form of product to buy, management needs to take into account many factors. The main factor is going to be price, but there are other selection criteria to be addressed. Does the operation have the skill to butcher the meat? Other criteria that need to be addressed are: Is there a place to butcher? Can byproducts be used? Management needs to do an analysis of whether it pays to have some-one with the ability on staff, or whether to outsource the work. This will be discussed further in Chapter 10.

The **butcher's yield test** is a tool used by the industry to find out the actual costs associated with buying larger cuts of meat and butchering (fabri-cating) it into smaller, ready to use cuts. A cost control factor that should be kept in mind is that when cutting meat, the ability to utilize the byproducts from the butchering will lower overall food cost. When fabricating large cuts of meat the end product is full muscles, or cuts of meat, and fat and meat that can be used for ground meat. An example is a leg of veal, which has seven dis-tinct muscles that are connected by fat. When fabricating the leg, besides the muscle there will be small scraps of veal that can be used for stew. Each of the individual cuts and scraps will have a value associated with them. By calculat-ing the costs associated with the byproducts, the actual cost of the product can be calculated. Another example is chicken. If the buyer procures a whole chicken, the cost per pound will be lower than if buying any of the parts indi-vidually. Part of this savings is associated with the labor cost of fabricating, but within the parts, the breast costs more than the legs, thighs or wings. If fab-ricating the chicken mainly for the breasts, the remaining products would be given a value, depending on what they would cost to purchase separately.

Figure 7.4 shows how management can figure out the actual cost of the chicken breasts when buying the bird whole. To start, the parts of the chicken are listed on the butcher's yield chart. When fabricating whole poultry, the end products include two each, wings, thighs, legs, breasts, as well as byprod-ucts (liver, gizzards, etc.), fat and bones. Each of these has a value to an oper-ation that practices 100 percent utilization. If the establishment does not use any of the components, the value associated with that product would be zero.

When butchering an item every piece that is removed from the carcass is individually weighed, and the amount is entered into the chart. The amount of product, for each line, is multiplied by the value associated with each item. In this example, the bird was purchased for $1.19 per pound; if the wings were purchased separately, they would cost $1.29 per pound.

FIGURE 7.4   Butcher's Yield Test for Chicken

Item: Chicken, whole			Grade: A				
			Weight: 4# 8 oz				
Total Cost: $5.36		Price per pound $1.19					
Breakdown	%	Weight Lb	Weight Oz	Purchase Value ($ Per Lb)	Total Value	Price for Usable Lb/Oz	Multiplier (per Pound)
Fat			2.5	.69	.11		
Bones			18.5	.59	.68		
Wings			7	1.29	.56		
Thighs			12.5	1.29	1.01		
Legs			12	1.29	.97		
Byproducts			5.5	1.49	.51		
Breasts	19.44		14		1.52	1.74/.11	1.46
Total		4	8		5.36		

EXAMPLE PROBLEM

$1.29/16 = $0.08 per ounce. The seven oz of wings are multiplied by the $0.08 per ounce creating a value of $0.56.

The same calculation is done with the remaining meat cuts and by products.

To calculate the value of the needed product, the breast, subtract all of the total values known, $3.84, from the purchase price, and the value for the breasts calculates to $1.52. Since the $1.52 value is for 14 oz of breast, the calculation for the value per pound needs to be done. This can be calculated two ways, either by calculating the value per ounce and multiplying that by 16, or calculating the percentage of a pound that 14 ounces represents and divide it by the $1.52.

EXAMPLE PROBLEM

$1.52 /14 = $0.11 Per oz
$0.11 × 16 = $1.76 or
14/16 = .875
$1.52 /.875 = $1.74

The minor discrepancy in this example is due to the rounding of the first example to $0.11 instead of the exact calculation of .1085714.

The multiplier is a percent increase in the value of the main product after fabrication. In this example, the cost of the breast has increased by 1.46 times (or 146%) after the other cuts are removed and accounted for. This calculation is done by dividing the true cost of the item, after butchering by the original cost per pound.

EXAMPLE PROBLEM

$1.74 / $1.19 = 1.46

This figure will allow for a quick calculation to find the new edible cost per pound of the main product when the as purchased price changes. In this problem, if the price of the whole chicken becomes $1.39, the cost of the breast will also increase. Rather than recalculating this entire yield test, all that needs to be done is to multiply the new as purchased price by the multiplier.

EXAMPLE PROBLEM

$1.39 × 1.46 = $2.03

$2.03 is the new cost per pound for the usable product. Without this information, the true cost of a dish and the new menu price would be very inaccurate. Two factors need to be taken into account when utilizing the multiplier in the future. The multiplier does not take into account if the values of the individual byproducts fluctuate. As the cost of the whole chicken changes, the value of each of the items may change as well. If the items do not change considerably, it may not justify recreating the entire chart, as each line is not a major percentage of the total weight and cost. For example if the cost of fat goes to $0.79 per pound, the total value of the 2.5 ounces will rise to $0.12 rather than the $0.11 cents it now represents. The second factor that needs to be taken into account is that for future calculations the product should yield the same percent of the main product. If purchasing by specification, all future purchases should yield chickens that have very close to 19 percent breast meat. This is calculated by dividing the weight of the individual item by the total weight purchased.

EXAMPLE PROBLEM

14 oz / 72 oz = 19.44%

In this example the specification should include that the breast should account for 19.44%, with a minor +/− variance of the total weight of the purchase.

TOTAL COST APPROACH

Many restaurants, especially high-end restaurants, will not utilize this method to calculate the cost of the chicken breast, or any other main entrée. Management may decide to absorb the cost of the whole chicken in the preparation of the two entrées represented by the breasts. In an establishment operating this way, the cost of each serving, and one breast, would be $2.68, rather than the $0.87 in the example above. In these establishments, since the entire cost of the product is absorbed and paid for by the entrée, it will lower the food cost for any dishes prepared with the byproducts. This technique is frequently used in steakhouses that purchase large pieces of meat, such as a full tenderloins.

The calculation is done as follows. If the full tenderloin cost $75 and it yields 10 filet mignons, each filet would cost $7.50, and the remaining meat and trim would cost nothing. If the trim were ground into hamburger meat, the hamburger cost would be minimal, only accounting for the bun and condiments. The scraps could be sold as a Beef Stroganoff, yielding a higher dollar sale, created with minimal costs.

BUTCHER'S YIELD

In Figure 7.5, the breakdown and actual costs can be viewed. A rib of beef is purchased weighing 30 pounds. It is purchased for $10.00 per pound, which gives a total cost of $300.00. After fabrication, all of the products are weighed and the chart is filled in. Loss in cutting is an intangible item that consists of blood or purge and scraps that are unaccounted for. The total weight of all the known products is subtracted from the purchased weight. In this example it is the fat, bones, short ribs, ground beef and prime rib. The ratio to total pounds column is calculated by dividing the weight of the item by the total weight.

EXAMPLE PROBLEM

An example of this calculation is the fat weight of 5 pounds is divided by the total weight of 30 pounds, equaling the ratio 16.67%.

5 / 30 = 16.67%.

The value per pound is what it would cost to buy the product. In the case of fat, certain companies buy the fat for use in cosmetics and soaps, among

FIGURE 7.5 Butcher's Yield Test

Item: Rib, primal	Grade: Choice					
Total cost: $300.00	Weight: 30 pounds Price per Pound: $10.00					

Breakdown	Weight Lb	Weight Oz	Ratio to Total Weight	Value per Lb	Total Value	$ Usable Pound	Multiplier per Pound
Fat	5	0	16.67	.13	.65		
Bones	1	0	3.33	.99	.99		
Short ribs	2	8	8.33	5.50	13.75		
Ground beef	3	12	12.5	1.29	4.84		
Loss in cutting	0	4	.83				
Prime rib	17	8	58.34		279.77	15.99	1.60
Total	30	0	100.00		300.00		

other uses. The value per pound is multiplied by the weight of product, and this is inserted into the total value column. Note that the product that can not be put on a scale such as blood is the loss in cutting and it does not have any value, as it is not something that can be used for anything.

EXAMPLE PROBLEM

As an example, the price being paid for fat is .13 is multiplied by the weight of 5, giving a total value of $0.65.

$0.13 × 5 = $0.65

All of the byproduct values are added up and subtracted from the total cost. This figure represents the total cost of the main product, the prime rib. The total value of the prime rib is $279.77 divided by the total weight of the prime rib, 17 lb 8 oz, and the result, $15.99, equals the cost per pound of the meat.

EXAMPLE PROBLEM

$0.65 + $0.99 + $13.75 + $4.84 = $20.23
$300.00 − $20.23 = $279.77
$279.77 divided by 17 lb 8 oz = $15.99 per lb

This process can be tedious, but once the calculations are complete, as long as the specification stays the same and the ratios of products remain the same, the calculations should not have to be redone. The last calculation is to figure out the **multiplier** per pound. The multiplier is a percentage increase in the cost of the product after trimming. This figure is calculated by dividing the actual cost per pound of the main product.

EXAMPLE PROBLEM

$15.99 \div 10.00 = 1.60$

This figure denotes that the actual cost of the usable product is 1.6 times, or 160%, of the cost of the product at its purchase price. This figure can then be used to calculate the actual cost of the main item when the original price changes. If the AP cost of the prime rib changes to $11.00 per pound, rather than having to recalculate the entire butcher's yield, multiply the new cost by the multiplier to come up with the new EP price per pound of the main product, in this case the prime rib.

EXAMPLE PROBLEM

$11.00 \times 1.60 = 17.60 per lb of prime rib

COOKING LOSS TEST

Taking this concept and working with beef, an additional yield test may be conducted, a **cooking loss test.** Certain items are sold using cooked weight as the standard, such as prime rib. In operations that fabricate their own meat, the prime rib starts as a rib of beef, gets trimmed to a prime rib, then is cooked and served. Most menus sell more than one cut of prime rib; they are differentiated by the cooked weight. To accurately calculate how much the meat costs, a butcher's yield and a cooking loss test are essential.

Now that the product is oven ready, the loss in cooking and any excess product after cooking—such as bones and trim—needs to be accounted for and deducted from the value of the meat. The first step is to fill out the cooking loss chart (see Figure 7.6) with the information from the butcher's yield test. The original weight and costs, 30 pounds and $10.00, are carried down from the above chart. The trimmed weight is also carried down and the loss in trimming is calculated by subtracting the trimmed weight.

EXAMPLE PROBLEM

30 lb − 17 lb 8 oz = 12 lb 8 oz

FIGURE 7.6   Cooking Loss Test

Breakdown	Weight Lb	Weight Oz	Ratio to Total Pound	Value per Pound	Total Value	Cost of Usable Lb	Multiplier per Pound
Original weight	30	0	100	10.00	300.00		
Trimmed weight	17	8	58.34	15.99	279.77		
Byproducts	12	8	41.66				
Cooked weight	16	0	53.33				
Loss in cooking	1	8	5.00				
Bones and trim	1	4	4.16				
Salable weight	14	12	49.17		279.77	18.97	1.90

After the rib comes out of the oven it is put on a scale and weighed. The weight is inserted into the cooked weight column. The cooked weight, 16 pounds, is subtracted from the trimmed weight, 17 lb 8 oz, to give the loss in cooking, 1 lb 8 oz.

EXAMPLE PROBLEM

17 lb 8 oz − 16 lb = 1 lb 8 oz

The meat is then trimmed and anything removed is added to the bones and trim column. The bones and trim, 1 lb 4 oz, is subtracted from the cooked weight, 16 lb, to get the salable weight, 14 lb 12 oz.

EXAMPLE PROBLEM

16 lb − 1 lb 4 oz = 14 lb 12 oz

To calculate the cost per pound of the cooked rib, divide the total value, which is the value of the trimmed weight, 279.77, by the salable weight, 14 lb 12 oz, to obtain the actual cost per pound of the cooked prime rib. These figures are used because the value of the meat that went into the oven is the value of the meat taken out of the oven. The loss in cooking and the trim have no usable purpose, so they have no value. As with the butcher's yield, the multiplier is a useful tool to avoid having to repeat this process when prices change, but only if the ratio of trim and cooking loss remains the same. As with the butcher's yield multiplier calculation, the cost per pound of salable meat, $18.97, is divided by the original purchase price per pound, $10.00, to get the new multiplier, 1.9.

EXAMPLE PROBLEM

$18.98 ÷ $10.00 = 1.90

When the price of the rib of beef changes from $10.00 to $11.00, the new cost is multiplied by the multiplier for the cooking loss test to get the new cost per pound of the salable prime rib (EP).

EXAMPLE PROBLEM

$11.00 × 1.90 = $20.90

In the event that the product is not butchered in house and is purchased in the oven ready form, the cooking loss test can be performed without the butcher's yield test. In that situation the multiplier would be calculated using the purchase price of the oven-ready meat, not the primal cut price.

EXAMPLE PROBLEM

$18.97 ÷ $15.99 = 1.19

WHY THIS IS IMPORTANT

Yield percent is needed when calculating how much to purchase, how much to prepare, and how much to sell an item for.

■

IMPORTANCE OF STANDARD PORTION SIZE

There are many reasons that the quality, quantity, and cost standards should be upheld. Although most of the factors are directly related to cost control, others may have an indirect relationship to cost control. The number one issue in calculating the correct value is that in many cases the menu price is established from the cost of preparing the dish.

EXAMPLE PROBLEM

If a dish is calculated to cost $1.00 and the establishment is utilizing a 25 percent food cost factor, the dish will be listed on the menu with a selling price of $4.00.

$1.00 / .25 = 4.00

If a restaurant sells the dish for $4.00 but the dish actually cost $1.10 to prepare, the dish should be selling for $4.40

$1.10 / .25 = 4.40

In this example, the restaurant should be charging 10 percent more for the dish than the menu indicates.

A second reason that standard portion size should be established and followed is due to the purchasing function within an establishment. After anticipating projected covers and menu mix, the purchasing department will create order quantities based on those numbers. If employees prepare dishes with 10 percent over on the quantity of raw product, they will only be able to prepare 90 percent of the forecast quantity.

A third reason to be diligent in the following of the recipe is for proper pre-production and customer satisfaction. If standard recipes or other guidelines are not followed, staff may need to stop work during a busy hour to prepare more products, or may be forced to tell a customer that they have run out of something. Additionally, if customers do not get a consistent product they may not return to an establishment. If a customer received a large portion on one visit and returns and receives a smaller portion, either from the same worker or a different one, the customer may not feel satisfied. A different scenario includes two people at the same table receiving different size portions for the same item. In any of these situations, establishing and following the three standards could easily eliminate a negative response from the guest.

FOOD COST EVALUATIONS

In the foodservice industry reports are generated frequently, aided by technology available to run the reports. If technology is not used in the operation, less frequent reports will be generated due to the high cost associated with the counting and comparing information needed. Food cost evaluations can be calculated using hourly, by shift, and daily calculations, as well as longer periods of time. Daily calculations may not give a true sense of what really is going on in the operation, but the timeliness of the reports can help correct inaccurate scenarios in the operation. If food cost calculations are done on a less frequent basis, inaccuracy or miscalculations will not be noticed or corrected for a long time.

Depending on the operation, there may be problems associated with a daily food cost calculation. In larger operations where inventory is requested daily, a daily food cost may prove to be more accurate than in a restaurant that has only one outlet. In the second scenario, since purchases are not done on a daily basis, there will be situations that can lead to misleading numbers. One example might be a restaurant that is closed on Sunday and receives most of the deliveries Monday for the entire week. The large cost of the deliveries needs to be spread out over more than one day's sales. The deliveries may be for a three- or five-day period, but the expenses were incurred on only one day. For this reason, a **food cost to date** figure will need to be calculated. Calculating costs to date and dividing by sales to date will accomplish this calculation. This calculation will eliminate the misleading numbers that would come from this scenario (see Figure 7.7).

In Figure 7.7, had management looked only at a daily food cost, it would most likely have been out of line with expectations on September 15 with food cost running at 36.03%. As the week went on and fewer deliveries were made and sales were generated from the deliveries from the first day, food cost percent came down almost 8 percentage points, to 26.27%. This figure is much closer to an industry standard, and negates the misread numbers as well as promoting a better view of the true numbers of the operation.

WHY THIS IS IMPORTANT

If only daily food cost is calculated, percentages will be skewed, unless all inventories are received on a daily basis.

■

FIGURE 7.7 Food Cost Today and To Date

Date	Direct	Stores	Transfers In	Transfers Out	Food Cost Today	Food Cost to Date	Sales	Sales to Date	Food Cost % Today	Food Cost % to Date
9/15	$321	$ 987	$17	$0	$1,325	$1,325	$3,678	$3,678	36.03	36.03
9/16	254	1123	27	12	1,392	2,717	4,385	8,063	31.74	33.70
9/17	168	875	38	14	1,067	3,784	6,340	14,403	16.83	26.27

SUMMARY

■ After the production schedule is created, production methods are created to follow quality, quantity, and cost standards. Techniques to accurately calculate yield percent and edible portion cost are explained and practiced. The concept of food cost to date was outlined and defined.

KEY TERMS

Menu mix
Real portion cost
Planned portion cost
Standard costs
Actual costs
Production schedule
Mise en place
Popularity index

Standardized recipe
Standard portion size
Standard portion cost
Recipe costing sheet
Butcher's yield test
Cooking loss test
Multiplier
Food cost to date

PROBLEMS

1. Why is a food cost to date calculation important in food service?

2. Using the following figures, calculate food cost for each day, food cost to date, as well as food cost %.

Date	Direct	Stores	Transfers In	Transfers Out	Sales
8/1	$128	$1,387	$32	$29	$3,678
8/2	0	923	65	46	3,385
8/3	76	690	28	34	2,840

3. Using the following figures, calculate food cost for each day, food cost to date, as well as food cost %.

Date	Direct	Stores	Transfers In	Transfers Out	Sales
3/1	$1,598	$3,292	$160	$ 67	$12,490
3/2	990	2,310	18	150	9,811
3/3	22	1,690	0	26	9,280

4. Using the following figures, compute the butcher's yield to find the multiplier, 25 pounds of prime rib purchased at 6.79 per pound.

	Breakdown	Value
Fat	2 pounds 4 ounces	$0.15
Short ribs	1 pound 4 ounces	$4.46
Bone	1 pound	$0.79
Ground meat	12 ounces	$1.39
Oven ready prime rib, 19 lb 8 oz		

5. Using the figures in Problem 4, compute the cooking loss test to find the multiplier.

    Bones and trim   12 ounces
    Loss in cooking   1 pound 4 ounces

6. What is the cost if serving an 8 oz portion?

7. What is the selling price for this portion of meat if food cost is set at 25 percent?

8. If the price changes to $6.99 per pound, how much will the new edible portion cost per pound be?

9. If food cost percent remains the same, what should the new selling price be?

10. How much meat needs to be purchased to serve a banquet of 189 people?

11. Why is the butcher's yield and cooking loss test important to understand?

12. Explain the total cost approach of calculating the cost of meats.

13. What are the advantages and disadvantages of using the total cost approach?

14. Why is a food production schedule important?

15. Why is standard portion cost important?

16. What are the three methods used to calculate standard portion size? Give an example of each.

17. If flour costs $0.67 per pound, how much does 3 lb 5 oz cost?

18. If 21/25 shrimp sells for $11.99 per pound, how much shrimp is in a 6-oz serving? How much does the portion cost? How much will it sell for if food cost is 28%?

19. If soup costs $7.75 per gallon to make, how much does a 5-oz portion cost? How much will it sell for if food cost is 22%?

20. In the example above, how much does an 8-oz portion cost? What is selling price with the same food cost percent?

21. When using the total cost approach, if a tenderloin costs $13.25 per pound, weighs 4 lb 6 oz and has a 70% edible yield, how much will a 6 oz steak cost to prepare?

22. If a banquet for 87 people is serving 2–3 oz petite filets for lunch, how many filets should be purchased?

23. Given the following information, how much does it cost to prepare Chicken Parmesan for 10 people?

    Chicken breasts @ $2.19 per pound
    Tomato sauce @ $2.99 per quart
    Mozzarella cheese @ $4.00 per pound

Recipe

10 ea 6 oz chicken breast
2 oz tomato sauce per breast
1½ oz cheese per breast

24. Given the following information, how much does it cost to prepare one bowl of French onion soup?

Onions @ $0.49 per pound
Butter @ $2.49 per pound
Beef stock @ $5.30 per gallon
Bread slices @ $0.07 each
Mozzarella cheese @ $4.00 per pound

Recipe: French Onion Soup   Yield: 1 gallon

Sauté 3 lb onions in 6 oz butter. Add 1 gal of stock and simmer for 45 min. Toast bread and add to bowl. Add 6 oz of soup into bowl and cover with 1 ea 1-oz slice of cheese. Melt under salamander and serve.

25. 5 pounds of tournéed potatoes are needed. Calculate food cost for the EP tournéed potatoes using the following information.

AP cost of potatoes: $0.39 per pound
Unusable potato skin: 18%
Potato scraps for mashed potatoes: 21%

26. Calculate for the purchase of two ribs of beef, U.S. Choice grade, weighing a total of 73 lb 12 oz, and purchased from a dealer at $5.39 per pound.

Fat	12 lb 4 oz	$0.09	Prime rib meat	45 lb 8 oz
Bones	7 lb 8 oz	$0.93	Bones and trim	3
Short ribs	3 lb 12 oz	$3.09	Portion size	10 oz
Ground beef	4 lb 4 oz	$1.19	Cooked weight	41 lb 12 oz

How many portions will this product yield?
How much beef do you need to order to serve 225 people a 10-ounce portion?
What is the EP cost of a serving?
What would the serving EP cost be if the AP price changed to $5.99 per pound?

27. An operation purchases a leg of veal weighing 41 pounds and costing $3.99 per pound. If the veal has 5 lb 3 oz of bones (valued at $1.99 per lb), 2 lb fat (valued at $0.18 per lb), 3 lb 11 oz of usable stew meat (valued at $3.99 per lb), how much does the edible veal cutlet meat cost per lb?

28. How many legs does an operation need to purchase to serve 390 people a 6-oz cutlet?

8

Controls in Beverage Purchasing, Receiving, Storing, and Issuing

Chapter Objectives

After finishing this chapter the student will be able to:

Identify the differences between a license and control state

Identify various alcoholic beverages within the three classifications

Identify purchasing standards

Differentiate among the three receiving standards

Distinguish receiving techniques

Distinguish storage principles

Distinguish issuing practices

Overview of non-alcoholic beverage purchasing

Introduction

This chapter follows the flow of beverages through an operation. It deals with the steps of purchasing beverages for an establishment and the controls needed to ensure profitability. The first part deals with purchasing, storing and issuing of alcoholic beverages. Due to the legislative authority over the distribution and production of alcoholic beverages, the amount of money that can be spent on them, as well as the amount of money that is generated by their sales, this will be the largest section of the chapter. The second section deals with the purchasing, storage and distribution of non-alcoholic beverages. Although there are fewer variables with non-alcoholic beverages, the flow of the beverages through the operation can help produce strong profits.

The flow of beverages through an operation is in many ways similar to the flow of food. Two of the most important differences in the purchasing, storage and use of beverages, as compared to food, is that food is more perishable than beverages and there are much more stringent state and federal government controls in alcoholic beverage purchasing, production, and sales. Although there are storage standards for beverages, there are very few beverages that degenerate as quickly as food products. Foodservice establishments need additional licenses to purchase and sell alcoholic beverages. There are also stricter controls in place for distributors of alcohol.

LICENSED VS. CONTROL STATE

A **licensed state,** like most states are, will issue a license to a distributor that allows them to sell the product (see Figure 8.1). In the licensed state there are many controls that the state has in place for the distribution of products

FIGURE 8.1   States That Control the Distribution of Alcohol

Alabama	Idaho	Iowa	Maine
Michigan	Mississippi	Montana	Maryland*
New Hampshire	North Carolina	Ohio	Oregon
Pennsylvania	Utah	Vermont	Virginia
Washington	West Virginia		

*Only Montgomery County is a control county in the state of Maryland.

and the many taxes that need to be paid by the distributor and the end user. Before selling alcohol it is advised to check the purchasing and distribution requirements of the state in which employed.

Although all states have some control over the distribution of alcohol, a **control state** has stricter controls over the distribution of alcohol, by selling alcohol through state-run distribution centers. This usually is on both the wholesale and retail levels of distribution. There are more advantages to purchasing from the licensed state than the control state (see Figure 8.2).

In a licensed state, there may be more than one distributor of each brand of alcohol. This allows for a competitive pricing structure for the buyer. Even if the state has only one distributor for each item, the buyer has competition among which brand to sell or which brand to establish as their pouring brand. In a control state, the only alcohol distributor is a state store.

In a licensed state, credit terms can and usually are established. This will allow the buyer to purchase the product and hold onto the money for a period or allow sales to be generated by the product before it is paid for. In a control state, the purchase of alcohol must be done on a cash basis, with the money available when the product is purchased.

In a control state, the buyer must pick up the product at the time of purchase, as compared to a licensed state, which allows the delivery of the product directly to the establishment that is using it. Unfortunately, businesses do not have the choice of which type of distributor to purchase; you cannot buy liquor in one state and transport it to another.

FIGURE 8.2   Advantages of a Licensed State

Licensed State	Control State
Credit available	No credit available
Delivery	No delivery
Ability to negotiate prices	No ability to negotiate prices
More competitive pricing	Less competitive pricing

WHY THIS IS IMPORTANT

Depending on where you live, different laws will affect your ability to buy and sell alcohol.

■

FRANCHISE STATE

An additional factor in beverage purchasing is the state's ability to enact a **franchise state.** In a franchise state, the state establishes procedures that allow only one distributor to sell a certain brand's product. Through this franchise agreement, the initial competition to distribute the product can be high, although some states have protection in place for the present distributor that make it very cost effective for a brewer or distiller to remain with their current distributor. Once the distributorship has been granted, the lack of competition will ultimately drive up the wholesale cost of the item and limit marketing dollars available to the packaged goods seller, as well as the drink retailer. Distributors still need to remain somewhat competitive, since establishments might elect not to carry an item or to limit distribution through many means—including not promoting the item—and, more definitively, not making the brand a pouring brand.

CLASSIFICATION OF ALCOHOLIC BEVERAGES

Alcoholic beverages are generally classified into three categories: beer, wines, and spirits. Within each category there are sub-categories to help differentiate the product. The controls in place for purchasing, storing, and issuing will be different for each classification.

Beer

Beer is created by the fermentation of grain, such as barley, and the addition of hops. One of the major differences between domestic and imported beer is the quality and strain of the hops used in its production. Beer is categorized into two major varieties: lager and ale. Lager style beers are more popular in the United States, as compared to ales, such as porter and stout, more popular in Europe. Beers are further classified as to whether they are filtered or pasteurized.

Wines

Wines have more classifications and differentiations than any other beverages. The major difference between wines is that they come from different grapes. Each distinct grape has a different flavor and sugar content; this gives a different flavor profile after the grape is made into wine. Wines can be made from one grape or a combination of grapes. If the bottle is vintaged, that means that all of the grapes used in production were from one year's harvest. A small percentage of wines are created using the grapes grown during one year, and these bottles have the distinction of putting the year on the bottle. Vintaged wine can carry a higher price, both wholesale and retail, depending on whether the year was a good year for wine or not. Factors for establishing a good year include the amount of sun and rain and the temperature during the growing season. All of these factors help create the flavor profile of the grape. The majority of wines produced are meant to be drunk within the first year of production, even if they have a vintage on them. A very small quantity of wine that is produced (less than five percent) is intended to be stored or aged under ideal conditions, to be consumed at a later date.

The region it is produced in also classifies wine. For a French wine to be called a Burgundy, it must have grapes that were grown and harvested in the Burgundy region of France. An additional classifier is the bottler of the wine. Certain bottlers purchase top quality grapes that produce top quality wines. When purchasing wines a buyer can create a profile of a wine without tasting it, by the producer and the region and the year of production.

Spirits

Spirits are fermented beverages that have been distilled, a process that heats up the fermented liquid into steam, which in turn separates out the alcohol. When the alcohol is cooled and re-liquefied, it is then usually aged in wood barrels to help establish the flavor profile. The production process helps regulate the amount of alcohol, and the end product is usually diluted to the proper alcohol content with distilled water. Spirits are generally purchased using the term proof (see Figure 8.3) to designate how much alcohol is in the product. Proof, which ranges from 0 to 200, is equivalent to two times the alcohol content; hence a 100 proof bottle would have 50% alcohol. Many brands have more than one alcohol content product; when purchasing, the buyer needs to be assured of getting the product that matches the specification written. Different color labels usually designate these two alcohol contents. Additional variations may include the difference between the duration of aging for different spirits. This will change the flavor profile of the product, as well as the price.

PURCHASING STANDARDS

The purchasing standards of alcohol are the same basic standards that are established for food: the proper quantity, quality, and cost. Due to the nuances of alcohol, the specifics may be different. One difference is the

FIGURE 8.3 What Is Proof?

Proof is another (older) measure of the strength of an alcoholic liquid. It had its origins in days when a simple test was needed to indicate that the liquor did indeed contain a "correct" measure (or more) of alcohol. And it was indeed a simple test. Some of the liquor was poured over a little gunpowder and ignited. If the alcohol content was adequate, then it would burn "just right" with a steady blue flame and eventually ignite the gunpowder. If there was insufficient alcohol, it would fizzle out and the gunpowder would be too wet to burn. The "just right" condition "proved" the liquor and it was declared to be "100% proof." This simple test was clearly cumbersome to perform and was later replaced by using a specially graduated hydrometer to measure the specific gravity. This was far more objective and allowed precise statements to be made as to how much it differed from 100% proof. This gave rise to "under-proof" and "over-proof" measures.

Source: www.ex.ac.uk/cimt/dictunit/notes6.htm. From "What Is Proof" from "Background Notes on Measures-6 The Alcohol Content of Drinks" from www.cleavebooks.co.uk.dictunit/notes6.htm. Reproduced by permission.

ability to purchase broken cases or mixed cases of alcohol. For certain products this is not available; in these situations you need to establish purchasing standards based on the periodic order system rather than the perpetual order system, as discussed in Chapter 5. The amount of product purchased is based on the amount needed for the length of the period until the next delivery. The amount will be different if the delivery timeline is pre-set, or based on the needs and timeline of the establishment.

Second is the quality standard. This is established through writing specifications based on the user's needs and the client's expectation. Some quality standards will include the brand name and vintage of wines, as well as the proof level of certain spirits (see Figure 8.4).

Third is the cost standard. In control states and states with strict franchise control, this is not a strong variable in the purchasing of alcoholic beverages. Due to the constraints placed on purchasing by the state laws, the buyer might not have any ability to control the costs associated with purchasing of these beverages. In non-controlled, licensed, states there is quite a bit of room to negotiate the costs associated with these beverages, especially if large volumes are purchased. One method of controlling the cost standard in any state is by purchasing alcohol in the largest size bottles. Purchase of 1.75 liter bottles is

FIGURE 8.4 Alcohol Packaging

Technology is playing a more important role in the packaging and marketing of alcoholic beverages. Mar de Frades 2003 Albario, a white wine from Spain, has a temperature indicator on its label that tells the consumer when it has reached the 52–55 degree ideal serving temperature. Iron City beer is bottled in aluminum long neck bottles to prevent light from inhibiting freshness and to create lighter packaging. Danzka vodka is packaged in metal bottles to help chill the vodka and maintain the cold temperature.

Source: Time, September 27, 2004, p. 21.

FIGURE 8.5 Common Bottle Sizes

Wine	Beer	Spirits
750 Milliliter	12 ounces; bottle/can	750 Milliliter
1.5 Milliliter	Keg (15.5 gallons)	1 Liter
	½ Keg (7.75 gallons)	1.75 Liter
	¼ Keg (3.88 gallons)	

the most cost effective method, although these bottles may not be appropriate and fit the specifications, depending on where the bottle is being used. The general bottle size used in front bars—those with customers coming up for drinks—is a one liter or 750 milliliter bottle (see Figure 8.5).

WHY THIS IS IMPORTANT

Although purchasing in the largest size container will usually be less expensive, it may not be the most cost effective.

■

RECEIVING STANDARDS

As with food purchasing, the standards for receiving beverages are based directly on the standards established during the purchasing of the product. The receiving standards are in place to ensure that the supplier has met the purchasing standards. The first standard of beverage purchasing is quantity. This means the first standard in receiving is to ensure that the quantity standard is being met. The receiver should count every bottle and case that comes in, checking against the purchase order to ensure that the product ordered is the product received. The receiver should also make sure that the product ordered is the same product, both quality and quantity, that is included in the invoice accompanying the delivery. With spirits, the method of receiving will include counting of bottles and making sure that the name and the proof is the same as ordered, as many brands make many products with multiple proofs. For beer, this will include counting of cases and weighing of kegs. Wine has the most details to check due to the many wineries, regions and vintages available for each grape and variety of wine.

Second is the quality standard, which should be compared to the specification written for the product. For beer, this may be to ensure that keg beer is refrigerated and date stamps, either born on or use by dates, are appropriate. For spirits, this includes ensuring that seals are secure on bottles. Again, wine has the finest distinctions. Wine must be stored at the proper temperature and humidity, and the cork must stay moist. This may not occur during transportation, so buying from an established and respectable company is imperative.

The third standard is cost. The receiving clerk needs to ensure that the costs on the invoice match the costs on the purchase order. If any of these standards are not met, the receiver needs to bring this to the attention of the delivery person. Any discrepancies should be noted on the invoice and adjustments made. In any situation in which the product delivered does not meet standards, the buyer should be notified while the delivery driver is still present to confirm if the delivered product is acceptable. The end users may need to be told immediately so they can adjust a menu or decide if the different product is acceptable.

STORAGE STANDARDS

Storage standards for alcohol are identical to those for food. Storage standards include the protection of the product's quality, accessibility and protection from theft. Beverage storage managers need to maintain the quality of the product. Storage for beverages is as diverse for each product as those standards for food. Storage standards differ between classifications and within each classification.

Storage for beer differs if the product is in a keg or in bottles or cans. Canned and bottled beer can be stored at room temperature, making sure to follow FIFO practices. The quality of beer stored at room temperature will lessen as time elapses. Bottled beer is best if used within three months. Keg beer has not been pasteurized, so the product should be stored in a refrigerator and used within one month. Storage for wines differs depending on the color classification.

Wines that are corked need to be stored on an angle to allow the cork to stay moist during storage. Wines (like fortified wines) that have a screw cap can be stored in an upright position. All wines should be stored with 75 percent humidity. The temperature for wines is very exact, depending on the type of wine being stored (see Figure 8.6). Storage for distilled spirits is much easier to control due to the limited requirements for storage. Distilled spirits are shelf stable and do not need refrigeration.

A second objective in the storage of alcoholic beverages is to make sure that the product is accessible. As mentioned in Chapter 6, the hours of oper-

FIGURE 8.6 **Storage Temperatures for Wine**

Port	66°F	Beaujolais, Rosé	54°F
Bordeaux, Shiraz	64°F	Sauternes	52°F
Red Burgundy, Cabernet	63°F	Chardonnay	48°F
Pinot Noir	61°F	Riesling	47°F
Chianti, Zinfandel	59°F	Champagne	45°F
Tawny/NV Port, Madeira	57°F	Ice wines	43°F
Ideal storage for all wines	55°F	Asti Spumanti	41°F

ation of the beverage storage area will dictate much of how the ordering process takes place. Beverages must be stored in an organized way, allowing easy access to filling orders and warehousing purchases. Most liquor storerooms are set up with like ingredients stored together. This puts all of the liquors together, and within that layout would keep the rums together and the gins together. There would be a separate section for wines, cordials, and beers.

The last goal of the storage is to have personnel to protect the product from theft. Alcoholic beverages are one of the most common items pilfered from a storeroom. As stated in Chapter 6, some of the controls in place include limited access and a stringent policy for removal of product. Additionally, beverage storerooms are often watched by security through video cameras.

WHY THIS IS IMPORTANT

Alcohol can be very perishable. Improper storage can lead to a loss of inventory. It is also one of the most "lost" inventory items.

■

INVENTORY TURNOVER

As with food, beverage storage is assessed by inventory turnover. The inventory turnover of beverages will show whether too much or too little product is on hand at any one time. If too much product is on hand, meaning the turnover is too low, this will tie up cash reserves as well as increase storage costs and take up storage space. If inventory turnover is too high, meaning that there is not enough inventory in stock, the costs of purchasing and storing might be too high, and inventory shortages or running out of an item may result. When purchasing beverages there usually is more leeway than when purchasing food, depending on the establishment, due to the nature of the product. Certain wines—less that 5 percent—are bottled with the intention of being held for future drinking. If the establishment has an extensive wine list, it may be purchasing bottles to cellar and hold for future use. This will increase the value of the inventory.

Another difference between wine and food purchasing is that a limited number of certain products may be available. Although, with food, the laws of supply and demand are present, when purchasing some beverages these laws become the most important factor. The vintages that are purchased may be prepared, or still available, in very limited numbers. This will increase costs and increase the need to maintain a larger inventory of these items. The same can be said of many spirits that take years to produce due to the aging requirement of the product, up to 20 years. These products may not be as plentiful as food products or other beverage products, so added inventory might be required.

The formula for inventory is the same as for food.

IMPORTANT FORMULA

$$\frac{\text{Opening inventory} + \text{closing inventory}}{2} = \text{Average inventory}$$

$$\frac{\text{Cost of goods}}{\text{Average inventory}} = \text{Inventory turnover}$$

The variable that needs to be taken into account when calculating beverage turnover and beverage cost is the amount of beverages that have been issued to the bar(s). Unlike with food, this amount will usually be a substantial amount of money; likewise, in situations where food issued has a great value, it too would be calculated.

EXAMPLE PROBLEM

Opening storeroom inventory	$100,000
Purchases	$200,000
Closing storeroom inventory	$90,000
Opening bar inventory	$10,000
Closing bar inventory	$9,000

$100,000
+ $200,000
+ $ 10,000
= $310,000 Cost of beverage available
− $ 90,000
− $ 9,000
= $211,000 Cost of beverage used

Generally accepted industry average for inventory turnover is 24 to 18 for beer and spirits per year. This number represents the number of times each year the average value of the inventory turns, or goes through the warehouse. The wine inventory turnover is less than an exact number, due to the nature of the wine industry and the storage potential of the product.

WHY THIS IS IMPORTANT

Since a bar needs multiple brands of almost every item it carries, liquor inventory can be very high if it is not controlled.

■

ISSUING STANDARDS

As mentioned in the last section, there is a very strong need to control the issuing of alcoholic beverages. Alcoholic beverages are the most abused item out of inventory in most establishments. When establishing standards for issuing, the two most common practices that are implemented are control from misuse and cost accountability of the product.

Control from misuse is a major component of the issuing standard. To control misuse, management usually limits the number of people allowed to requisition alcohol. Only certain managers have the ability to requisition product from inventory, and they are only allowed to requisition product that is permitted in the bar or outlet that they supervise. For this to be effective, management needs to assess the needs of every bar and create a list of products that each bar uses, based on the needs assessment of that outlet. Every bar will have different needs based on the clientele of the bar, and whether it is a front of the house bar or a service bar. Other factors will include whether the bar is established for a banquet, dinner, or social gathering. This limitation gives management further control.

The second standard is cost accountability. This is easy to control in an operation that computerizes the inventory. Through computerization, every bottle or product that leaves the inventory area can be charged out to the appropriate end user. If products leave the warehouse without proper paperwork, hard copy, or computer movement, the accountability of the product is lost. A procedure often used to control issuance is the added step in which employees need to turn in an empty bottle to receive a full one out of storage. Through a process such as this, every bottle is accounted for before another bottle is issued. Many establishments also implement systems similar to those used in warehouse stores, where someone's job is to check the order that leaves the warehouse. This checkout system helps staff account for all products in inventory and ensures that the end users are getting all of the product they have requisitioned and are being charged for.

WHY THIS IS IMPORTANT

Alcohol creates high profit margins. Without control of inventory, financial misconduct can occur.
■

NON-ALCOHOLIC BEVERAGE PURCHASING

There are as many factors with purchasing non-alcoholic beverages as with purchasing alcoholic beverages. Usually, more time and effort are spent on purchasing, receiving and issuing of alcoholic than non-alcoholic beverages due to higher expenses associated with purchasing and the higher sales that are generated from them. The storage of alcoholic beverages is much more detailed than the storage of non-alcoholic beverages, as well as the storage of food.

There are many selection and cost control factors associated with the purchasing of beverages such as sodas and juices. There are many incentives towards selecting one brand over another. There is a higher level of competition among non-alcoholic brands than alcoholic brands, which results in buyers and management having the ability to bargain for brands, and the ability to receive promotional material when selecting one brand over another. There is a strong competition between Coca-Cola® and Pepsi-Cola® branded soft drinks. This allows the buyer to work one company against the other. If business style allows, changing brands frequently can work in a company's favor.

One factor to consider when purchasing non-alcoholic beverages is the size of container being purchased. When purchasing in larger containers, prices are usually much lower. But if all of the product cannot be consumed before a change in the quality, it is not financially prudent to purchase a larger quantity. Other factors to keep in mind when purchasing is whether to purchase the product in its final form, pre-mixed, or a post-mix product (which allows the restaurant to mix as much as they need for a certain period of time). Although this is usually a factor when purchasing carbonated soda, juices as well as other items can be purchased this way. Products that come in a concentrated form and are mixed after purchase are usually cheaper to purchase due to lower delivery costs. These products will take up less storage, but space may be needed for equipment to prepare the product for sale.

Many beverage brands, including coffee and soda, will install and maintain equipment in any operation that sells their product. This deal usually includes an exclusivity clause, mandating that the operation sell only their brand. If there are any problems with the equipment, the company will make the repairs. In many cases, such as with soda, the equipment is proprietary, which means that you can only purchase product from whichever company supplied the equipment. This type of program can lower the costs associated with generating the sale of the beverages.

WHY THIS IS IMPORTANT

Even in operations that sell alcohol, non-alcoholic beverages substantially add to sales. Taking advantage of a competitive beverage market can lower costs and add to profitability.

■

SUMMARY

■ Terminology about beverage purchasing is discussed
■ Differences between a license and control state are discussed
■ Alcoholic beverages are classified and described
■ Purchasing, storage, and issuing standards are described
■ Beverage inventory turnover is discussed

KEY TERMS

Licensed state   Franchise state
Control state

PROBLEMS

1. What is the average inventory turnover for wine?
2. What is the average inventory turnover for spirits?
3. What is the average inventory turnover for beer?
4. How can a franchise state affect the costs associated with alcohol?
5. What are the main differences between a control and a license state?
6. List two examples of issuing control.
7. Do you live in a licensed or control state?
8. Do you live in a franchise state?
9. What are the differences between food and alcohol purchasing?
10. Why is the 1.75 liter bottle the most cost effective way to purchase alcohol?
11. What is the cost of beverage issued in the following example?

Opening storeroom inventory	$ 56,478
Purchases	$123,503
Closing storeroom inventory	$ 48,580
Opening bar inventory	$ 11,670
Closing bar inventory	$ 10,523

12. In the above example, what is the inventory turnover?
13. Explain an equipment program.
14. What are the storage principles for wine?
15. What are the storage principles for bottled and canned beer? For keg beer?
16. What are the storage principles for spirits?

9
Controls in Beverage Production

Chapter Objectives

After finishing this chapter the student will be able to:

Distinguish the value of beverage production control

Differentiate among different bars

Distinguish between different glassware and the value of this in beverage production

Identify different production controls

Calculate beverage inventory

Identify government controls for beverages

Explain dramshop laws

Differentiate between well brands and call brands

Identify different methods of inventory valuation

Evaluate the positives and negatives of extensive wine service

Introduction

This is an important chapter for any establishment that sells alcoholic beverages. If beverage sales are a large percentage of overall sales, this chapter is even more important. The controls that management puts in place will help ensure that all sales are accounted for and that all products are used for the correct purpose.

BEVERAGE PRODUCTION CONTROLS

Controls in beverage production are extremely important because beverage sales and costs are a large component of a profit and loss statement. Profit margins for beverages are much higher than that for food and the expenses associated with beverage sales are much lower. Even though a very high profit margin can be attained through beverage sales, without controls in place, beverages can cost an establishment a lot of money in sales and potential profit.

Controls over beverage production vary from operation to operation, and can vary within one operation. In many hospitality establishments, there is more than one type of bar represented. Each bar may have a different standard and expectation. Some of the different bars in an establishment may include a front bar, where customers sit and order drinks or come up to the bar and order. The expectations for this bar will be different than those for a service bar, which does not deal with the interaction of the customer; only servers utilized this bar. Another type of bar with different standards is a catering bar; another is a nightclub bar. Some of the differences among them include par levels and types of alcoholic and non-alcoholic beverages.

Another very fundamental difference is the size of the bottle used in each establishment.

WHY THIS IS IMPORTANT

Different bars have different needs to be addressed.

■

TYPES OF BARS

In a front bar, bartenders pour in front of a customer, so it is very rare that a 1.75 liter bottle is used. Although a 1.75 is considered the most cost effective bottle due to the highest yield and lowest price of any sized container, it is not used frequently in the front bar due to the awkwardness of working with the bottle. When establishing the varieties and brand names of liquor to be served at this bar, management needs to look at the preferences of the clientele expected to be purchasing drinks. The pars for this establishment will vary depending on the clientele and the volume of business. In a service bar, the pouring is usually done behind the scenes, which allows the use of the higher yielding 1.75 liter bottles. Not all beverages are available in this size, but usually the largest available is used, unless it is a very slow selling beverage that is needed for one reason or another.

The kinds of liquor are also established by the clientele, but may be different from those used at the front bar. Establishments that have both bars may put the premium brands in the front bar for visibility; servers need to order them from the front bar rather than the service bar. This exhibits the high quality liquors, and the establishment will not have to stock multiple bottles of expensive brands. The par levels will also be different between these two bars depending on the mix of sales through servers and bartenders. Some pars will be higher at the front bar and others at the service bar.

In the catering bar, the selection will usually be smaller and the options limited by space or customer preference. Catering bars can be arranged in many ways, with differences for cash bars, open bars, and host bars. Other differences will include whether the bar is permanent or portable. Permanent bars usually can be stocked with more merchandise than portable bars, and they are usually closer to a storeroom selection of more inventory. Replacement of inventory and special requests are usually easier to arrange from a permanent bar than a portable one. Cash bars need room for a register and usually have a limited menu, while inventory methods for a host and an open bar allow for larger selection.

In a nightclub bar, the clientele will again mandate what inventory is stocked, but this may change more frequently than the clientele for other aspects of the hospitality industry. When forecasting inventory needs to develop pars, it must be remembered that patrons have more loyalty to beverages than they do to food. As the clientele changes, due to day of the week or group booking, so do the variety and the pars for different beverages.

ISSUING CONTROL

There are many controls that management can implement, physical as well as policy, to help control staff during the production of alcoholic beverages. One control used commonly in the industry is the bottle exchange program for replacing empty bottles. Management can help ensure that bottles are added to the bar inventory through the stockroom, but only if they employ a policy of turning in an empty bottle to receive a new one from inventory. If the warehouse does not receive an empty bottle, they do not issue another one. This helps control bottles being brought in from the outside and added to inventory.

WHY THIS IS IMPORTANT

Beverage sales create an excellent opportunity for dishonest people to steal from an operation.

■

BEVERAGE PRODUCTION CONTROL MEASURES

One of the most effective controls that management can set in place is a standardized recipe. As discussed in Chapter 7, a standardized recipe allows for a consistent product that will yield customer satisfaction, per drink cost accountability, and purchasing and storage control.

Another piece of equipment that helps control production and inventory is an **automated beverage-dispensing machine.** This machine can be used in both alcoholic and non-alcoholic beverages, and saves both product and labor. This is not usually done in a front bar, as the aesthetics for the customers may not be what management wants to display. An advantage of this type of system is that every drink is mixed according to management's specification; and customer satisfaction should increase. With this system, the bartender uses a point of sale system to input an order. The guest check is processed prior to the machine adding the ingredients and mixing the drink. High volume fast food restaurants use systems such as this for high volume drive through lanes.

Another beverage service technique that allows management to control production standards is the **service gun.** Although this was used mainly in behind the scenes bars in the past, it is now commonplace to see this in any bar in a hospitality establishment. Liquor is controlled from a beverage storage room and is pumped through plastic tubing to a gun at the bar. When an

FIGURE 9.1   Approximate Number of Glasses in a Half-Barrel (15.5 Gallons)

Income From 1/2 Case Barrel of Beer						
There are 1984 ounces of beer in any 1/2 barrel. The table below indicates the approximate number of glasses of shell, pilsner and other types of glasses that should be obtained from each 1/2 barrel.						
Type of Glass	**Size**	**1″ Head**		**3/4″ Head**		**1/2″ Head**	
		# Glasses	**Act Oz.**	**# Glasses**	**Act Oz.**	**# Glasses**	**Act Oz.**
	8 Oz	343	5.78	325	6.10	283	7.01
Sham	9 Oz	292	6.79	279	7.11	260	7.63
Pilsner	10 Oz	265	7.49	245	8.10	223	8.90
	12 Oz	221	8.98	204	9.73	186	10.67
	8 Oz	305	6.50	292	6.79	275	7.21
Tulip	10 Oz	248	8.00	230	8.63	207	9.58
Goblet	11 Oz	227	8.74	209	9.49	185	10.72
	12 Oz	210	9.45	191	10.39	167	11.88
	8 Oz	325	6.10	292	6.79	280	7.09
Footed	9 Oz	282	7.04	259	7.66	245	8.10
Pilsner	10 Oz	250	7.94	233	8.52	215	9.23
	7 Oz	360	5.51	336	5.90	315	6.30
Shell	8 Oz	315	6.30	292	6.79	279	7.11
	9 Oz	270	7.35	255	7.78	243	8.16
	10 Oz	245	3.10	236	8.41	220	9.02
	10 Oz	264	7.52	248	8.00	233	8.52
Hour	11 Oz	235	8.44	220	9.02	205	9.68
Glass	12 Oz	220	9.02	204	9.73	189	10.50
	13 Oz	198	10.02	184	10.78	173	11.47
	10 Oz	248	8.00	233	8.52	223	8.90
Stein	12 Oz	203	9.77	189	10.50	176	11.27
	14 Oz	169	11.74	158	12.56	153	12.97
	16 Oz	149	13.32	140	14.17	134	14.81
	9 Oz	378	5.25	331	5.99	294	6.75
Heavy	10 Oz	330	6.01	296	6.70	264	7.52
Goblet	12 Oz	248	8.00	220	9.02	204	9.73
	14 Oz	209	9.49	194	10.23	172	11.53
		1″ HEAD		**1.5″ HEAD**			
	54 Oz	47	42.21	50	39.68		
Pitcher	60 Oz	39	50.87	42	47.24		
	64 Oz	35	56.69	38	52.21		

Source: Courtesy of Dr. Donald Bell.

order is placed, the bartender hits a certain button and the ordered product is delivered into the glass. The gun will control the quantity ordered and can be set up to automatically ring up on the Point of Sales system. Some of the older models posed limitations on the variety of liquors dispensed, but now there are systems that can deliver an almost unlimited variety of liquors.

Additional measuring tools do not control the amount given, if a bartender wants to over pour, but can help the bartender measure the appropriate amount of liquor. These devices include a **shot glass,** which when purchased can be ordered in many sizes and can be lined or unlined. The standard recipe indicates which size shot glass should be used to ensure that the drink is made according to management's standards. Lined shot glasses give an impression of over-pouring due to the thickness of the glass. When looking at the glass at eye level, the meniscus—the lower part of the bubble—should be on the line. When looking down at the glass the liquid level will appear higher in the glass. This gives the customer a feeling of getting something for nothing, while in reality it is the correctly measured shot. Another measuring tool is a jigger. A **jigger** is a two-sided measurer that has a handle and two cups at the end. The two cups are different sizes, each being a size used to measure liquors according to management's specification.

The method of mixing drinks with the least amount of management control is **free pour.** Although it is used in smaller independent operations, it is being seen less and less frequently in larger or corporate operations. With free pour, there is the potential for inconsistency in products and in controlling the actual costs of the drinks. Although a bartender may be consistent from drink to drink, the differences between bartenders' pouring styles may interfere with customer satisfaction due to an inconsistent product. One control that can help with free pour, and should be added to all standardized recipes no matter the pouring style, is glass size. If a bartender is free pouring a drink on the rocks, if an appropriate glass is filled with ice and the beverage is poured to the top, there is some control over the quantity served. This method is not accurate and should not be used, but if there are no other systems in place, this can help control production (see Figure 9.1).

WHY THIS IS IMPORTANT

If all alcohol is not accounted for and used correctly in drink preparation, true sales value will not be realized, and costs will not be controlled.

■

MONITORING BEVERAGE PRODUCTION

Monitoring of a bar area is essential in the control process of beverage production. There are many ways for a dishonest person to make money through a beverage operation. Many scams have been reported in this industry, which has led to technological advances in the control of inventory and revenue.

FIGURE 9.2   Common Methods of Bartender Theft

1. **Over-pouring** to get a larger tip
2. **Under-pouring to build a bank of liquor,** which the bartender will later sell and pocket the difference
3. **Bringing in his/her own liquor** and pocketing the sales from that bottle
4. **Complementary (comping drinks** to get a bigger tip)
5. **Giving free drinks** to friends
6. **Ringing bottled beer as draft** and pocketing the difference
7. **Ringing a sale on the comp or "no sale" key,** then pocketing the difference
8. **Leaving the cash drawer open after ringing the sale,** which gives the bartender a chance to make a few sales without management's knowing
9. **Claiming someone walked out without paying,** when the bartender is actually pocketing the difference
10. **Faking a broken bottle,** then selling the contents of the bottle and pocketing the difference
11. **Making a drink wrong,** then selling it to someone else after it's returned and pocketing the difference
12. **Circumventing a pouring spout control system** by bringing in his/her own spouts, leaving spouts off certain bottles, putting electronic spouts in the microwave to fry them (really!), or dozens of other ways that have been devised to beat spout systems.

Source: www.g4tech.com/products/accubar/scams.asp. From "Your Bartender's 'Retirement Plan'" from www.accubar.com. Reprinted by permission of AccuBar Inventory Systems.

Bartenders can be in a position to take money from an establishment. There are many ways money can be pilfered from an establishment, and in many cases the bartender may work with a very large cash flow. See Figure 9.2 for some of the ways bartenders have available to them to remove inventory or money from an establishment.

BEVERAGE INVENTORY

One of the biggest differences between food inventory and beverage inventory is that within the beverage department, there are usually two inventories to be completed when one is doing a physical inventory. The first inventory is the same as with food, done usually on a monthly basis, where one counts and adds a value to the inventory in stock. The second inventory, not usually done with food, is where the inventory of beverages in the bar is also calculated. Food inventory issued to the kitchen but not yet used is generally a small amount of inventory, depending on the facility. Beverage inventory issued to a bar can have considerable value, depending on the establishment, and when one is doing a physical inventory on a regular basis, the value of inventory issued to the bar is added to the value of inventory in the warehouse. In many establishments bar inventory is measured on a daily basis, due to the nature of the beverage industry.

Bar inventory can be measured in many different ways, depending on the bar and the training of the staff. Many bar managers are trained to look at a bottle and calculate how much liquid is inside. This is not the most accurate method, especially if the bottles are not transparent, but if the same manager is calculating the inventory on a regular basis, the count can be somewhat accurate. A more accurate method of valuating inventory in a bar is to weigh the bottles and take off the tare for each bottle. One of the negative aspects of this method is that not every bottle weighs the same. Many types of liquor are currently being produced in plastic containers, which weigh differently than glass bottles; even two glass bottles with the same capacity may weigh differently between brands.

GOVERNMENT CONTROLS

A major difference between the sales of alcoholic beverages and most every other item is the stringent control the government has on the distribution of liquor. In Chapter 8, we discussed some of the laws in place for purchasing alcohol on the wholesale market, but it would be a mistake to forget about the controls in place for the retail distribution of alcohol. Liquor license laws vary by community and state, but in every jurisdiction there are laws concerning the sale of alcohol. Every state has a federally mandated age at which someone is allowed to purchase and consume alcohol, but many jurisdictions include additional laws for the distribution of alcohol. Many counties are considered dry, which means that no alcohol can be sold in the county, and others have blue laws, which prohibit the sale of alcohol and other items on Sunday mornings, or all day Sunday. Some communities allow bars that serve alcohol also to sell packaged goods, unopened alcohol for consumption off premises.

For the restaurateur, the most important law about liquor licenses is the number and type distributed in a community. Many communities limit the number of licenses available, tying this to the number of citizens in the community. Sometimes liquor licenses are issued one for every 2,000–3,000 community members, and sometimes there are no limits to what the market will bear. In the former case, liquor licenses are considered a commodity and retain a value, since a limited number are available. In situations like this, liquor licenses are considered an asset in a business and can be sold with the establishment. Liquor licenses have sold for as much as $1,000,000 in a marketable location where there are no more available.

Many communities have different levels of liquor licenses. Each license has different costs associated with it and different regulatory controls in place for each type of license. Some of the different varieties of license include beer and wine, or just beer. Many communities require a license for customers to bring their own wine into an establishment. Many establishments that have

FIGURE 9.3 Typical Requirements for Properties Serving Alcohol, Found on Many State Websites

Through financial and inventory audits, the ABC Commission's Audit Division ensures that permit holders comply with ABC laws and rules. ABC permittees are required to maintain certain qualifications that are monitored through required reports and verified by routine visits to a business location. All ABC businesses are subject to being audited, but those that possess mixed beverage permits receive the most scrutiny. ABC rules require all mixed beverage permittees to maintain full and accurate monthly records of their finances and to submit reports on their financial and inventory on a schedule set by the Audit Division. In addition, ABC statutes require businesses to meet certain criteria. For example, mixed beverage restaurants shall have gross receipts from food sales of not less than 30 percent of the business's total gross receipts. Once the application requirements are met and a retail ABC permit is issued, an ABC auditor will visit the location to discuss the regulations.

Source: From "Mixed Beverage Audits" from North Carolina Alcoholic Beverage Control Commission, www.ncabc.com. Used by permission.

this limited license charge a corkage fee for the privilege of bringing in one's own beverages and not purchasing from the restaurant. Additional licenses may be for a full service bar, and depending on the community, there also may be a packaged goods license that allows the sale of unopened liquor.

The list can go on and on, but that is not the purpose of this book. The main thing to learn is that prior to opening a facility that sells alcohol, research is imperative if you want to be successful (see Figure 9.3).

DRAMSHOP LAWS

Additional legislation that has changed the way the hospitality operates is the creation of dramshop laws. **Dramshop laws** are laws that pertain to third party liability. If a server or bartender serves a patron who then hurts someone due to intoxication, the server and the establishment can be held responsible for the liability due to the accident. Many establishments, private and especially public corporations, have strict rules and training to support and control the serving of alcohol to patrons who appear under the influence of alcohol. Besides the personal loss and the negative publicity that comes with an incident, dramshop laws have placed a heavy financial burden on the insurance coverage of hospitality operations (see Figure 9.4).

FIGURE 9.4 States Without Dramshop Laws

Delaware	Kansas	Maryland	Nebraska
Nevada	South Dakota	Virginia	

WHY THIS IS IMPORTANT

Every jurisdiction has unique laws and guidelines in place to control and implement taxes on the sale of alcohol. Ignorance of the law can lead to closure, fines, and/or imprisonment and the loss of a job.

■

WELL BRANDS AND CALL BRANDS

One distinction that needs to be made is the difference between **well brands** and **call brands** in the bar industry. Well brands, named for the "well" they sit in for easy access, are used when a patron asks for a drink without specifying a brand name, for example, vodka and tonic. As mentioned earlier, when management is deciding the clientele for the establishment, one aspect that needs to be evaluated is, what is the well brand for each of the major liquor varieties to be served? Well brands set a standard for an operation. If the well brand is a higher quality item, customers will recognize this as quickly as if the well brand were of lower quality. Well brands generally are cheaper than call brands, where the customer calls out the name of the liquor (for example, they may say "Absolut and tonic"). If the establishment has a high quality well brand, and a customer orders a brand name that is lower priced, the call brand drink may be cheaper than the well brand. The cost differences between brands may not be so prohibitive as to deter having the higher quality product. If bottle A costs $10.00 wholesale, and produces 20 one oz drinks, each drink costs $0.50 to make. If bottle B costs $14.00 and produces the same number of drinks, each drink costs $0.70.

TRANSFERS

When discussing food, the topic of transfers is very extensive when compared to beverages. Within beverage production, there are fewer opportunities to transfer goods, but the total cost of the goods transferred can be higher. There are few operations that transfer alcoholic and non-alcoholic beverages between different locations. Many state and federal laws prohibit the transfer of goods from one establishment to another, even if the same company owns them. Since establishments that sell alcoholic beverages are some of the most regulated and controlled industries in this country, every purchase of alcohol needs to be backed up by records that indicate how much in sales was generated by the issued beverages. Alcoholic beverage commissions (ABCs) require monthly reports that explain how much inventory is in the establishment, how much was sold, and how much sales revenue was generated. Due to these in-depth controls, many states prohibit the transfer of alcoholic inventory between different establishments. This is not the case within a property that has multiple outlets that vend alcohol.

Due to the limitations of external transfers, this is not as big a factor as it is with food. Transfers may occur between outlets in the same property, and transfers may occur between the outlets and the kitchens; this needs to be documented. In some larger properties, inventory may not be duplicated in every outlet, so when a product like wine is ordered, it may come from another outlet. Another example would be when one outlet has a run on a particular brand; they may requisition it from another outlet. The kitchen also may not purchase its own alcohol used for cooking; it may requisition it from a front of the house venue. Some of the alcohol used in the kitchen may include beer for beer batter or cooking wine, or certain alcohols used in the production of desserts and sauces.

WINE SERVICE

Many establishments invest a lot of money and resources in establishing an extensive wine list for a restaurant. An extensive wine list has both pros and cons in the restaurant business. This investment should not be made until one establishes that it would be appropriate for the clientele of the restaurant. Although the investment could be large, the rewards can also help an establishment to become successful and a destination property (see Figure 9.5).

MONITORING BEVERAGE OPERATIONS

There are three approaches to monitoring beverage operations. The first method is the **cost approach.** In the cost approach, a monthly inventory is taken to determine value of the inventory. This value can be calculated using the same methods as described with regard to food. As with food, adjustments are made taking into account transfers to and from the kitchen, as well as any other plus and minus calculations that are needed. At this point, total dollar value of closing inventory is determined. As with food calculations, opening inventory plus purchases, plus and minus adjustments, minus closing inventory is equal to the cost of beverages used.

FIGURE 9.5

Pros of an Extensive Wine Service	Cons of an Extensive Wine Service
Higher check average	Financial outlay
Prestige	Storage costs
More sophisticated clientele	Higher labor cost
Marketing	Training
High profit item	Spoilage

IMPORTANT FORMULA

> Opening inventory
> + Purchases
> + Adjustments and transfers in
> − Adjustments and transfers out
> − <u>Closing inventory</u>
> = Cost of beverage used

This calculation may be done for total beverage costs, or it may be separated by the different categories management has established, such as some of the common divisions including draft beer, bottled and canned beer, wine and spirits. Using this information, costs may be used to compare the actual cost of beverage sales to the standard cost of sales that has been previously established. These standards are based on beverage cost percents and standard recipes. The data is then used to create daily calculations as well as period to date calculations.

The second method is the **liquid measure approach.** With this method, also called the ounce control method, a daily physical inventory of every bottle is completed and the actual usage in ounces is compared to the ounces sold. This method, although not used widely due to time constraints and the tedium of counting, is finding a return in the industry. This is due to the use of automatic alcohol dispensers, which give an accurate count of what alcohol has been used.

The third approach to monitoring beverage operations is the **sales value approach.** In this approach, management calculates how much in sales each bottle should generate by multiplying the drink cost times the number of drinks a bottle should generate.

IMPORTANT FORMULA

> If a bar is using a liter bottle, and the drink size is one ounce, each bottle should generate 33 drinks at the set per ounce selling price.

EXAMPLE PROBLEM

If management has established that the selling price of each ounce of a certain brand of vodka is $2.50, and they are pouring out of liter bottles, each bottle should generate:

$33 \times \$2.50 = \$82.50$

In this method, the **beverage differential** needs to be accounted for. The beverage differential is the difference in sales generated by selling a mixed drink, as compared to an ounce measure of the liquor. Beer sales do not generate a beverage differential unless the establishment sells pitchers of beer. Bottled and canned beer is sold "by the each," so every can or bottle will generate a sales value that is easily calculable. When selling keg beer, the amount of money generated by beer sales is not as consistent, due to pouring techniques—including spillage and head—and if the product is sold by the glass or by the pitcher.

Wine sales are similarly less affected by beverage differential than liquor because many establishments do not sell wine by the glass. If wine is sold by the bottle, the amount of sales is easily calculated, but if it is sold by the glass other factors become important when forecasting sales. If wine is purchased solely for by-the-glass sales, a value can be calculated as to the total amount of sales generated by the bottle. However, if that same bottle can be sold whole, a different sales value will be calculated. One of the most important variables in individual glass of wine sales is whether there is any waste during production. Wine spoilage, which can occur more frequently during individual glass sales, will create a difference in forecast sales.

Beverage differential most affects sales forecasts of liquor. When calculating sales value of a bottle of liquor, unless all prices are the same and all serving sizes are the same, the bottle may have a very great difference in the sales value associated with it.

EXAMPLE PROBLEM

If a bar sells one-ounce shots of liquor that comes in a liter bottle (33.8 oz), it can be assumed that the bottle will generate 33.8 drinks. For ease of calculation, assume that there is a small amount of waste and exactly 33 drinks are poured from this bottle. If the bottle costs $10.00 to buy, each drink would cost 30.3 cents. If beverage cost percent were 20%, the selling price for each drink would be $1.51. The calculation for sales generated from the bottle is 33 × 1.51 = $49.83. This is the sales value of this bottle if all sales were done as one shot with no additional cost items included in the sale, such as when selling a shot of liquor.

Most establishments do not sell an entire bottle of any type of liquor in shot form. Most include mixers, ice and/or other alcoholic beverages. When this is calculated the sales value of the bottle will change, unless unusual situations occur. If the selling price of a mixed drink is adjusted only to take into account the increased cost of the mixer, then sales value will be the same for the bottle. In the normal course of business this does not often occur, since the mixed drink prices usually run a lower beverage cost due to the amount of labor involved in the preparation of the drink and the perceived value of the mixed drink as opposed to the straight shot. Another difference between the two is that quantities of alcohol may differ between a straight shot and the amount of alcohol used in a mixed drink. Many establishments will pour a one-ounce measure of liquor when a shot or an on-the-rocks drink is ordered, while pouring a $^3/_4$ ounce shot when they are adding a mixer.

Drink prices may also vary depending on the mixer, as juices will generally cost more than soda, depending on the establishment. This will affect both the sales value of the bottle and the beverage cost percent associated with the liquor. If sales value of the bottle has a very large discrepancy, it makes it very difficult to forecast anticipated sales and to control revenue produced from the bottle. Through an analysis of the clientele and the type of establishment, management may be able to estimate sales value of a bottle; however, this can be a very inaccurate method. A better way to forecast sales value of a bottle is to use historical data to forecast the beverage differential per bottle. When looking at past sales, management can identify the percentage of drinks that are sold as straight shots and the percentage that are sold as mixed drinks. This information is much easier to access through computerized data sources such as a POS system than through hand counting of drinks sold over a period of time.

EXAMPLE PROBLEM

If management calculates that the liter bottle generates 10 drinks that sell for 1.51, 13 drinks that sell for $2.00, and 10 drinks that sell for $1.75, then the sales value of the bottle become $58.60 instead of the $49.83 calculated in the previous example.

WHY THIS IS IMPORTANT

Control of inventory is essential to create profitability in the bar industry.
■

SUMMARY

- Identify the different controls for different bars
- Identify beverage production control techniques
- Identify bartender theft techniques
- Identify beverage inventory techniques
- Identify government controls in beverage sales
- Identify states with dramshop laws
- Differentiate between well and call brands
- Identify methods of monitoring beverages

KEY TERMS

Automated beverage-dispensing
machine
Service gun
Shot glass
Jigger
Free pour
Dramshop laws

Well brands
Call brands
Cost approach
Liquid measure approach
Sales value approach
Beverage differential

PROBLEMS

1. Why do establishments need production control?
2. What are some pros and cons of extensive wine service?
3. Why would the bottle size change from one bar to another?
4. Why is issuing control a major factor in the beverage industry?
5. Explain three measuring devices for alcohol.
6. What is standardized recipe?
7. Why is glass size and shape important when selling keg beer?
8. Why is free pour considered a limited control technique?
9. Explain the pros and cons of an automated beverage-dispensing machine.
10. Explain three of the potential methods for bartender scams.
11. List and explain some government controls over alcohol.
12. Explain dramshop laws. Does your state have dramshop laws?
13. What is the difference between well brands and call brands?
14. Explain the three methods of monitoring beverage operations.
15. What are the licenses needed to sell alcohol in your city?
16. What is the beverage differential?

10
Costs in Labor

Chapter Objectives

After finishing this chapter the student will be able to:

Differentiate among the salaried and hourly employees

Describe the high turnover rate in the industry and some methods to lower it

Describe the costs associated with high employee turnover

Explain ways to save labor dollars

Calculate labor cost percent

Examine forecasting for labor needs

Use an operating budget

Explore various compensation techniques

Introduction

This chapter introduces labor cost in the hospitality industry. Issues on labor cost control, such as employee turnover and the various ways of spending and saving money in the labor column of the operation budget are discussed. Some of the many ways to compensate employees are discussed, including direct and indirect payments, as well as deferred and current compensation, including wages and benefits.

LABOR COST

One of the major expenses in operating a foodservice facility, or any facility in the hospitality industry, is the cost of labor. Labor costs vary depending on the operation, but usually they are offset by the cost of food. In many operations the cost of labor can run into the high 30 percent to 40 percent range. Generally speaking, for these establishments to earn a profit they need to offset the higher labor cost by running a lower food cost, in the low 20 percent range. Another variation in the industry is the restaurant that runs a higher food cost, in the 40 percent range, while keeping labor costs down to the 20 percent range, which brings the costs into balance. Fast food restaurants typically run higher food costs, due to the low menu price, but many of the employees are students or others who are usually working for close to minimum wage. On the other end of the scale, restaurants that have a higher check average will run lower food cost percents. This is due to the higher menu price; these establishments will have higher skilled labor that will make more than minimum wage.

When calculating labor costs, the figures will be broken down into many categories. The first category is **overall labor cost.** This is calculated by dividing total cost labor in labor by the total sales amount. This gives a comparative figure that can be used to help calculate profitability in a restaurant. Once this figure is calculated, additional numbers should be looked at: labor cost of servers, cooks, prep cooks, dishwashers, and management. When these figures are calculated, the resulting labor cost percent is used to make sure that all expenses are in line with forecast labor costs.

WHY THIS IS IMPORTANT

The understanding of one-third of a hospitality operation's expenses, and the knowledge of how to control those expenses, is crucial element to profitability.

■

TYPES OF EMPLOYEES

Labor costs in the food industry are divided into fixed and variable expenses due to the type of employees used within the industry. Every facility needs to have salaried employees and hourly employees to compete successfully.

Salaried employees are considered fixed and non-controllable expenses, as the cost associated with them does not change with changing sales. If an employee is salaried, expenses are carried every pay period no matter how many hours are worked. This will usually include management positions such as chef or maître d'.

Hourly employees are considered variable and controllable wage employees. The cost associated with these employees will vary greatly with fluctuations in business. The industry is heavily supported by these employees. Hourly employees typically make less money than salaried employees, and when times are slow, schedules can and will be adjusted to save labor cost money. The cost savings associated with variable cost earners in the hospitality industry is a major consideration when schedules are created.

REASONS FOR TURNOVER

One factor that adds expenses to the bottom line in the hospitality industry is the extremely high **turnover rate** of employees. Turnover, the percentage of employees that leave an establishment compared to the number of employees for the establishment, historically runs around 100 percent for the hospitality industry. This is in comparison to an average rate of 21 percent for the government or 14 percent (Department of Labor statistics) for the manufacturing industry. There are many reasons for the high turnover rate in the industry: the number of opportunities that constantly present themselves with new operations opening and closing, the nature of the industry with the focus on customer service, the hours of operation and the consolidation within the industry.

A chief cause of turnover is improper training of employees. If the establishment does not properly train the employee, the chances of successful long-term employment are minimized. The type of training will vary, but a clear explanation of company goals and the methods to reach those goals must be explained to all employees. If training does not occur, this can affect the employment from two perspectives. If the employee is not trained properly, it will be hard to show success at whatever task is being done, because management has not told the employee what the proper result should be. This can lead to dissatisfaction at work, and the desire to leave a job. If the employee is not trained properly, management will look at the output and find more discrepancies between the work and expectations.

Whatever the cause of the turnover, the costs associated with it can affect the profitability of any operation. The main costs associated with turnover are the cost to find, replace, and train a new employee. Depending on the operation, the type of employee, and the responsibilities and knowledge required for the position, the replacement of key employees can be expensive and time consuming. Depending on the economy, many positions may have people waiting for an opening, but in many segments of the industry, and in many geographical locations, the replacement of key and non-key employees may be difficult.

Many establishments have in-house human resource departments that hire employees as positions become available. Often the work of hiring the correct employee is outsourced to companies that find employees for many operations. In either case, the costs to bring in a new employee can add up to a considerable amount of money, depending upon the variables associated with that hiring. If a business has a human resource department, it usually has additional functions within the property, but if the turnover rate is high, too many of these resources will need to be spent to recruit workers.

Once an employee is hired, possibly at considerable expense, additional costs are incurred in their training. Most new employees need to go through some form of training, depending on the operation and the type of position. Costs can include a full time trainer or a current employee working with a new hire. Either scenario adds expenses to the operation. If an employee, not a trainer, is teaching a recruit how to follow the company's policies, usually they cannot complete their own work too. Training levels will vary greatly depending on the position. A chef may understand how to cook food, but might not know how the inner workings of the operation are carried out. In this scenario, the training can be very minor when compared to the server who has never carried a tray.

Hiring and training employees can be very costly, but an additional expense associated with the high turnover rate is the cost of **unemployment insurance.** Unemployment rates are directly related to the amount of turnover in the industry. With the high turnover rate for the hospitality industry, the unemployment insurance rate is one of the highest. This insurance is a percentage charged on wages of all employees of every establishment.

WHY THIS IS IMPORTANT

Employee training is a crucial element in retaining employees. If employee turnover is high costs will rise due to such causes as hiring, training and employee error.

■

PAYROLL BUDGET

Prior to the scheduling of employees, an analysis of needs must be completed, and then it must adhere to the allotted **payroll budget.** The first step in scheduling employees is to **forecast** needs. This is done in every segment of the hospitality industry, whether in the kitchen, dining rooms, front desk or housekeeping. Forecasting will be covered in Chapter 14, but it needs to be discussed with regard to scheduling. When creating a schedule, the scheduler needs to have an estimate of the needs for the department. In the rooms department of a hotel, this may include how many check-ins and check-outs are scheduled. In food and beverage, this would be how many reservations are expected and how much preparation for these dishes is needed. Once the need is determined, the scheduler needs to be aware of the quantity expectations of each employee in the department. How many rooms can an attendant make up? How many tables can the server effectively cover? How many meals can the cook prepare, and how many dishes can the employee clean? Once these questions are answered, the schedule can then be made. The job of scheduling employees for this industry is not as easy as in other industries. If the forecast says 200 customers should be dining during the shift, it should be taken into account that they will not be spread over an 8-hour shift, but more likely will come within 3 hours. If a server can handle 25 seats, the additional calculation needs to be: How many will come in at the same time? If the guests come in evenly spread over the 8-hour shift, one server can handle the entire dining room, but that is unlikely. This is unlike other industries, such as manufacturing, where the flow of work is consistent throughout an entire shift.

OVERTIME VS. PART TIME

When staffing an operation some of the factors to be acknowledged are the use of part time employees. Part time employees are an integral part of this industry because the hospitality industry has a large number of seasonal workers; part time employees generally are cheaper to hire, as they usually do not receive full benefits; the costs associated with paying overtime to full-time employees as compared to part-time employees are higher. Overtime costs are higher than labor costs during normal work time; this needs to be considered while scheduling employees. Overtime laws are set as a standard by the federal government, but states may enact higher levels of overtime laws, laws that will pay the employee more money. The Fair Labor Standards Act (FLSA) has established that overtime is considered over 40 hours in a fixed consecutive 7 day / 24 hour period. Overtime payments are a minimum of 1 1/2 times the wages paid. It is important that management investigate state overtime laws to see whether they include time and a half after an 8-hour workday, time and a half after a 40-hour week, or any other variations.

The FLSA also addresses the overtime pay for salaried employees.

> Salary for Workweek Exceeding 40 Hours: A fixed salary for a regular workweek longer than 40 hours does not discharge FLSA statutory obligations. For example, an employee may be hired to work a 45-hour workweek for a weekly salary of $300. In this instance the regular rate is obtained by dividing the $300 straight-time salary by 45 hours, resulting in a regular rate of $6.67. The employee is then due additional overtime computed by multiplying the 5 overtime hours by one-half the regular rate of pay ($3.335 × 5 = $16.68).

This example from the Department of Labor website illustrates why management employees have successfully sued many fast food and other restaurant companies in recent years. Many articles have been written detailing these cases, including *"Workers' Winning Claims for Back Overtime Shake Employees," Nation's Restaurant News,* September 24, 2001, Special Report, p. 1 (byline: Alan J. Liddle).

There are situations that show that scheduling employees and paying overtime is a good alternative. In many employment situations, the costs of 1 1/2 times the rate of pay may be more beneficial financially to an establishment than hiring an additional employee, raising the hours of another part-time employee who makes more money, or making another employee work enough hours to qualify for benefits. The overtime pay may be substantially less than the alternative.

The Department of Labor has recently changed the regulations that define what duties and positions are exempt from overtime pay. At the same time, they are changing the salary minimums for workers to qualify automatically for overtime pay from $155 per week to $455 per week, or $8,060 to $23,660 annually.

PLANNING FOR LABOR SAVINGS

Whether planning an operation from the ground up or just upgrading an operation, planners need to take into account any labor cost savings that can be utilized. This includes more expensive labor saving equipment and supplies, menu design and service style, and more efficient facility design and layout.

One way to reduce labor costs is to purchase equipment that can take the place of a number of employees. This can include dish machines that are more labor efficient or equipment that will cut food instead of having items hand cut, as well as pre-prepped or pre-cooked items. This concept is expanding in the hospitality industry, as the labor force available is smaller than the positions available. When menu or design planning takes place, the number and quality of employees should be evaluated. If employee numbers are expected to be low, convenience foods and effective equipment purchasing may be the only way to prepare the quantity and variety of needed food. Machinery exists that will peel potatoes and cut them any way wanted. Also, instead of the labor involved in making sauces from scratch, products can be purchased that require only adding water. Many properties purchase products pre-portioned or pre-cut to the size and shape that management specifies.

Many major national chains prepare foods at a commissary location and then send products to smaller locations completely prepared; they need only to be reheated. Through the technological advances created with sous vide, vacuum packaged, preparation and handling system, food can be prepared according to managements needs. Any employee, with or without culinary training, can reheat the food and serve it to the guest. The advantage of this is that the product is prepared according to management's specifications and it is prepared in a large quantity, allowing the establishment to purchase in a larger quantity, usually creating a lower cost. In any commissary system, an additional advantage is that when an employee is preparing a product in a large quantity, repetitiveness will increase productivity. In large hospitality operations with multiple food outlets, much of the preparation work is done in a communal preparation area; the product is then transferred to every outlet that uses the item. This commissary system saves additional money in that usually these employees are compensated less per hour than those in gourmet rooms or outlets that generate sales and profits for the operation.

Another technique for labor savings is to limit the diversity of the menu, allowing for a limited number of employees to prepare and cook the food. This diversity will allow for a limited variety of equipment needed to prepare the menu mix. Additionally, when planning a facility and the menu, management can select a service style that will incur limited labor costs.

Kitchen layout is another factor in labor cost savings. When designing a kitchen or any back of the house operation, layout can add or save in the costs of doing business. Workflow will avoid employees taking extra steps to get the job done. If a chef does not have a refrigerator in the workstation and needs to walk to another location for product, labor is not effectively being utilized. In the MGM Grand Hotel in Las Vegas, Wolfgang Puck has a full time employee whose only job is to pick up product at the loading dock and bringing it back to the kitchen. The layout of the property shows that the loading dock is almost a half mile away from the restaurant; yet enough deliveries come in to warrant a full time employee. If the layout allowed, and the restaurant were better situated, less labor might be required to keep food in the restaurant.

WHY THIS IS IMPORTANT

Proper restaurant and kitchen design can help keep employee productivity high, if the proximity of supplies is near the production area. Efficient kitchen design will also maintain quality of products due to proper storage space near production areas. Proper design can also help maintain sanitation principles, eliminating the need to dispose of product.

■

OUTSOURCING

The **outsourcing** of goods and services is one of the fastest growing labor saving concepts being implemented in the hospitality industry. This concept has been utilized for a long time for the human resource sector; many companies have used headhunters for searching for and hiring employees. Hospitality operations have typically outsourced many facets of the operation, including waste disposal, decorating, pest control, linen supply, advertising, and landscaping.

One of the advantages of outsourcing is the ability to keep costs under control. It may not be efficient financially for a food service establishment to keep accounting staff on hand full time; this cost could be decreased by hiring a company to do financial services for the company. Outsourcing can help companies avoid this costly cash drain. Outsourcing allows an organization to strengthen employment capacity without increasing personnel. This gives organizations access to experts with skills and expertise to embrace new technologies immediately. Most important, outsourcing of services allows organizations to focus on their core business objectives. This enables them to concentrate on strategic planning and responding to market opportunities.

WHY THIS IS IMPORTANT

Outsourcing has become one of the largest trends in many parts of the industry. Some operations outsource all food and beverage operations, while some outsource various components of their operation.

■

COMPENSATION

The costs associated with employees can be broken down in many ways. When hiring employees, or scheduling them, the many different forms of **compensation** need to be considered. The first criterion to look at is whether the employee is earning wages or a salary. Wages are defined as an hourly pay multiplied by the number of hours worked. This is the variable rate employee, who may have hours and shifts adjusted higher or lower depending on the volume of work available. Salaries are a set amount of money earned independent of the amount of work produced. If an establishment has salaried employees and wage earning employees, when business slows down, the hourly employees might not be given many hours, while the salaried employee might have to work additional hours. If the expense of the salaried employee is being paid, the need to spend extra money on additional hourly employee wages is not in the best financial interest of the establishment.

The second criterion to keep in mind while hiring and scheduling employees is how the compensation will be paid. In most cases, most compensation is considered **current compensation,** meaning that it is paid to the employee within a short period of time after the performance of the employee's duties. Current compensation includes wages and salaries as well as certain short term benefits, such as insurance. Additional compensation may be classified as **deferred compensation,** meaning that the costs associated with the expenses do not come until the future, usually after the separation of employment. This includes stock options and pensions. Although these expenses are incurred, they are not necessarily added to the expense column until the future date that the expenses are actually incurred. In the case of Social Security or a pension, the expenses are added at the time, but the compensation is deferred until the employee is eligible to collect it.

The third criterion to keep in mind is that compensation can be **direct compensation** or **indirect compensation.** Direct compensation is the money given to the employee in a paycheck. Indirect compensation includes everything the employee is given except for the paycheck; this includes the many benefits that may be available to the employee. Benefits can add a large expense to the cost of labor. If an employee is earning an hourly wage of $10.00, you need to calculate how many additional costs are associated with scheduling that employee. Some of those expenses include payroll taxes, which every employer needs to pay for every employee. Additional expenses depend on the benefits offered by the establishment. These benefits can include—but are not limited to—health insurance, sick leave, vacation days, discounts, and retirement benefits. These expenses can add up to 25 percent or more of employee earnings. In the case of the employee making $10.00 per hour, the cost with benefits may make the actual wages $12.50 per hour (see Figure 10.1).

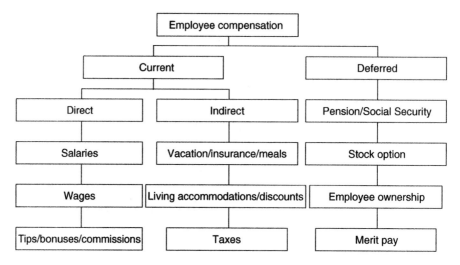

FIGURE 10.1   Employee Compensation Organizational Chart

The best way to ensure that labor costs are controlled is to train the employees properly and to have a clear objective of how to train them. A well written, clear, concise job description will allow an employee to be trained correctly and have full knowledge of the expectations of the job. These concepts will be covered in depth in Chapter 11.

WHY THIS IS IMPORTANT

How and when employees are compensated can affect profitability over an extended period. How and when employees are compensated may also be a factor when hiring employees.

■

ADDITIONAL FORMS OF COMPENSATION

Some forms of compensation either are required by law or required to keep an establishment competitive in the market for employees. These may include:

Taxes. Different forms of taxes will be paid in different states and jurisdictions. Federal taxes will be the same across the nation:
Social Security: currently 6.2%
Medicare taxes: currently 1.45%
Unemployment: will vary by state and industry

Insurance
Health: 8–10 percent of payroll amount
Dental
Life insurance
Long term/short term disability

Paid holidays
May include only national holidays or include additional days
Paid vacation: accrued after one year or pro-rated monthly
Sick leave: accrued after one year or pro-rated monthly

Educational assistance. Offered to help improve employee knowledge and skills, and repaid to the employee after successful completion of the course and upon receiving a pre-agreed upon grade. The course might need to be related to the current job description.

Some forms of compensation may add very little cost to an establishment, especially if they already offer some of the services to guests, such as:

Concierge service. This is becoming very popular as employees are spending more time at work. May include dry cleaning, shopping and making reservations.

Exercise facility. Many studies have shown the benefit to the well being and ability to handle an increased workload if employees maintain good physical fitness.

Childcare. Studies show that many potential employees cannot work due to family obligations, by offering on premise, or reduced cost, child care the potential workforce will increase.

Meals. The employee cafeteria may be considered a benefit if it is subsidized to the employee.

Flexible schedules. Employers may need to check local overtime laws to decide whether to implement a schedule such as 4–10-hour shifts.

Telecommuting. Although this is not used much in the restaurant industry, the hospitality industry has many positions in which employees may be able to work from home, or at a remote location.

Some forms of compensation are used to lure people into taking jobs, such as:

Moving expenses. This can be either a flat rate or exact expenses.

Signing bonus. Many times bonuses are given after an initial employment period, or spread out over a timeframe to ensure that employees stay with the company.

Housing. This is usually offered in high rent areas or areas that hire many seasonal employees.

Some forms of compensation that have been used for key employees have recently proven to be non-cost effective:

Low interest loans. Used to help raise the compensation of higher executives by giving them money at a reduced rate. This has been outlawed, for future loans, through the Sarbanes-Oxley Act, signed into law in 2002.

Golden parachutes. Used to ensure that it is very expensive to re-place upper management in case of management changeover.

WHY THIS IS IMPORTANT

Many employees, especially those in upper management positions, may require different forms of compensation to entice them to join an organization. Many operations may be able to take advantage of in-house perks, free meals or hotel stays to add compensation.

■

SUMMARY

- ■ Labor cost calculations were discussed
- ■ Industry turnover rate was explored
- ■ The pros and cons of overtime were discussed
- ■ The concept of outsourcing was investigated
- ■ Forms of compensation were evaluated

KEY TERMS

Overall labor cost

Salaried employees

Hourly employees

Turnover rate

Unemployment insurance

Payroll budget

Forecast

Outsourcing

Compensation

Current compensation

Deferred compensation

Direct compensation

Indirect compensation

WEBSITES

http://www.bls.gov/home.htm

http://www.dol.gov/

http://money.howstuffworks.com

http://restaurant.org

PROBLEMS

1. Explain why the forms of compensation listed at the end of the chapter would fall under the deferred or current category.
2. Explain why the forms of compensation listed at the end of the chapter would fall under the direct or indirect category.
3. Why do most establishments need both hourly and salaried employees?
4. How does the Fair Labor Standards Act affect the hospitality industry?
5. Explain the concept of outsourcing.
6. What is the value of outsourcing?
7. What criteria can an establishment use to decide whether or not to out-source?
8. Why is the turnover rate higher in the hospitality industry than in other industries?
9. How can turnover of employees be lessened in the hospitality industry?
10. What is the government's definition of overtime?
11. How can a new hotel operation plan for labor savings?
12. How can a new foodservice operation plan for labor savings?
13. What benefits are most important to you? Why?
14. Why are salaried employees considered fixed costs?
15. How do restaurants balance food costs and labor costs?
16. How are unemployment rates calculated?
17. How does forecasting affect labor costs?

11
Controls in Labor

Chapter Objectives

After finishing this chapter the student will be able to:

Differentiate between varieties of quality standards

Differentiate between varieties of quantity standards

Evaluate the cost standard of labor

Distinguish between the hospitality industry and other industries with regard to productivity standards

Use an organizational chart

Differentiate between a job analysis and a job description

Identify appropriate corrective actions

Introduction

This chapter gives an overview of the standards associated with labor cost. The first step in establishing these standards is to create an organization chart. This chart is a direct result of the task analysis and the creation of the job description. Once this is done, quality, quantity, and cost standards can be established. After these standards are established, employees are trained. Monitoring of the employees is essential to success, as is corrective action when the standards are not met.

LABOR COST CONTROL

The first step in the control process of labor is to establish performance and productivity standards for every position in the establishment. Some industry accepted performance standards include: quality, quantity and cost. Before the first step can be taken, management will need to establish which positions are going to be required in the hospitality operation. These positions will be based on the clientele that is expected at the establishment.

ORGANIZATIONAL CHART

After the clientele is established, management needs to perform a needs assessment for the facility which should include all of the positions and jobs needed for the property, including management, front of the house, back of the house, and support positions. In Chapter 10 outsourcing was discussed. Part of this process included the creation of the three standards of labor: quantity, quality and cost.

TASK ANALYSIS

Prior to the creation of the **organizational chart,** a task analysis needs to be completed. A **task analysis** is completed through answering a series of questions related to what should be done, when it should be done, and how is it should be done. When establishing the quantity standard, management will need to look at all the tasks and decide what the level of service will be, the number of employees that will be needed, and the amount of work each employee will be responsible for. An example might be how many servers in the restaurant, or how many seats each server will be responsible for. Another example is how many cooks will be needed, and how many stations each will be responsible for. In both of these cases, the answer will tie into both the quality and quantity standard. As the quantity standard increases, in most cases the quality standard will decrease, whether it is how many tables a server has, or how many rooms a housekeeper needs to clean in a shift. Once these two standards are created, a cost standard will be created.

This is the point at which management would need to complete a **cost-benefit analysis.** This analysis is done to decide which tasks should be performed in house and which ones an outside company can do. A cost-benefit analysis is used to compare the costs associated with doing a task and the benefit realized if the task is outsourced. It is imperative that management ensure that any outsourced positions, or tasks, are competitively bid on; that a work specification is written so that the quality of the work is the same for every bid; and that the quality of the work is up to the standard established to serve the clientele (see Figure 11.1).

Once management has decided which tasks should be performed in house, it can start to create **job specifications.** Job specifications are needed to effectively hire employees, train them, and to ensure that they are doing the correct task, both efficiently and effectively. Detailed job specifications will allow management to make sure that all the work that should be accomplished is assigned to an employee, and that the employees will know how to do the jobs they are enlisted to do (see Figure 11.2).

With the brigade system, or any other organizational chart, the job description will be very detailed and will include what should be done. The

FIGURE 11.1 Examples of Tasks That Can Be Outsourced

Butchering of meats	Usually outsourced to a degree rather than buying a whole carcass
Trash removal	Most common outsourced task
Linen service	Many operations are not large enough to support their own laundry
Landscaping	Many operations do not have landscapers
Baked goods	Many operations do not support an on-site bakeshop

FIGURE 11.2 Escoffier's Brigade System

> Auguste Escoffier is the chef who created the kitchen brigade system, which gives every employee a title and a list of jobs they are responsible for completing. Prior to the implementation of this system, no one had any specific duties in the hospitality industry and everyone did whatever they wanted. Escoffier's brigade system, although adjusted to the needs of the individual restaurant, is the system still used in many kitchens and most classical French restaurants.

more exact this description, the more likely it will be followed to management's expectation. If the description is not detailed enough an employee without the required skills may be hired for a job.

WHY THIS IS IMPORTANT

Understanding the needs of an operation allows for proper staffing.

■

ESTABLISHING STANDARDS

Before writing the job description, management needs to take the task analysis and create the standards the employees must attain. The quality standard is the first standard to be established. This standard should be directly related to the type of clientele expected in the establishment. Management will establish what employee expectations are after establishing what type of

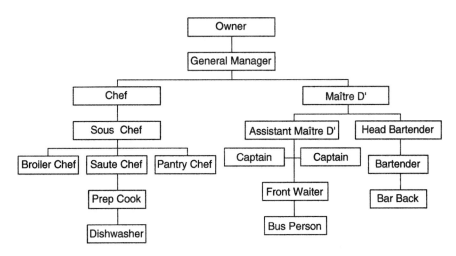

FIGURE 11.3 Sample French Restaurant Organizational Chart

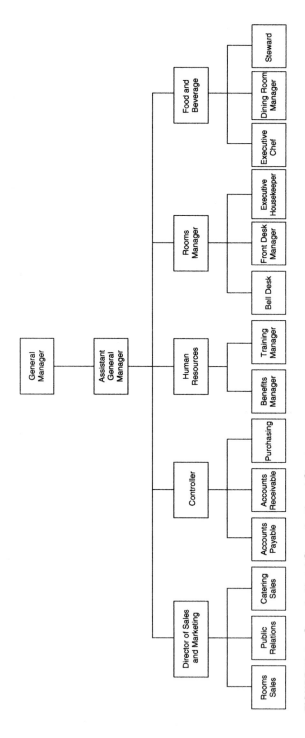

FIGURE 11.4 Sample Hotel Organizational Chart

restaurant is being created. If a formal French restaurant is being created, the quality of the employee's skill level will be increased as compared to the quality expectation of a French bistro or a casual family style restaurant. In the formal restaurant, a service employee may be expected to perform certain tableside cooking techniques, which will bring in a different worker than for the more casual restaurant. In the back of the house, a formal restaurant will include a larger number of employees who are specialized in the preparation of a certain category of foods, as compared to an employee who will cover many stations. The more specialized position might require a more experienced or trained employee. In the hotel end of the industry, a four- or five-star or diamond property may require the employees to be better experienced in customer relations, or the working of front desk computers.

The quantity standard will be established after the quality standard, and is recognized as the amount of work an employee should manage during a particular timeframe. Quantity standards can be assessed by the hour, by the shift or for any given timeframe. For servers this may include how many tables or seats they can effectively service at any one time. The number of customers served throughout the shift may be less important to management, if they cannot cover an entire station during a rush period.

The more formal the restaurant, the larger the quantity of employees needed, due to the varied nature of each of the positions and the more diverse and specific job skills each employee will need. In the hotel industry the overall number of employees per room has declined in recent years. This increases the quantity of work that each employee is expected to generate. Industrywide, the ratio of employees to rooms has gone below 2:1, the exception being the high-end hotel market, which has maintained an employee to room ratio of 1:1.

The last standard is the cost standard. This will be established after establishing the clientele, the quality and the quantity standards. If an employee were expected to work intensely, the cost standard, or pay scale, would be higher than for an employee who works a station that is not as busy. An additional factor is the skills and education needed by any employee, which will have a strong influence on the costs associated with filling the position as well as filling the position with a specific employee. Management may have input in the creation of this standard, but in many cases management will have very little input in the cost standard. Labor unions, local laws, and the effects of the economic theory of labor supply and demand will also influence the cost standards (see Figure 11.3 and 11.4).

JOB DESCRIPTION

Additional components of an effective **job description** are the inclusion of when and where the task needs to be performed. In many cases the "when" for a task can be an apparent answer, but in many tasks the timing of the task can be an important element in the success of the task. Many tasks in the

FIGURE 11.5 Sample Job Descriptions

Ineffective Job Description	Effective Job Description
. . . be able to work a broiler	. . . effectively work the broiler keeping track of 6 different broiled meats, cooked to a variety of doneness, and 3 chicken and fish entrées
. . . work the front desk	. . . check in a minimum of 15 guests an hour
. . . clean rooms	. . . clean 8 rooms an hour
. . . cook breakfast foods	. . . and operate a minimum of 6 omelet pans simultaneously

hospitality industry are sequential, with one task to be completed before another can be started. This may include housekeeping, where the order of cleaning a restroom will matter in the successful cleaning of the facility. Other jobs may not need to be done at a specific time, but the job description should indicate this.

Another element of the job description is where the task is to be completed. Certain tasks can be completed in any environment, but others must be completed in a specific location in the facility, for example the dish area. Although dishes can be washed in a three-compartment sink, they usually are not. In a job description for a dishwasher it may indicate that dishes are to be cleaned in a dish machine, while pots and pans are to be cleaned in the sink. Many establishments will allow pots and pans to be completed in the dish machine, while others will not. When hiring and training a dishwasher, this factor will be essential to ensure that management's standards are met.

The final component of the job description is completed once all of the standards are established. At this point measurable performance criteria should be created (see Figure 11.5).

WHY THIS IS IMPORTANT

Understanding the needs of the operation based on the clientele will allow an operation to prepare for the guest. Having clearly defined job descriptions and organization charts allows all employees to perform their jobs effectively and efficiently.

∎

TRAINING

A critical task for management in the hospitality industry is the training of employees. Training can take many forms, depending on what needs to be taught, and how much previous knowledge the employee has. All new employees should have some form of training, even if merely an explanation of the philosophy of management.

Smaller operations may do less formal methods of training, such as on the job training, while larger establishments and multi-unit operations may have training managers who direct the education of the employees. This department is usually a component of the human resources department. Training done through human resources may be training for the organization rather than training for a specific job. After this initial training, additional training may occur once an employee enters the department that person will be working in.

Besides new hires, there are many instances in the hospitality industry that require present employees to have additional training. As technology advances, organizations may update their equipment with newer technology. With this update, they may need to train the entire staff, or only those using the equipment directly. In many operations the standards may change, due to costs or profit, and employees may need to be trained to the new standard. Many restaurants change menus frequently, as often as daily. In these situations employees need to be trained to prepare the new menu items. This training may take only a few minutes, but it is essential that all affected employees get it. Another use of training for present workers is when an employee is cross-training for another position. Cross-training may be within a department, or within a hotel. Cross-training of employees is an essential part of the industry, helping employees better themselves, and ensuring employee growth and feelings of contentment.

TRAINING METHODS

Training methods will vary depending on the job specification and the previous knowledge the employee may possess. One method of training frequently used in the hospitality industry is **on-the-job training.** On-the-job training consists of the employee either entering the work force completely, or following another employee for a pre-determined or un-determined time. Employees learn the needed skills and standards by watching or working with present employees. Management needs to ensure that present employees working around newly hired employees are familiar with, and use, the standards. There are many jobs in the field that allow for successful training using this cheap and easy method of training. Jobs that can use this training may include dishwashers, servers, porters or office help.

Certain positions may need a more formal or extensive training than on-the-job allows for. In these cases there may be formal standards established for more extensive training, but often the additional training will be based on the specific needs of the employee. When establishing this additional training, certain decisions have to be made. One decision that has to be made is where the training is going to take place. Many companies prefer on-site training by present employees or experts in the field. Other establishments may elect to teach the material off site, at a location that may be centrally located if the company has multiple locations. Off-site locations may also allow for the training to not interfere with business at the worksite.

A very common method of training is distance learning, where via the Internet or videotapes, an employee can train at home or at any location. An advantage of distance learning is that the resources for the training can be spread over a large number of people and places. While this may work for certain jobs, cooking skills, among many other jobs, are not as easily learned through this technique

Training decisions will also include additional factors, such as if the training will be for one individual or for many learning the same material. Another factor is that certain material may require extensive training that may include a more formal setting, such as a college, either community or four year.

The objectives of training are to ensure that employee's mission meets your mission, to maintain consistency for your products and services, make employees more confident because they want to do a good job, to promote safety on the job, to allow a person to contribute to and feel part of the team sooner. Management must remember that training is an investment in the employee that will ultimately help the establishment.

MOTIVATING EMPLOYEES

A major component of a positive workplace environment is employees who are happy at their jobs. A cornerstone to this is to link individual employee goals to the company's objectives. Employees "buy in" to the philosophy and goals of management, they are more likely to be successful and happy at their job. Successful employees can help management reach their goals. Not every employee will buy into the job, and many do not consider their job their career, so many times external rewards will have to come into play. Some of these rewards may cost the company money, but there are many motivation and reward methods available to open minded managers to use for employees who are not necessarily long-term, company minded.

Some of the non-financial techniques that can help to motivate workers include having positive and comfortable work surroundings. Although it may not be possible to paint the kitchen a soft color, there are many things that make the surrounding more comfortable. Neat and orderly environments can make employees feel more satisfied with the job. Additionally, employees who feel an ownership in the operation are more motivated to do a good job. When management allows for employee empowerment, most workers will be more organized and goal oriented.

A very common reason for employee dissatisfaction and an unmotivated work force is working for an establishment that does not have an open communication policy. Employers should always keep staff informed about what is going on in the business that is relevant to them, whether it is a possible manager change or a change in company standards. Employees should create a true open door policy that allows for a safe two-way dialogue between management and non-management employees. Through this open communication policy, employees are allowed to communicate work and non-work related situations that may affect them. This can lead to the implementation of a corrective measure for many of these situations. Even if the problem might not be related to work, some work solutions may help relieve it, such as a change in work schedule or a change of position. Through this open door policy managers should ask their employees what they want as a motivation tool. Many people will not ask for a lot, but by being asked they will feel that they are a wanted and needed part of the work process. If the employee asks for something reasonable, management should go out of its way to try to accommodate them.

Management should care about, and respect, employees and if it truly does, it can make a work situation much more pleasant for workers, leading to higher job satisfaction. One adjustment might be to have flexibility when scheduling for employees, especially part time workers who may have another job or might be enrolled as a student. If management personnel look employees in the eye rather than avoiding them, they will build up trust, which will further enhance the work environment.

All management should set a good example in everything they do. If management does not show people respect, many employees will follow suit. Every employee wants to be complimented, and this minor motivation factor can build up self-esteem and workplace competencies in many employees.

All of the previous motivating tools may not cost much for the establishment. There are also many financial tools that can be used to motivate people. Employees can be motivated with comp time, or added benefits. One of the biggest motivating tools is money, and this can be tied into motivating employees by offering bonuses to work above and beyond the job description.

Besides a positive work site and a more successful operation, one of the biggest benefits to motivating employees is that it will lower turnover rate in your facility. With a lower turnover rate, success will be perpetuated through not having to spend the money to hire and train new employees, and the present employees are much more educated about your standards.

PRODUCTIVITY

Hospitality, unlike most industries, does not have a steady work pace that allows for consistent and easy control over productivity. **Productivity,** as described by *Webster's Dictionary* (www.m-w.com), is the "quality or state of being productive or yielding results." Without consistent, continual work-flow, management needs to assess many hospitality workers' and positions' productivity through alternate means, such as over a longer period of time, not minute by minute. One effective tool used to monitor employees is a count of items completed. This may include sales per hour, number of dishes prepared, number of rooms cleaned, or guests checked in.

Although this is an efficient method, worker productivity can also be measured through less concrete methods, including outside operations to assist in the observation of employees. Most of these options are for front-of-the-house employees so traditional methods may be engaged for employees not in a direct interactive position with the guest.

WHY THIS IS IMPORTANT

Proper training needs to be based on the needs of the operation, the job and the job appli-cant. Motivating employees creates higher productivity.

■

Monitoring Productivity

For a manager of any hospitality operation, especially food service, it is imperative to maintain careful and diligent observation of the facilities and operation. This observation can and should come in many forms to ensure compliance to the standards established. An effective means of observation is the use of management to monitor company personnel. One of manage-ment's crucial roles is to monitor employees' actions to safeguard against loss or abuse of company assets. Although this is a very effective tool, often this observation needs to be complemented with some form of external observa-tion and evaluation.

One effective way to monitor any operation is with a **mystery shopper.** Mystery shoppers are trained individuals who use the services of a company

FIGURE 11.6   Sample Mystery Shopper Survey Sheet

Y/N	Service	Y/N	Quality
___	Were you cheerfully greeted by the employee?	___	Was the temperature of the meal satisfactory?
___	Did the server "up sell" or suggestive sell any items?	___	Were proper condiments supplied?
___	Were the dishes clean?	___	Was portion size satisfactory?
___	Did the server return within two minutes of food delivery to check on the order?	___	Was presentation of your food satisfactory?

FIGURE 11.7 Guest Satisfaction Form

Were you greeted properly?	Yes	No
Was your room ready at check in?	Yes	No
Was your room clean?	Yes	No
Will you stay here again?	Yes	No

and monitor the success or failure of the operation. Mystery shoppers are trained to keep their observations from being detected by staff members. They can be hired either as individuals or through companies that perform mystery shopping. There are hundreds of companies that specialize in this type of outsourced productivity tool. Many large companies have their own departments that travel around and visit corporate or franchised operations within a brand and rate the property according to management's expectations.

Mystery shoppers are usually given training to allow them to take note of characteristics that the company is shopping for, usually including personnel issues as well as facility issues. Some of the categories that may be shopped for include exterior, interior, service, quality, atmosphere, restrooms, staffing and value. Many shopper reports include a negative value associated with each infraction, and a positive value for above level service.

Another non-management tool used to assess an employee's ability to follow management's guidelines is a guest satisfaction inquiry, index or survey. This form, shown in Figure 11.7, is a measuring tool that can come in many forms, depending on management's needs and the type of customer being asked. These forms can be on the table or in the room, and patrons fill them out and turn them in to an employee. Another variation has postage included on it and the patron can fill the form out after they leave, at their leisure or without the pressure of an employee's being aware of what they are saying. Other forms of the guest satisfaction index may be sent to patrons after they have left the property. Chains, wanting to find out how their prop-

FIGURE 11.8 Food and Sanitation Inspection Report

Establishment Name Manager's Name		Address Date of Last Inspection
Number	**Demerits**	**Infraction**
1	2	Food from approved source
2	1	Food labeled properly
3	1	Food contact surfaces clean
4	6	Food cooled properly

erties are performing, more commonly use this resource. Many establishments also offer these forms, which can be completed on line. Typical customized customer surveys are designed to measure overall satisfaction, product-level satisfaction, timeliness of delivery, customer service process satisfaction and interest in new potential products and services.

Another non-management tool used to assess an employee's ability to follow guidelines is the government health department report. Every jurisdiction may use a different form, but the commonality of the form is that the establishment is meeting minimum health and safety standards established by the local government. The form includes categories such as food, personnel, pest control, and plumbing, among others. If the health report is filled out with demerits, unless management has set standards too low, employees are not fulfilling their job descriptions. This tool can lead to management realizing it needs to raise their standard, or needs to ensure that employees are following the set standards. In many jurisdictions, health ratings are publicized in the newspaper or on television, and are also available on the Internet (see Figure 11.8).

Less formal and less exacting is a review written by a newspaper or other media source critic. Although critics can evaluate any establishment, they may not be aware of the standards that have been established by management. These reviews may not be written to the audience, or clientele, that management aspires to reach. When readers, or listeners, hear a review of any establishment they should be aware of who the critic is, and previous reviews from that critic. In many situations, the point of view of the critic may not be the same as for others, so the reviews should be filtered before major changes are implemented.

One of the most influential non-management tools for the hospitality industry are the rating systems that belong to many organizations. Many rating organizations are national, with the same standard used in every establishment. Consumers should be wary of many ratings that can be arbitrarily given to an establishment. Some of the more recognized rating organizations include Mobil and AAA (see Figures 11.9 and 11.10).

FIGURE 11.9   Mobil Rating Guide

Ratings are assigned according to the following scale:	
* * * * *	One of the best in the country
* * * *	Outstanding—worth a special trip
* * *	Well appointed establishment, with full services and amenities
* *	Comfortable establishment with expanded services and amenities
*	Clean, convenient establishment with limited services

FIGURE 11.10 Stars and Diamonds: How are hotel and restaurant ratings determined?

How are hotel and restaurant ratings determined? Who gives them? Who takes them away? How are they similar? How are they different? MOBIL awards stars; AAA awards diamonds. Both bestow ratings on a scale of 1 to 5, 5 being the highest, denoting the ultimate in luxury, service, atmosphere, and price. There are many similarities in the way these organizations determine ratings, and some significant differences.

Both conduct annual on site physical inspections. AAA employs a full-time staff of more than 50 inspectors; Mobil uses some part-time inspectors and some contract personnel. Both organizations have very detailed rating criteria that are available to the industry.

AAA publishes its ratings in 23 regional *Tour Books* that are free to the 40-million-plus AAA members. Mobil *Travel Guides* are sold to the public in bookstores.

Both AAA and Mobil provide inspections, evaluations, and ratings free of charge to hotels and restaurants. Approved establishments may pay a fee to display the copyrighted AAA logo and may purchase advertising space in the *Tour Books.*

Our clients often ask us which rating is better; which is more credible? Despite my background with AAA, I must be totally honest and objective. In my professional opinion, they are of equal merit. In my personal opinion, stars may be better known and more widely recognized as the universal symbol of quality and excellence. This is due primarily to the generic meaning of the word.

Basically, a AAA 4 diamond hotel and a Mobil 4 star hotel are very much the same thing, as both ratings have been awarded through similar evaluation processes and guided by similar physical and service standards. One must remember that both AAA and Mobil rating criteria are based on industry standards and reflect guests' expectations, not on the personal whim of the inspector.

Source: www.hoteljobresource.com/menu/article4815.html. "Feature—Stars and Diamonds: How Are Hotel and Restaurant Ratings Determined" by Harry Nobles and Cheryl Thompson Griggs, from www.hoteljobresource.com, January 15, 2003. Used by permission.

WHY THIS IS IMPORTANT

Outside monitoring of operations allow for unbiased, customer-based critiques of employees and procedures.

■

CORRECTING MISTAKES

One of management's most important functions is the implementation of corrective action when the established standards are not being adhered to. The first step in this process is to identify the problem. Once the problem is known, a process is established to teach the employee the correct standards. In many cases, the first step is to inform the employee that they are not meeting the standard. Ideally, this would be the last step of the correction, as the employee is now informed as to what they should be doing. If the employee knows the standard, but does not know how to reach it, management needs to enact training for the employee. This can be done quickly on the spot for many tasks, but also may include other forms of training such as a class or any of the methods mentioned earlier in this chapter.

DISCIPLINE

The last step in labor control is to discipline employees who do not follow the established standards. Discipline is a last resort after training and correcting mistakes occurs. If employees do not amend methods of performance to meet the standards that management expect, discipline in one of many forms needs to be administered. Discipline corrections can come on many levels and can include loss of hours, demotion, and in the worst-case scenario, termination of employment. The extent of the discipline will be directly related to the problem that initiated the discipline, as well as the position the employee holds.

FOOD COST VS. LABOR COST

Labor cost standards are directly related to food cost standards, in most businesses. Generally speaking, the higher the food cost, the lower the labor cost. This works the other way as well: The higher the labor cost, the lower the food cost. By balancing these two numbers, establishments can maintain profit margins after fixed and variable costs. Take fast food, for instance. When the profit and loss statement is analyzed for a fast food establishment it is generally considered a low labor cost average. Fast food establishments are known to hire high school students and employees who have recently graduated. In many instances these employees are earning minimum wage or just above it. With the average check for fast food, especially with the 99-cent menu, the cost of food is generally going to be higher than the cost of labor associated with the sale. At the other end of the spectrum, although a formal French restaurant will have a larger staff to guest ratio—and generally, they will be higher paid than in other segments—due to the higher check, average labor costs will be a lower percentage than food cost. If you cost out a menu in a French restaurant, you will find that the types and quantities of ingredients will raise food cost to a higher percentage than labor cost. In both examples, both food and labor cost percents should be maintained within an acceptable level to ensure profitability after other expenses are deducted.

These standards are employee expectations that span the entire operation. Every employee will have a job description that will explain minimum workload expectations, both with regard to quality and quantity. Once the standards are created for an individual establishment, forecasting for work schedules can begin. The first step is to forecast how many guests are expected during a period of time. Once the total number of guests is calculated, that information will be used to establish the number of employees needed for every position in an establishment. This forecast will be used to estimate employees needed in both the front of the house and back of the house positions. Using the forecast data, management needs to anticipate how many of each classification of employee are needed—bussers, servers, line cook positions, dishwashers, as well as every other position in the facility.

One of the next decisions to be made by management is the use of full time or part time employees. This may include the use of seasonal workers or workers who work less than a predetermined, full time number of hours. One of the advantages of using these types of employees is that they do not receive certain benefits to employees; some of these benefits will be discussed in Chapter 12.

SUMMARY

■ The organizational chart is introduced, and the steps to creating one are explained

KEY TERMS

Organizational chart	Job description
Task analysis	On-the-job training
Cost-benefit analysis	Productivity
Job specification	Mystery shopper

PROBLEMS

1. List some quality and quantity standards for a variety of hospitality related jobs.
2. Why is an organizational chart an important element for labor cost control?
3. Explain a cost-benefit analysis.
4. Why would a brigade system be implemented?
5. Why is a job description needed?
6. How does a task analysis help in the creation of job descriptions?
7. What factors can influence the cost standard for labor?
8. Write an effective job description for a hospitality related position.

9. Explain an employee motivation tool not discussed in the book.

10. List and explain four methods of monitoring employees.

11. Explain three employee scenarios that would lead to on-the-job training.

12. Explain three employee scenarios that would mandate formal training.

13. What is the value of hiring a mystery shopper?

12
Controls for Other Expenses

Chapter Objectives

After finishing this chapter the student will be able to:

Identify controllable and non-controllable costs associated with
   Restaurant operations

Business operations
Facilities
Occupancy

Introduction

Throughout this book the costs associated directly with preparing and selling food and beverage have been analyzed. For an operation to be successful, the realization that there are many peripheral expenses associated with the foodservice business is imperative. After analyzing these additional expenses, cost control principles should be administered to ensure that these costs do not become an obstacle to success and profitability. Many of the costs identified in this chapter are one time expenses, or expenses incurred infrequently. Other expenses, such as utilities, will be ongoing expenses that require constant managing.

COSTS: RESTAURANT OPERATIONS

There are many additional costs associated with food and beverage that must be analyzed. Many of these costs are necessary components of the restaurant industry. The quality, quantity, and cost standard associated with them should reflect the clientele and the price point of the restaurant. It would not be appropriate to serve food in a fast food restaurant on china, any more than it would be appropriate for service to utilize paper or plastic in a fine dining establishment. After establishing clientele, the standards for all of the following costs should be determined. The pattern and style should be selected. Many of these expenses will be a one-time shot and the cost can be depreciated over a long period of time. But many will continue to cost over an extended period: for example, expensive silverware. If purchased, it may be expected to last the lifetime of the restaurant; a cheaper grade might have to be replaced yearly; disposable silverware needs to be replaced every time it is used.

Linens

One of the first decisions to be made about linens is whether to have them in the establishment or not. Most restaurants do not see the need to put down tablecloths. Many restaurants, such as Romano's Macaroni Grill, replace a costly tablecloth with butcher paper or some other less expensive table covering. Many tables are finished with a high quality finish that does not require a tablecloth, but they cost more than a table that is designed to use a cloth.

Once it is decided to use a tablecloth, the next decision to be made is whether to buy the tablecloths and napkins and clean them in house, or to rent the linen and have a service that cleans them. An advantage to renting linens is that when you want to change the color or style, or if the product is wearing poorly, you do not need to re-buy the entire product; the linen company will bear the burden of cost. Another big advantage to renting linens is you are not responsible for washing and pressing the items. Many large operations, especially ones that include other outlets for linen, can justify the costs associated with self linen, while most operations doing a cost-benefit analysis will find that it is cheaper to outsource this task. The disadvantage of renting linens is that the product will cost you more every time you use it than if you own it yourself.

Flatware

Another large expense in the hospitality industry is the costs associated with flatware. When deciding which flatware to use there are many variables to consider, including weight of the item, design pattern, material used, and variety of utensils needed. As the menu is being decided, management needs to decide the quantity standard for the utensils. Will there be a separate fish fork (usually with fewer tines) or will an across-the-menu entrée fork be appropriate? Another question is, can the same fork be used for appetizer, salad and dessert? Once the quantity standard for the variety of utensils is resolved, how many of each utensil will be needed is calculated using the number of seats, the turnover, and the established quantity of backup needed.

Then other variables need to be decided. The next biggest expense variable is material and the weight of the utensil. As a rule, the heavier the weight of the utensil, the higher the cost of the product, but that depends on the costs of the raw material. Prices will vary greatly among silver, silver plate, stainless steel, or any of the other materials that utensils can be made of, including plastic, if appropriate for the establishment.

Decorations

A potentially high cost item in any establishment is the cost of decorating the dining room and any public areas. These costs could vary from a marginal expense to a huge outlay, depending on the décor selected to go with the menu and the clientele. Restaurants may put fresh flowers on the table, or fake (cheaper) flowers that can be reused for an extended period. It would be cheaper still to use free marketing material from suppliers who want to

FIGURE 12.1   Costly Restaurant Decorations

Picasso Restaurant at the Bellagio Hotel in Las Vegas opened their doors with 11 original paintings, as well as some rare photos of Pablo Picasso. Currently they exhibit nine paintings on the walls of the restaurant for diners to enjoy. At the Renoir Restaurant at the Mirage Hotel in Las Vegas, four original paintings by Pierre Auguste Renoir and six by his contemporary painters adorned the walls. The value of the paintings has been estimated to be millions of dollars.

advertise their items. Other decorations such as wall hangings can vary, from a coat of paint, to posters, to original works of art (see Figure 12.1).

Cleaning Supplies

One controllable expense that can cost a restaurant a large amount of money is the costs associated with cleaning supplies. Cleaning supplies are an integral part of the industry, as sanitary conditions are a requirement for a successful operation. With proper quality cleaning supplies and proper training, the costs associated with cleaning supplies can be controlled and maintained at the proper level. The costs of unmanaged cleansers can add up to a lot of money. Many of the industry standard cleaning supplies come in concentrated form. If employees are not properly trained on how to dilute the chemicals they could use too much product which, besides adding to the cost, will lessen the effect of the chemicals.

Utilities

Certain utility expenses are unavoidable and uncontrollable, such as air conditioning, heat, and lighting, but many can be contained with proper planning and oversight. Many of the costs, such as refrigeration and cooking fuel, are required and in many cases unavoidable; however, through proper design techniques efficiency can be maximized. Although most operations operate using natural gas as the main cooking fuel, some operations use electricity. Equipment costs may be higher if an establishment is switching to gas, or purchasing the initial equipment, but the cost of running equipment using natural gas can be half as much as using electricity. Walk-in coolers should be large enough to hold the amount of product needed, while allowing for proper air to circulate; in this way, establishments can keep electric bills low. When doing preparation work, timing may allow for ovens to be on for shorter periods of time if proper mise en place is practiced. Electronic thermostats can control the amount of air conditioning and heat running when the establishment is closed and no employees are on staff.

Menus

One expense for most operations is the costs associated with the physical menu. Menu costs can be very high or very low, depending on the operation. Many establishments only have a menu board; once the outlay is made, there are no other expenses. Other operations have leather bound menus that are very costly to create and which require frequent efforts to keep clean and usable. Others create daily menus which can be cost effective or not, depending on the material used. Expenses associated with the menu will vary, depending on the type of operation, the type of food, the service style, and the clientele.

Franchise Fees

Many foodservice operations are franchised by national or regional companies which allow other operations to sell a product that they have created or individualized. In these operations, the **franchisee,** the restaurant owner, has to pay the **franchisor,** the developer, for the right to sell its product. The franchisee usually needs to pay money up front, as well as a percentage of sales to the franchisor, for the right to sell its product. They may also be required to pay a percentage of sales to the main office for advertising the brand; this may not be a lot of money, but in some cases the amount may be large (see Figure 12.2 and 12.3).

Product Testing

A critical component of the foodservice industry is the updating and expansion of the menu. This is done through the trial and error practice of mixing different ingredients to create an acceptable tasting product with the appropriate appearance. The costs associated with research and development have

FIGURE 12.2 Franchise Fees for Restaurants

Restaurant	Franchise Fee	Royalty and Advertising Fee
McDonald's	$45,000	12.5%
Subway	$12,500	8.0%
Dairy Queen	$35,000	6.5%
TCBY	$20,000	4.0%
Applebee's	$35,000	7.0%
Denny's*	$40,000	7.0%
TGI Friday's**	$75,000	8.0+%

*Minimum net worth of 1 million dollars
**Minimum net worth of 3 million dollars

FIGURE 12.3 Franchise Fees for Hotels as a Percent of Sales

Courtyard	9.50
Crowne Plaza	9.60
Doubletree	9.00
Embassy Suites	8.90
Hilton	10.10
Marriott	11.30
Residence Inn	8.10
Sheraton	8.80

to be absorbed into the costs of any operation. In national chains, the research and development of new products is done on the corporate level, and the expenses are included in the fees for franchising (or they come out of the corporate profits). In the single unit operation, the costs have to be taken from the profits generated by the operation.

Outsourced Services

Many operations are required to outsource certain tasks; many others choose to outsource other tasks. Many local health departments require that foodservice operations maintain a contract with a licensed pest control operator for extermination. The operator, due to the training needed and the types of chemicals used, usually cannot do this job. A service more commonly outsourced in many hospitality operations is the accounting for the operation. Many places outsource the payroll operation, as well as the positions of accounts payable and accounts receivable. Larger operations do this in house, but smaller operations without the expertise to perform these tasks hire companies to complete them. Other jobs that can be performed by the operation may be outsourced due to the nature of the specific task, such as trash removal.

WHY THIS IS IMPORTANT

There are many additional expenses incurred while running a foodservice organization. If attention to detail in all of these expenses is not maintained, profit margins will disappear.

■

Licenses

There are many costs associated with the hospitality industry that are not directly related to food and beverage. Some of these costs cannot be avoided, such as licensing fees. Many localities have fees for business licenses, as well as health department fees. Every year the fees need to be paid and the costs included in the operating budget (see Figure 12.4).

FIGURE 12.4   Sample Licenses Needed for a restaurant in Wheeling, Illinois

1. Special use permit (see Planning Department)
2. Sign permit (see Building Department)
3. Liquor license (if applicable, see Licensing Clerk)
4. Building permit (see Building Department)
5. Certificate of occupancy (see Building Department)
6. Business license (see Licensing Clerk)
7. Vending machine (see Licensing Clerk)
8. Metropolitan Water Reclamation District of Greater Chicago (see Engineering Department)
9. Health permit (see Health Personnel)
10. State of Illinois Food Service Manager's Certification (see Health Personnel)

Source: http://www.vi.wheeling.il.us/Services/CommunityDevelopment/PermitsInfoAndRequirements/RestaurantPermitsAndLicenses.htm.

Marketing

Marketing expenses for an operation depend on the size of the operation and the demand for the operation. Marketing—getting out the word about the operation—can be very expensive, depending on the type of marketing being performed. A marketing budget can include expenses for such things as free meals, mailers to potential clients, newspaper advertisements, coupons, and television ads. Larger operations might also include the services of a public relations person, either full time or as an outsourced service. The marketing budget can also include the expenses for signage around an operation, as well as menu design costs.

Music and Entertainment

Some operations have live music, and the costs associated with the performers must be taken into account. Besides the cost of the musicians, there are some costs such as meals that must be included. Operations that have music in the background have expenses associated with this. All restaurants and businesses are required to pay royalties to music organizations such as ASAP, BMI and SESAC whenever they have music playing in the establishment. These expenses will vary depending on the size of the operation.

COSTS: BUSINESS OPERATIONS

Small businesses may be able to function without additional employees who are not directly related to the production operation, but larger operations will need support positions to help with the flow of the operation. In smaller operations the manager may be able to complete schedules for employees, but in larger operations support positions may be required to complete the added paperwork and recordkeeping needed. Many establishments hire an office manager or business manager to orchestrate all of the non-production related issues. With this employee comes the expense of having an office equipped with furniture and supplies.

WHY THIS IS IMPORTANT

There are many added expenses and permits needed to run any operation. These costs must be realized and added to operating costs.

■

COSTS: FACILITIES

One of the largest initial expenses of any restaurant is the cost for the furniture, fixture and equipment (FFE). This cost will be very large in any new establishment. Many establishments will create opportunities to help offset the costs associated with the initial purchase of FFEs. One way to help minimize this investment is by purchasing a previously owned facility. This allows for the initial costs, and depreciation, to be absorbed by another organization. The problems with this include that since the products are used, they may be in disrepair; as an investor, one would have to investigate why the previous operation did not succeed; and (the biggest factor) the design and standards may not be exactly the specification written for your restaurant.

There are many ways to purchase these products that can help to minimize the costs associated with them. In some cases, you may need to have flexibility when determining quality. Many times equipment—especially kitchen equipment—can be purchased either reconditioned or rebuilt. Although these products are not new, many times they include a limited warranty, which can create a higher level of confidence. Another way to acquire used equipment is through auctions, but in this case you may not know the quality of the product. Even if the product is guaranteed to be working at the time of the sale, it is usually unknown how the product was treated when it was in service.

Other options include purchasing demonstration equipment. Although this equipment has been used, it is usually fully covered by a manufacturer's warranty. Demonstration items might not appear as new, but the mechanics usually work as new. This may not be an option for a front of the house piece of equipment. Whenever purchasing equipment, especially used equipment, management needs to keep in mind the expenses associated with maintenance of the items. If there is no in-house maintenance department, the costs of repairs—especially for products no longer being manufactured—can be prohibitive. Even with an in-house department, these costs need to be budgeted for (see Figure 12.5).

FIGURE 12.5   Average Allocation of Budgeted Costs, All Type of Hotels

13% for land
11% for development and soft costs
61% for site improvement and building construction
12% for furniture, fixtures, and equipment
  3% for pre-opening and working capital

Furniture and Fixtures

Furniture in the hospitality industry can be very expensive. Since this product is the focal point of a room, the quality—especially the visual quality—must meet the standards for the anticipated guests. These costs may be very high for a high-end operation, while they will not necessarily be low for a lower end facility. Foodservice furniture includes tables and chairs, although many operations use a higher cost banquette or booth for seating guests. Other front of the house furniture can include a greeter stand; lounge and waiting area seating; and a bar. Back of the house furniture and fixtures will include office furniture, fixtures, and storage shelves.

In hotel operations, the costs and assortment of furniture and fixtures will be much greater. In these operations, additional furniture needed will include the lobby area, which must make the guest feel welcome. Additional hallways and meeting rooms have to be furnished, as well as the guest rooms within the property. These costs will add up and can be very high in higher quality operations (see Figure 12.6).

Equipment

Whenever purchasing major equipment, the concept of **lifetime costs** needs to be taken into account. When purchasing expensive items, management needs to consider the trade-in value of any old equipment that the new product will replace, delivery costs, installation and testing costs, relevant operating costs, trade-in value of the new FFE when it is replaced, and—one of the most important in times of short labor supply—the potential operating savings from the product. Many products are manufactured to include a large amount of labor and energy savings by creating more efficient, automated equipment. When contemplating new equipment, one should take into account all of these factors. Although the initial cost may be higher than for other products, sometimes the lifetime costs and operating savings can make a product more beneficial to the operation.

One way to reduce costs when purchasing large equipment is to purchase directly from the manufacturer. Bypassing the distributor or retailer, a

FIGURE 12.6 Hotel per Room Development Costs

Type	Land	Development	Construction	FFE	Pre-Opening and Working Capital	Total, Project
Economy						
Average	$7,200	$1,200	$31,700	$6,400	$2,400	$48,900
Percent	15%	2%	65%	13%	5%	100%
Mid-Priced						
Average	$13,000	$9,000	$65,400	$10,800	$3,600	$101,800
Percent	13%	9%	64%	11%	4%	100%
Upscale						
Average	$19,500	$16,100	$110,100	$20,200	$6,200	$172,000
Percent	11%	9%	64%	12%	4%	100%
Luxury/resorts						
Average	$48,500	$60,500	$202,100	$52,000	$12,400	$375,500
Percent	13%	16%	54%	14%	3%	100%

Source: http://www.hotel-online.com/News/PR2003_2nd/May03_HotelWaterParkStudy.html. Prepared by JLC Hospitality Consulting (507-261-7474) using survey data from HVS International, 2001. Costs are per room.

designer, architect or end user can save money by avoiding one markup in the chain of distribution. If this link is not used the product may be cheaper, but the service offered from the distributor is not available. This service may include the expediting of custom made FFEs, which can add an extended time to the making and delivery of the product. Conversely, larger distributors may have the volume of business actually to lower the price of the goods.

Commercial foodservice equipment is a competitive business. Many times a buyer can negotiate for better deals from manufacturers if management agrees to use only equipment from one brand. Many equipment companies give very low interest loans to restaurants that use only their equipment, and some may lend money to a startup establishment that they think will be successful. Many suppliers of food and beverage may include certain equipment needed to sell their product: for example, a soft drink company giving a restaurant a soda dispenser if it sells only that brand, or a coffee company giving a facility a coffeemaker so it can brew and sell their coffee.

When purchasing major equipment, a buyer may want to look at the versatility of the equipment to see if it can be used for more than one meal period or food item. Many fast food operations use the same equipment, or can easily convert some equipment, so they are able to prepare both breakfast and lunch on the cooking line. Another factor that should be kept in mind is whether the equipment has add-on capabilities for potential growth. Technologically advanced equipment may cost more money for the initial investment, but over time may save on both labor and food costs. Some technology—such as combination ovens—will help minimize food shrinkage, while other types of equipment—such as an automatic soda dispenser—may save on labor costs.

Equipment maintenance.   Major expenses for older restaurants are the costs associated with maintaining the equipment in the kitchen. Although commercial equipment is built to work harder, longer, and more efficiently than models for residential cooking, the fact that equipment is used for longer periods of time in the commercial kitchen can lead to disrepair. Many operations run 24/7, and some of its equipment is expected to be in use during the entire shift. Operations that do not run 24/7 will usually be open for preparation and production for many continuous hours. If equipment is not properly maintained, it will no longer work efficiently, and may end up costing more for lost labor than for repair. Money should be budgeted to make any necessary repairs on equipment to make them more efficient, as well as safe for employees. Many operations have departments, or staff, that can make repairs on equipment, while many smaller operations have maintenance contracts with repair companies. This may not be cost effective for many operations that may be able to make some repairs or hire repair people as needed.

WHY THIS IS IMPORTANT

Furniture, fixture and equipment costs are a large component of the costs of opening a business.

■

COSTS: OCCUPANCY

Land and Building Ownership

The largest expense associated with facilities is the facility itself. There are many options for the facility depending on the location and the type of operation. Facilities can include a freestanding building with the ownership of the land, which is one of the more expensive choices. Other options include leasing the land for a building or leasing space for the operation. Although building ownership adds to the assets of the operation, the costs associated with it may become an obstacle to its success.

Rent

Many establishments do not buy a building, for many reasons. Some include the high cost to purchase in many cities, the additional need and costs to maintain the building, and additional liability. In these cases the owner will rent the facility from others. Most rental agreements are a fixed cost, with the monthly fees the same for the length of the contract, or with incremental increases, but many are based on a percentage of the sales volume. In these cases, the higher the sales, the higher the rent. This situation can work for both parties, but if sales dollars are forecast to be very high it may be more advantageous to the landlord. Many establishments that have long-range high-volume goals may need to get into a facility with a lower cost; this arrangement may be beneficial.

Insurance

The insurance policy types that are needed for foodservice establishments, and the amount of coverage needed, will depend on the type of business and its location. Many types of business insurance are optional, while others are required either by law—such as workers compensation insurance, mandated by many states—or by a lending agreement. For example, if a mortgage lender has the title to the building, it may require property and liability insurance.

Required insurance includes comprehensive property insurance, which will cover damage due to fire and other business misfortunes. Additionally, a restaurant will need liability insurance, which gives coverage for injuries that occur on the property, or are caused by employees. Most states mandate that employers purchase workers compensation insurance, which is coverage in case employees are injured while on the job. If the business uses cars, trucks or any other vehicles, these will require mandatory insurance, and may include optional coverages.

Even though certain insurance policies may not be required, many types should be purchased to protect the business from any unexpected losses, extra coverage for a variety of contingencies that aren't covered in a policy. For example, the business might need to pay more to get coverage for flood or other water damage, or to have windows and other glass fixtures repaired or replaced under specific circumstances.

Depending on the kind of business, and where the business is conducted, it is very likely that an additional purchase will be made to protect against losses not covered in a standard policy. As an example, off site catering may require additional insurance policies, or business-interruption insurance, which helps offset some of the losses a firm would suffer if a fire or other disaster forced it to shut down or cut back operations while cleaning up or rebuilding. This kind of insurance provides money to make loan payments and pay employees while management is regrouping. Policies are also available to compensate a restaurant if a liquor or business license is lost.

Hotel operations require the same types of insurance. They may purchase additional insurance to cover business operations such as guest cancellation, and coverage for personal possessions of guests. Other types of insurance for the hotel industry include personal accident cover for guests, accidental damage to buildings and contents, and loss of entertainment and liquor licenses.

Landscaping

Restaurants that are independent buildings need to plan for the expenses associated with landscaping for the facility. As buildings are designed, landscape architects are planning for what the outside of the building will look like. During this planning, future expenses need to be kept in mind. If grass is part of the design, owners should be aware of the future costs associated with the grass. One expense is the cost of watering the grass, as compared to a rock landscape. Another expense associated with grass is the cost to maintain it. If it is anticipated that employees will maintain the landscape, money must be budgeted for this expense. If the task is to be outsourced, that money needs to be budgeted as well. Restaurants that are part of a large building or complex may not be required to spend additional money during construction, and additional money for upkeep of landscaping, if this is included in the lease payment, but they may have to pay a landscape fee to a management company.

Parking Lot

Parking lot expense can be very high in many cities, but in any location with a parking lot there will be added fees. Many higher end operations outsource the parking lot and valet services to minimize the expense and liability associated with a parking lot. Depending on location, parking lots may need periodic upkeep such as snow removal, repaving and repainting of lines. Other expenses associated with a parking lot are the lighting and security associated with the parking area. Although many operations might not justify the expenses associated with maintenance and upkeep of a parking area, one should always remember that this will be the customers' first and last impression of their experience at a restaurant or hotel.

Building Maintenance

With a freestanding building, and less so with a connected unit, there are many costs associated with upkeep. A landlord may pay many of these expenses, but some of them will be paid by a lessee of a property. These expenses include costs such as the cleaning of windows on the property, snow removal, costs associated with maintaining signage, and costs associated with keeping the physical building safe, up to date and working properly. These expenses can be very large, and many are mandated by city building codes and health department regulations: maintenance or replacement of heating and air conditioning units, fixing leaking ceilings, and maintaining proper plumbing for city, state and health department criteria.

Taxes and Legislation

As with most businesses, the hospitality industry needs to pay local, state and federal taxes based on the rates established in the community, and based on the volume of business and profit generated. If an establishment serves alcohol, the taxes paid will be considerably higher than if no alcohol is served. One tax issue that is currently a big issue with the hospitality industry is the taxing of gratuities for employees who receive them.

Legislation that affects the hospitality industry includes both federal and state legislation, so many items are consistent across the country, and many must be researched on a state-to-state basis. These laws may not directly affect the cost control of an operation through higher fees, but many will require an operation to increase spending to comply. Some legislation that is in place, or being negotiated, includes issues that will lower fees and costs for the hospitality industry. On the federal level, industry-positive legislation currently includes bills addressing issues such as protection from lawsuits about obesity, and protection against frivolous lawsuits. Federal legislation that could cost the hospitality industry includes laws to increase the minimum wage for employees, laws that will increase the amount of overtime that establishments must pay, and mandatory health insurance. Other regulations that are in place include issues related to food safety and the Americans with Disability Act.

Legislation will vary depending on the state involved. State issues include the use and regulation of teen labor, as well as the sales impact from lowering of the blood alcohol content (BAC). Additionally, many state and municipal governments are creating legislation to control smoking in restaurants, bars, and other buildings. Many state and local government are also tackling issues such as increasing of fees, nutritional labeling and the expansion of gaming.

WHY THIS IS IMPORTANT

The decision to rent or own the land and building will add considerable costs to an operation.

■

SUMMARY

■ The controllable and non-controllable expenses associated with restaurant ownership are described. Most of these costs vary widely depending on the quality, quantity, and cost standard that is established for an operation. Once the standards are established, the design and implementation of the building and décor can begin. Many of the expenses discussed are costs that are incurred after operations begin; through employee training and management controls, these costs can be minimized.

KEY TERMS

Franchisees   Lifetime costs
Franchisor

WEBSITES

www.restaurant.org   http://www.eeoc.gov/facts/
                                                        restaurant_guide.html

PROBLEMS

1. List and explain three of the costs associated with restaurant operations.
2. List and explain three of the costs associated with business operations.
3. List and explain three of the costs associated with facilities.
4. List and explain three of the costs associated with occupancy.
5. How can you minimize some of the operating expenses within restaurant operations?
6. How can you minimize some of the operating expenses within business operations?
7. How can you minimize some of the operating expenses within facilities?
8. How can you minimize some of the operating expenses within occupancy?
9. List and explain additional controllable and non-controllable costs for restaurant operations.
10. List and explain additional controllable and non-controllable costs for business operations.
11. List and explain additional controllable and non-controllable costs for facilities.
12. List and explain additional controllable and non-controllable costs for occupancy.

13. What licenses are needed to open a restaurant in your city?

14. What licenses are needed to open a hotel in your city?

15. What are franchise fees?

16. List each of the expenses listed in the text. Explain if they can be controlled, and if so, what steps can be implemented to control them.

13
The Menu
as a Marketing Tool

Chapter Objectives

After finishing this chapter the student will be able to:

Evaluate a menu as a marketing tool
Evaluate menu design techniques and
principles, including:
    Physical menu characteristics
    Focal point
    Methods of emphasis

Menu diversity
Signature dish
Menu layout
Menu descriptions
Perform a menu analysis
Analyze data from a menu analysis

Introduction

One of the most important techniques that any retail establishment must practice, and perfect, is the ability to market an establishment successfully. There are many methods of marketing; one of the most effective for the foodservice industry is the use of the menu as a marketing tool. Since every establishment must have a menu, if it is created using correct and effective design principles, it can make great strides toward ensuring return customers and bringing in future clients. It is said that the menu can be considered three uninterrupted minutes of marketing for an establishment. There are many ways to market a restaurant and many of them, including the menu, can be done in house. If employees can design a menu that will effectively sell the restaurant and sell the dishes that management wants sold, other forms of marketing can be eliminated, or expenses greatly decreased.

MARKETING

The menu is not the only method of marketing an establishment, but it is one of the most effective once a customer enters an establishment. There are many situations that will place the menu as the most effective way to draw customers in, but generally it is not the tool most used to bring them into the restaurant. Once they are in an establishment, it is the second most effective selling tool, after the well trained server. Through the implementation of effective design principles and suggestive selling, management can influence the guest to order what management prefers to sell.

Menu planning, design, and implementation should all begin with the client in mind. Creation of the menu should be focused on the intended users and their expectations, using all design components. This can include the wording of the document as well as the paper it is printed on, and the menu items selected for the operation. Many operations try to serve a very broad range of customers, but as with any hospitality operation, the most success-ful restaurants are those that focus directly on their target audience and can dedicate their operation toward one sector of its potential clientele. Once this clientele has been identified, the marketing and promotion of the property can begin. The marketing plan should be engineered toward the target audi-ence through appropriate print and media methods to which the potential clientele is exposed.

WHY THIS IS IMPORTANT

Marketing, whether for an entire operation or for a specific menu item, helps increase sales and profitability.

■

TYPES OF MENUS

The menu is broken down into two design and service concepts; **table d'hôte** and **à la carte menus.** With a table d'hôte menu, dinners are priced combin-ing multiple courses and including a starch and vegetable with every entrée. An à la carte menu prices every item individually. Many restaurants combine the two menu concepts or offer a modified table d'hôte menu; these restau-rants will pair a starch and vegetable with every entrée, while not including other courses (see Figure 13.1).

Some advantages of the table d'hôte menu are that price changes are rel-atively simple; consumer decisions are easier to make because of limited choices, increased turnover due to faster customer decision making, and with limited combinations, quicker kitchen preparation. Some disadvantages of this type of menu include possible waste of food if guests receive something they would not have ordered; prices are usually higher than an à la carte menu; and guests may feel that they are not in charge of the meal.

Some advantages of an à la carte menu include the ability to increase check average by selling add-on items; customers can choose how much food they want to eat, and this gives total choice to the customer. Disadvantages of this type of menu include the extra purchasing and preparation needed for the various menu options that are available; and the added requirements for management needed to control production and service.

A common menu type for institutional foodservice establishments is the **cycle menu.** A cycle menu will repeat itself when the timeframe of the menu is complete. Cycle menus are usually designed for a weekly, two-week or monthly cycle. Every day the menu changes, but on every day one of the cycle, the same items are sold. This type of menu is very efficient for buyers and kitchen staff. Many restaurants include a cycle menu component in a dif-ferent style menu. An example of this mixed menu is when a menu includes a daily soup: every Friday, New England Clam Chowder will be served.

FIGURE 13.1   Menu Styles

Table d'Hôte Menu	A la Carte Menu
Advantages	**Advantages**
Price changes are easy	Possible check average increase
Increased turnover	Customer choice
Limited variety in the kitchen	
Disadvantages	**Disadvantages**
Possible food waste	Extra purchasing and preparation
Higher menu price	Added controls needed
Guest feels less in charge	

An additional menu design principle is whether a menu will include more than one meal period. If a restaurant is open for breakfast, lunch, and dinner—or any combination—management needs to decide if foods from all meal periods will be available throughout the entire day. If the menu items are available, the menu should include all of the menu items. If the menu items are not available throughout the day, management needs to decide whether to create menus for each meal period or whether to use one menu and make some items not available to the guest during certain meal periods.

Some restaurant concepts may include the need for additional menu design principles. These will include ethnic restaurants, based on cultural traditions, which need to include additional explanations and translations so that all customers understand what the menu items consist of. Theme restaurants, based on a unique concept or character, have to coordinate menu names and descriptions to fit the theme of the establishment.

MENU DESIGN

When designing a menu there are some basic features that need to be taken into account to help market the foods that management wants to sell. The first is the **focal point** of the menu. The focal point is the place on the menu that the eye of the reader automatically goes first. The location of the focal point will depend on the type of menu that is being devised. If the menu is a single sheet, the focal point will be just below the centerline of the menu (see Figure 13.2). In a two page side-by-side menu, the focal point is on top of the diagonal line on the second page (see Figure 13.3).

The focal point of the menu is the first place that patrons look when they open or scan the menu. This is not the only way in which to highlight items. Another is to **emphasize** the menu item through another means, such as changing the font size of the menu item. If the font size is changed subtly the menu designer can draw the attention of patrons without their knowing

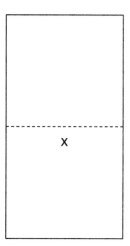

FIGURE 13.2   Focal Point, One-Sided Menu

that they were influenced. If the designer wants to ensure that the customer sees the emphasis, it can be changed to a larger, more pronounced font. Additional forms of emphasis can include using different colors, bolding of words, designs around menu offerings, or pictures.

FOCAL POINT

What items belong in the focal point? To utilize the focal point effectively, management needs to perform a **menu analysis** of the existing menu and decide which items should be sold more frequently to help profitability. A mistaken belief that management wants to sell the highest cost item can make the establishment lose money in the long run. The selling price of the item can be misleading with regard to creating profit, due to the costs associated with preparing the items. Certain high cost items cannot be marketed and sold at the same mark up level that other that can be used with other

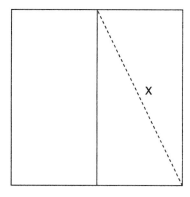

FIGURE 13.3   Focal Point, Two-Sided Menu

items. Some items require special skills or training that add costs to their preparation; these factors need to be included in the analysis. Chief to be taken into account when deciding what items should use a focal point effectively are the items that contribute the most to the contribution margin. Remember: The contribution margin includes fixed costs and profits, which will help the bottom line more than high selling price items.

WHY THIS IS IMPORTANT

Putting a more profitable item in a focal point will increase sales of that item.

■

MENU ANALYSIS

Periodically, management needs to evaluate the menu and decide which items should stay on the menu and which should either be removed or revamped to further management's ability to create profits. The first step in this analysis is to evaluate every item on the menu, within each category, and calculate sales figures and contribution margins for each item. Once these figures are available to management and the analysis starts, the menu items can be broken down into four main categories:

> Unpopular/unprofitable
> Unpopular/profitable
> Popular/unprofitable
> Popular/profitable

To calculate whether an item is popular or not, an industry accepted calculation is used.

IMPORTANT FORMULA

All menu items are added up and the percentage that one menu item represents is multiplied by an industry-accepted 70%. If an individual items sales percent is higher than the number that was calculated, it is considered a popular menu item.

EXAMPLE PROBLEM

If there are 20 menu items, 1/20 = .05 × .7 = 3.5%

The sales of each of the 20 items are divided by the total sales. All items that have a number higher than 3.5% are considered popular. If the individual percent is below 3.5% it is considered unpopular.

For the contribution margin, the circumstance that makes the item either profitable or unprofitable is whether the contribution margin of each specific dish is greater or less than the average contribution margin. If it is higher, the dish is considered profitable; if it is lower, it is considered unprofitable.

The first category, the unpopular and unprofitable items, should be removed from the menu. These items do not sell in large quantities and when they sell they, do not generate a profit. They are sometimes left on menus due to a few customers' liking or if a staple of the menu, even though not sold frequently. These menu items do not help the contribution margin. In many cases, management feels the need to keep them on the menu maybe for nostalgic reasons, but at almost all cost they should be removed.

The second category, the unpopular but profitable items, are an untapped item for which management needs to create additional sales. These items do not sell well, due to either poor marketing or salesmanship. Since these items generate a large contribution margin, and therefore lead to profit, management needs to create strategies in which to promote them. Some methods to promote the sales of these items might include running an item as a special to promote more customers to purchase it; including the item in future advertising; giving samples to guests; promoting the sale of the item through the use of a pre-shift meeting and menu tasting; or running sales contests among the selling staff. *These items should be the ones emphasized on the menu.*

The third category is the popular item that is unprofitable. These items are customer favorites; removing them will cause dissatisfaction among your clientele. But leaving these items on the menu will harm profitability of the establishment. Since many customers order such an item, and it does not add an equitable amount of contribution margin, every sale you make is taking away from the potential sale of an item that can create a larger profit. These are the most important items that management needs to re-evaluate, implementing either change in the quality, quantity, or cost standard associated with the dish. If customers want these dishes and are willing to buy them but they do not generate a substantial profit, management needs to decide whether to remove them or not. If such an item remains, either the quality or quantity standard of the dish will have to be lowered, or the menu cost will need to be raised.

The last category is the popular and profitable items on the menu. These items will usually be left alone, as they are doing what they should be doing. The customer likes them and they generate an ample amount of money toward the contribution margin of the establishment. These are the money-making items for the establishment, and may include signature dishes, which allows management to charge prices that do not reflect the actual food cost percent. These are also the items that do not have to be emphasized on the menu, because they already are creating ample sales.

The popular and profitable group is one of the dishes that management likes to sell. This is not the category that the menu designer would put into the focal point or emphasize through one of the other techniques. This item sells well on its own and does not have to be emphasized on the menu or through suggestive selling. If this item were to be left alone, sales would be high and every sale would generate an acceptable contribution margin.

The popular but unprofitable item is the selection that you can not take off of the menu because you have a customer loyalty toward it—if you removed it your clients would miss it—but you cannot mark it up high enough to generate an acceptable contribution margin. This may be an item such as a hamburger that you need to have on the menu for your customer, but you have to sell it at a lower price than you would like due to your competition's pricing strategy. You cannot remove it, but you do not make much profit from it.

The unpopular yet profitable item is the number one choice to emphasize or put in the focal point because this is the item that would contribute a large contribution margin if sold. For some reason it is not selling as well as management would like. Management needs to explore reasons why it is not selling, and decide how it can make it sell in larger quantities. Sales may improve if the item is placed in a spot that is looked at first, and sales may improve if the servers are effectively selling it, but it may be something that does not get the attention or satisfaction of the customer, so it is not being purchased.

The unpopular and unprofitable items are the items that must be removed from the menu. The diners do not like these items, and they do not help create profit for a restaurant. There are a few examples of restaurants that have to keep some of these items on the menu, either for historical value or for a few valuable guests who frequent the establishment. Otherwise, these items should be removed from the menu (see Figure 13.4).

In Figure 13.5, there are four items so to calculate the popularity index multiply .25 (1/4) × .7 = 17.5. In this example, Item B is the only item considered not popular. The average contribution margin is $7.27. Items A and D are below the average contribution margin.

> Item A: popular and unprofitable
> Item B: unpopular but profitable
> Item C: popular and profitable
> Item D: popular but unprofitable

In this scenario, management should leave Item C alone, and try to boost the sales of Item B. This would be a candidate for menu emphasis or discus-

FIGURE 13.4   Menu Categories

Item	Sales	Profit	What to do
Unpopular/unprofitable	↓	↓	Remove
Unpopular/profitable	↓	↑	Sell more
Popular/unprofitable	↑	↓	Change recipe
Popular/profitable	↑	↑	Keep the same

FIGURE 13.5   Menu Analysis

Menu item	Number Sold	Menu Mix % (mm%)	Item Food Cost	Item Sales Price	Item Contribution Margin	Total Costs	Total Menu Revenue	Total Contribution Margin
Item A	16	19.75%	$2.10	$8.95	$6.85	$33.60	$143.20	$109.60
Item B	12	14.81%	$2.20	$9.95	$7.75	$26.44	$119.40	$93.00
Item C	32	39.51%	$2.14	$9.95	$7.71	$71.68	$318.40	$246.72
Item D	21	25.93%	$2.29	$8.95	$6.66	$48.09	$187.95	$139.86
TOTALS	*81*	*100%*				*$179.77*	*$768.95*	*$589.18*

Average Contribution Margin $7.27
Popularity Index 17.50%

sion with staff, to see if they can improve sales. Items A and D should be re-evaluated either by raising the prices or lowering the costs. If neither of these methods can be used, the item should be removed from the menu.

This type of analysis is the same type that is done in many industries throughout the world: as an example, take the automobile industry. At the end of the selling season, management evaluates which cars have sold and which ones have not. Management's role is to investigate why these items did not sell, and establish a way to increase sales from that point. Management can market and sell the car, or it must remove the model from production. If the car does not make money (profit), it should remove it from production. There are many models of automobile that are directly connected to a brand; management may feel the need to keep a model going, even if it cannot maintain the same profit margin on the car that it would like. If it is going to market the car, it will be doing a product emphasis, or putting the car in the focal point of the consumer.

WHY THIS IS IMPORTANT

Understanding menu analysis will allow an operation to redesign a menu and create one that will lead to more profits.

■

ADDITIONAL FACTORS IN MENU DESIGN

Other factors associated with menu design and the marketing of the menu include the physical placement of food items in the menus. There is much psychology included in the design principles of creating an effective menu, including the placement of the items by price points. If a menu is designed with the lowest priced items listed first, a customer may reach a predetermined maximum price for the course and stop looking at the other menu items. This could limit the average check per person and lower the overall sales of the restaurant. As mentioned earlier, just because a menu item is more expensive does not necessarily mean that it is adding a higher contribution margin. This pricing structure may also interfere with the guests' enjoyment, if they do not look beyond the item that has reached their high point in spending.

Menu layout design should also be established taking into account the many psychological components that the industry has researched over many years. There are many reasons for the placement of each category within the menu, as well as the placement within each category. Another concept that needs to be kept in mind is that categories of items should not be separated onto two pages. If a menu category starts on one page, it should finish on the same. If two pages are used, patrons usually stop reading the menu items when they finish the first page, not continuing to the second. Many of the physical aspects of the menu in regard to design and marketing will vary greatly depending on the type and quality of the restaurant. Background, pictures, illustrations, font size, and paper designs should also be appropriate to the restaurant and the clientele, as well as the material used for the cover and any cover design (see Figure 13.6).

Another factor to consider when designing the menu is the expectation of the length of service for the menu. If the menu is expected to last for a long period of time, the quality of the paper and any binder should be high enough to last and be cleanable for an extended period. Many restaurants laminate menus that need to be in service for extended periods. If the menu changes daily and is reprinted every day or frequently, quality does not need to be as high. The placement of menu items on a daily menu can be adjusted on an individual basis, depending on the need to sell each item.

FIGURE 13.6   Sample Font Sizes Affect the Readability of a Menu

7 Point

8 Point

9 Point

10 Point

12 Point

14 Point

16 Point

Menu Diversity

There are many factors to be taken into account while creating the various menu options. One is the variety of items offered. When contemplating menu items, diversity of items needs to be great enough to attract a variety of customers, while not being so diverse as to overwhelm the kitchen. Menu design and kitchen design need to be thought of at the same time, because planning one without keeping the other in mind will lead to a potential downfall for the operation. When planning menu items, the capabilities of the kitchen staff may inhibit the ability to complete certain dishes successfully. If the menu includes preparation styles above the skill and knowledge level of the kitchen staff, either a new employee will need to be hired, or the dish will not be prepared correctly. Some issues may go beyond staffing, and may be directly related to the physical layout of the kitchen. Without certain equipment available, the restaurant may not be able to prepare certain dishes. An example of this might be a kitchen that does not have enough room for a smoker. If smoked dishes are added to the menu, they will have to be outsourced for the smoking to take place.

A second factor that needs to be kept in mind is that restaurants should make sure to include enough diversity in the menu to allow for different main entrée items and preparation styles. Without an available variety of entrees—such as beef, chicken, pork and fish—as well as diverse cooking methods, the establishment may not be able to satisfy everyone: for example, large groups might not find something for everyone, and decide to go to a different restaurant. On the other hand, a menu that is too diverse creates the potential for over-purchasing and over-production due to the many items that customers can choose. Menu items should include different products that allow for total utilization of raw products; an example would be if a restaurant only used chicken breast meat, it would be forced to purchase the product in its butchered end use form, which is much more expensive than purchasing a whole chicken and butchering it. If a facility can purchase and butcher a whole chicken, they can utilize the less expensive cuts of meat for other dishes. This brings overall food cost down because the cost of the whole chicken is much less than the boneless breast.

WHY THIS IS IMPORTANT

Menu diversity can lower food cost and improve customer satisfaction.

■

SIGNATURE DISH

Many foodservice and hospitality companies place a strong emphasis on the ability to differentiate themselves from their competition. One very effective method that is often implemented is the creation of a **signature dish** or service. A signature dish is any product that is unique to an establishment, and cannot be—or is not—re-created elsewhere. The value of the signature dish is realized when business is created by a loyal following for the unique product. The value will also be recognized when the lines of supply are affected, or the demand for the product changes. The economic theory of supply and demand within purchasing states that when the prices are high, product producers want to carry out more production, but there is less consumption by the consumers. When lower prices are created, this discourages production by the producers, but the lower prices encourage consumption by the consumers. When prices increase due to lower production, the differentiated product may avoid the rising prices because it is a different product: When beef prices increase, chicken restaurants may be able to keep their costs down.

Another big advantage of the signature dish is the ability to market the product, and the operation, as unique. In the food business, this can include a product that is prepared differently, even if everyone sells a version of it, or the differentiation may be the cooking method or the chef who created the operation and recipes. In the hotel business, a differentiated product may be a five star quality, or boutique designed, hotel.

An additional benefit of creating a **differentiated product,** one based on different ingredients than most other operations use, is that it helps a restaurant survive the economics of supply and demand fluctuations in price. If there is a downward trend due to supply or negative publicity of an item, the operation with a differentiated product will be able to survive or increase business due to the negative situations of other operations who use the same ingredients. Within the fast food industry an example of this is, if the beef supply is short or negative publicity about health risks is in the news, sales at chicken restaurants will generally increase. Chicken restaurants have differentiated their product from the hamburger chains.

MENU DESCRIPTIONS

As a marketing tool, the menu must sell the items that are listed on it. The most effective way to sell these items is to create and write descriptions that sell the item listed. An effective menu description is a strong component of selling add-on items, those which consumers did not think they would order before they were given the menu. To sell additional items, the effective description should be used for all courses and menu items, not just the entrée.

There are some basic guidelines to be followed when writing descriptive copy for the physical menu. Descriptive copy will help to describe the main entrée item, as well as secondary items and preparation styles. Some menu items may not require a detailed description; having one will allow the guest to have a better understanding of the overall dish, including the ingredients, preparation style or accompaniments (see Figure 13.7).

FIGURE 13.7   Sample Menu Descriptions

Ineffective Menu Description	Effective Menu Description
6 oz NY steak	Mesquite grilled, 6 oz boneless New York strip steak
Chicken in mushroom sauce	Boneless chicken breast sautéed in butter and olive oil and served with a mushroom demi glace.
Onion soup with a crouton and melted cheese	Sautéed Walla Walla onions simmered in a combination of chicken and beef broth, served with a French bread crouton and covered with melted provolone cheese.

Some of the basic guidelines for menu writing include keeping the description simple, while describing the dish effectively. Sentence structure should be short and concise, while using eye-catching descriptive words. If the menu copy is too long, guests will lose interest while reading. Grammatical consistency is very important when writing menu copy. Standard writing rules may not apply while writing a menu; whatever standard is established needs to continue throughout the document. An example is the use of a period at the end of the description. Many menus do not end the description with a period, which is an accepted style in writing menu copy. If the period is not to be used, it should not be present on any entrée or menu item. Another example is the use of capital letters. Many menus capitalize all words in the menu copy, contrary to grammar rules.

WHY THIS IS IMPORTANT

Effective menu description will sell a dish and add to the dining pleasure of the customer.

■

TRUTH IN ADVERTISING LAWS

While there are no local or state laws that require restaurants to list every single ingredient, menus must tell the truth. Truth in advertising laws are designed to protect consumers from fraudulent food and beverage claims. With truth in advertising laws, accuracy in a menu involves a great deal more than honestly and precisely stating a price. Accuracy also entails care when describing food attributes, such as the preparation style, ingredients, portion sizes, and health benefits. Another component of the laws includes the point of origin of the product. Point of origin can influence the quality expectations and physical product being served. Some examples of quality expectations of a product based on geographical location include Alaska salmon or

FIGURE 13.8 Truth in Advertising Components and Examples

Point of origin	Certain items can only be produced in certain geographical locations: For example, balsamic vinegar can only come from Medina, Italy.
Weight/size	Serving size or product size (shrimp) must be accurate
Preservation	Fresh or frozen
Grade	Meat, produce, or dairy products
Preparation style	Made on property, as compared to being purchased, or if an item is listed as prepared with a more nutritional method than actually prepared
Standard of identity	Government guidelines to call certain items certain names—such as jelly, jam, and preserves—or how much pepperoni is needed to call the dish a pepperoni pizza
Dietary claim	If listed on the menu they need to be substantiated (see Figure 13.9)

New Zealand lamb. Examples of a product being different based on the harvest or production location includes a Maine lobster, which differs from warm water lobsters. Maine lobsters are crustaceans that include claws, while Australian, Florida or Mexican lobster—also called spiny lobster—does not have edible claws. When consumers purchase a lobster, they have an expectation of what will be served on the plate. There are other menu components that fall under the truth in menu laws and must be followed when designing the menu (see Figures 13.8 and 13.9).

FIGURE 13.9 Nutritional Descriptions

Nonfat	Less than 0.5 grams (g) fat per serving
Low fat	Contains 3 g of fat or less per 100 g, and not more than 30 percent of calories from fat
Light and lite	Foods that have at least one-third fewer calories or at least 50 percent less fat per serving than original version
Light/lite in sodium	Food must have at least 50 percent less sodium than original version
Lean	Food has less than 10 g of fat, less than 4 g of saturated fat, and less than 95 milligrams (mg) of cholesterol per serving and per 100 g
Extra lean	Food has less than 5 g of fat, less than 2 g of saturated fat, and less than 95 mg of cholesterol per serving and per 100 g
High/good source	Food must contain 20 percent or more of the Daily Value for that nutrient in a serving
Good source	Food contains 10 to 19 percent of the Daily Value for the nutrient

Source: www.cfsan.fda.gov

SUMMARY

- How to make the menu into a marketing tool
- The different types of menus
- Menu design principles
- Analyze a menu for successful and unsuccessful items
- The value of the differentiated product
- Effective menu copy
- Truth in advertising guidelines

KEY TERMS

Table d'hôte	Emphasize
À la carte menus	Menu analysis
Cycle menu	Signature dish
Focal point	Differentiated product

WEBSITES

www.cfsan.fda.gov

PROBLEMS

1. How is a menu a marketing tool for a restaurant?
2. What are the advantages and disadvantages of a table d'hôte menu?
3. What are the advantages and disadvantages of an à la carte menu?
4. Where is the focal point on a one-page menu? On a two-page menu?
5. What item should be placed in a focal point?
6. Prepare a menu analysis using the following information. What should be done with each item?

Item	Sales	Food Cost	Selling Price
Item A	44	8.56	17.99
Item B	37	5.89	16.99
Item C	15	7.90	18.99
Item D	17	4.86	15.99
Item E	21	7.75	17.99

7. Describe the four types of menu items characterized by the menu analysis.
8. What should management do with menu items in each category?
9. How does font size effect menu sales?

10. Why is menu diversity needed in most restaurant operations?

11. What is a signature dish? How does it help a restaurant realize profitability?

12. What is a differentiated product? What is the value of a differentiated product?

13. Write an effective menu copy for an entrée, dessert and appetizer.

14. List four ways to emphasize a menu item.

15. How do truth in advertising laws help the consumer?

16. Prepare a menu analysis using the following information. What should be done with each item?

Item	Sales	Food Cost	Selling Price
Item A	22	12.38	33.00
Item B	41	10.78	29.00
Item C	49	15.34	38.00
Item D	5	12.98	29.00
Item E	30	9.66	27.00
Item F	26	11.48	30.00

17. Prepare a menu analysis using the following information. What should be done with each item?

Item	Sales	Food Cost	Selling Price
Item A	25	11.46	29.99
Item B	35	10.81	29.99
Item C	22	12.50	29.99
Item D	44	14.21	29.99

14

Forecasts in Sales; Controls in Sales and Revenue

Chapter Objectives

After finishing this chapter the student will be able to:

Understand the steps to forecasting

Differentiate among qualitative and quantitative data

Examine POS data

Calculate a menu analysis

Explore various sales control techniques

Explore methods of theft protection

Introduction

This chapter will help the student to create a work production schedule based on the anticipated needs of the establishment and the customer. It includes information on how to predetermine total sales and how to determine sales of individual items. The chapter concludes with an overview of theft protection techniques that should be implemented in any hospitality establishment.

FORECASTING

An essential step in any successful operation is to forecast potential sales accurately. Through successful forecasting, management can control production, which leads to correct use of both labor and food supplies. A step toward profitability is in the control over waste and excess production.

While large properties may have a department that will forecast sales, this is not necessarily cost effective for a smaller property. If the property does not have anyone with the ability (or direct access to the information) to perform the forecasting themselves, many chambers of commerce have the information needed to assist. They may not be able to tell how many customers your type of business will draw from expected guests, but they should be able to provide some demographics on expected guests. Many companies sell computer software that can be used for vague forecasting, and with a qualified employee relevant data may be extrapolated from the software forecasts. To be successful in the industry, the ability to take the raw data and through knowledge and experience calculate potential sales is essential.

DATA USED FOR FORECASTING

The information used to calculate any forecast can be broken down into two categories. The first category is **quantitative data,** which includes historical data. **Historical data** comprises information amassed during the history of

FIGURE 14.1   Forecasting Data

Timeline	Data Used	Alternate Data Used
Perpetual	On-going since business started	On-going for fiscal year
Previous year	Since the beginning of the fiscal year	Previous 365 days
Month	Past 30 day period	Same month last year
Week	Last week	Same week last year
Daily	Same day last week	Same day of the week for the last month or other period

the operation: previous sales separated by shift, product variety, day of the week, as well as any other relevant factors. The ability to track historical data has become very easy with the technology that is available to management. With the advancement and popularity of **point of sales equipment (POS)**, data can be available by the touch of a button on a POS computer. If the technology used does not allow for this easy step, management should have a system in place that will facilitate the hand counting of patrons and the quantity of individual menu items sold. If advanced technology is being used, it may also keep track of other factors such as group preferences and spending habits, which is data used in forecasting (see Figure 14.1).

The second type of data used for proper forecasting is **qualitative data,** which includes weather (good or bad), the type of clients expected during the forecast period, road conditions, and other non-specific factors related to quality. This type of data is not as clear and concise as the quantitative data, so further analysis will be required. Historical data is factual, but it can be misread when analyzed for future expectations. The ability to interpret quantitative data correctly and, more so, the ability to read and anticipate qualitative data correctly is what makes for successful forecasting. If an establishment does not have a forecasting department, the ability to anticipate future business successfully is needed by every department manager.

STEPS OF FORECASTING

There are six steps to proper **forecasting:**

1. Predict number of customers
2. Check surroundings
3. Establish total expected sales
4. Use popularity index (menu mix)
5. Prepare production schedule
6. Monitor/ reconcile and correct for the future

FIGURE 14.2   How to use Forecasted Data

Forecast the same as previous period
Average the data from multiple periods
Calculate the percentage increase or decrease during the previous period and anticipate
the same change for the upcoming period

The first step in proper forecasting is to analyze the historical data for as many relevant characteristics of the time period as possible. Many factors need to be taken into account: one is how many **covers** are normally served on the given day of the week being forecasted. When forecasting for Sunday dinner service, how many covers were served last Sunday, and the last four Sundays, will be used as a starting point to predict this Sunday's service. If a business averaged 100 covers for the last two months, one can assume that it should do around 100 covers this Sunday. This is only a starting point toward accurately forecasting total sales. In most segments of the restaurant industry, Sunday dinner will serve a different number of covers than Friday dinner. For this reason, most aspects of the hospitality industry will forecast for weekly covers, but they will also forecast for daily covers and meal period covers (see Figure 14.2).

This first step is the same step that would be used in any industry to anticipate future business. The hotel industry looks at the number of guest rooms sold in the past to start the calculation for how many rooms will be booked in the future. As with food, adjustments will be made after reviewing changes that may occur, such as conventions. A big advantage to forecasting any business within the hospitality industry, as compared to other sales businesses, is that a very large portion of the industry has the added luxury of accepting reservations. Although a reservation gives additional data to the forecaster, data that would not be available to other retail businesses, a reservation does not guarantee the customer will show up. If reservations are accepted, an added calculation of the percentage of reservations that will be no-shows should be added into the forecasting operation. For a truer estimate of guests, the establishment should also forecast the percentage of customers that walk in compared to those having reservations.

One of the easiest forecasts to make in the industry is that needed for the catering end of the hospitality industry. Since much of the catering business is booked far in advance, forecasts can be completed much earlier than in facets of the industry that are decided closer to the time of the event.

Once the average number of covers expected is established through the use of historical data, this number must be adjusted to account for events and situations that occurred during that period, as well as those that are occurring currently. This can include weather; there are many industries that have extreme fluctuations of sales if weather conditions change, which may add or subtract from the total covers expected. If rain is forecast, this may raise the forecast for a hotel restaurant, while lowering the forecast for a national park foodservice facility. In analyzing historical data, numbers are not the only part that is looked at; one must also analyze the situations occurring during the previous time period. This is why management should keep supplemental logs, although many POS systems can programmed to record this data.

Besides weather forecasts, events occurring in the area will have a great impact on forecast sales. Local meetings may not increase room sales, but can increase restaurant sales. Many conferences or conventions will increase sales at certain restaurants, but not at others, depending on the clientele. When analyzing a group of people coming into the area, one needs to analyze the spending habits of the guests. Many conferences are known to spend more money on drinking than food, and others will eat at expensive restaurants while lower priced restaurants may not see an impact in sales based on the group. Another aspect of conferences is how many and which meals might be eaten in a business or pleasure banquet. Historical data is usually available for many groups that frequent resort areas.

Local environmental conditions also should be taken into account when forecasting. This includes construction in the area and any other factor that may alter sales from a previous time period. This can include the opening or closing of other facilities in the same market as you and positive or negative reviews for the establishment. This is only a partial list of the possible factors that can affect forecasting (see Figure 14.3).

WHY THIS IS IMPORTANT

Without forecasting, over- or under-preparation can occur. This will lead to higher costs or customer dissatisfaction.

■

FIGURE 14.3 Forecasting Irrelevancy

When evaluating any data compiled, management must take into account the relevancy of certain past data. Depending on the situation and the clientele, some of this data may be more important to the future than other information. An example would be an Olympic host city. It is estimated that two million people visited the Atlanta Olympics in 1996. In this scenario, a sales history for that period would be irrelevant to the 1997 business forecast. Additionally, the forecasting for that event used the previous summer Olympics data, but large adjustments needed to be made to take into account that the event was in the United States, not in Spain. Neither of these venues helped in 2000, when the Olympics were on yet another continent, only this time with a much smaller population than either North America or Europe.

Menu Analysis from the Menu Mix

Once total covers are forecast, the data should be used to forecast sales of individual items. This is the first step in preparing a **production schedule** that will allow for the kitchen to prepare products that will allow for speed and accuracy, as compared to over-production that can lead to waste. To prepare the correct number of individual items, management must prepare a **menu analysis.** This calculation will give an idea of how many of each item will be sold, based on total sales. Menu analysis will be used to create the popularity index.

IMPORTANT FORMULA

A menu mix is the calculation that divides the total number of items sold by the number of each item sold. This gives a percentage of sales for each individual item. This is done for every item on the menu, calculating how many of each entrée is sold compared to how many total entrées are sold. It will also be done for appetizers, desserts and side dishes. These calculations are also done to calculate how many desserts or appetizers will be sold compared to the number of entrées. This will also be done for beverages, as well as any other category management decides to explore.

EXAMPLE PROBLEM

If the historical data shows that of 100 entrees sold;

25 are chicken
27 are fish
33 are steak
15 are vegetarian

it can be calculated that 25 / 100 = 25% have ordered the chicken, 27% have ordered the fish, 33 % the steak, and 15 % the vegetarian dish. If the sales mix remains the same, the percentage of each item will remain the same. This may not occur exactly every time, but it is a starting point for forecasting. Management needs to decide any adjustments, either higher or lower, to the forecast that should be included in the production schedule to avoid running out of items or over-producing items if the forecast is not 100% accurate. After calculating menu mix, one needs to take into account that many factors will affect the actual sales numbers. One mistake that can be made during this calculation is if management uses overall sales for a period and does not take into account the varied sales mix that will occur depending on the day of the week. A majority of restaurants will have different sales on weekends and weekday. Management additionally needs to take into account the characteristics of the forecast guests. If a conference of vegetarians is in the area, one can presume that the menu mix of the vegetarian entrée should increase. This difference can be remarkably noticeable when calculating a beverage forecast.

EXAMPLE PROBLEM

This same concept is utilized for the calculation of dessert items. If 37 desserts are sold on any given night that serves the average 100 covers, management can presume that 37% of the covers, 37 / 100, will order dessert. Once the total sales forecast is made, menu mix of desserts is calculated and total forecast sales for each dessert is then arrived at. The next step is to take into account local conditions, including characteristics of the anticipated guest. This is then repeated for appetizers, sides, and beverages.

Forecasting is not an exact science. Although the history shows the amount and percentage of sales being averaged to a certain number, this does not mean that under all circumstances these will equal the same number in the future. There are probabilities that certain numbers will repeat themselves, or come close to previous numbers, but other variables might interfere with those odds. The important role that management plays in forecasting is using their knowledge and experience, to help predict any variations in the numbers for the future, and make adjustments accordingly. One such variation is if business is experiencing a business-increasing trend or an overall decreasing trend.

Once forecasts have been created, purchasing quantities can be determined. If accurate sales numbers are forecast, the correct amount of supplies will be purchased—enough to cover sales, but not too much to create over-investment or spoilage. Additionally, once forecasts have been created, kitchen management can create production schedules to ensure that the proper amount of food is prepared and available to cooks, so that they do not run out of food in the middle of service or have to stop production and plating of food to perform additional pre-preparation.

Once sales forecasts are made, they can be analyzed further to help the establishment with further planning. Total sales can be broken down into sales per shift, sales per server and sales per cooking line position. This information is then used to assist in the scheduling of employees. This will help determine the number of employees needed, and the positions those employees will cover. In the front of the house, a serving station may have a certain number of seats, or the sizes of the tables may be larger or smaller than at another station, or the quality of the employee covering that station may be adjusted. In many kitchens, the specific employee scheduled to work may be based on how many covers the employee can successfully achieve. Since employees do not work every shift, the ones that can handle busier shifts are scheduled for those shifts, and other employees cover the position during slower times. Sales mix per line position is also a factor in preparing sales specials for the shift. If the sales forecast shows that a particular position is going to be preparing more covers than normal, specials will not usually come out of that station.

The last step to the forecasting system is the re-evaluation of the data. After the shift or timeframe has passed, management needs to review what actually occurred, and compare this data to the forecast numbers. If there are any discrepancies, management needs to examine the process and determine what can, and should, be done differently for the next period. There are many situations that management can not account for such as if an unanticipated busload of customers pulls up to a hotel or restaurant, but in many cases the review process can correct, or adjust, a present course of action in the review process, which can then lead to a more accurate forecast for the future. These discrepancies need to be noted in the supplemental log or POS system.

One of the biggest advantages of an accurate sales forecast is that it leads to accurate revenue estimates. This is the first step in creating an accurate operating budget and creating profitability. This also leads to accurate production schedules and employee scheduling. The most financially important aspect of accurate sales predictions is the ability to accurately purchase the correct amount of food and beverage. Due to the perishability of food products, if over-purchasing is done, the potential for loss due to spoilage is greatly increased. If food spoilage occurs, it takes money directly out of the profits generated by the establishment. If losses are controlled, this can lead to lower sales prices due to efficient usage of supplies. If forecasting is done correctly, it will lead to higher profitability and shareholder value. There is a growing industry in the creation of computer forecasting software and forecasting consultants who can be used in the place of the manual steps of forecasting.

CONTROL OF SALES REVENUES

Once the sales have been made, it is imperative to control the revenue. The best way to do this is to have responsible and reliable people in the positions that include cash handling. One way to ensure this is to have your employees **bonded,** but this is not common in the hospitality industry. Establishments may have certain employees who are trusted with making large cash deposits bonded, but it is very rare that others on the payroll will have this insurance. If bonding of employees is not feasible, background checks, previous employment checks, and reference checks are a must for all employees handling cash. Previous employment checks may not be the most reliable source for checking on employees because many companies have policies that forbid the passing of any information about present or previous employees, due to potential legal ramifications. Many companies do not document or prosecute employees who are accused of theft because of the negative publicity that can come with prosecution. Often employees are given the opportunity to resign rather than face being fired. None of this may appear in an employment record. In the third method, employee references,

FIGURE 14.4 Pre-Employment Screening Tests

Integrity	Reliability
Sales ability	Drug
Personality	Credit
Job placement	Energy
Verbal/numerical and reasoning ability	Sociability
Independence	Management ability
Attitude	Assertiveness

the names are hand picked by the applicant so they may have a bias when talking about that person. Hiring companies that perform background checks on potential employees may be the most effective way to screen. Many companies also give pre-employment screening tests, which can work toward ensuring integrity and reliability, as well as positive personality traits of employees (see Figure 14.4).

ISSUING CHECKS

The guest check is an integral part of the cost control of food and the control of sales and revenue. With a guest check system, controls are in place to ensure that food does not leave the kitchen without first being rung up and eventually paid for. With a guest check system in place, a server would need to submit a copy of an order, allowing for a duplicate copy to be held by the server. This system allows the cooks to prepare the food, ensuring that the server cannot use the check again. In systems that are computerized, the server rings up the order on the point of sale system, and the order is printed in the area that is going to prepare the food or beverage. In establishments with an employee expeditor, the expeditor will get the "dupe," the printout, and call the orders out to the individual worker who will make the dish. In other establishments, the orders will print at the printer located nearest the employee preparing the items: the bartender, the pastry department, the broiler cook, or salad maker. If the orders print at various locations, an expeditor may be used to ensure that all of the food items for each table come up at the same time. Without someone in place to ensure that all the food goes out simultaneously, line cooks have the added responsibility of getting the hot food out hot and the cold food out cold. A point of sale system facilitates that no food leaves the kitchen without a computer-generated order coming in. In this system, the need for conversation between the front-of-the house employees and the back-of-the-house employees is minimized. Since conversation is minimized, the chance for unaccounted food leaving the kitchen is also minimized. The expeditor, if there is one, has the responsibility to ensure that only the food ordered leaves the kitchen, and leaves it correctly.

Numbered guest checks add an additional level of security in controlling revenue. The employee is given a specific number of checks, and the check numbers are recorded. At the end of the shift every check is accounted for, either with a sale, or returned empty. This is very effective in situations where employees are self-cashiers. In establishments that have cashiers, this will add an additional level of checks and balances not present in self-cashiering establishments. If checks are issued without numbers, there is less control in their use and possible abuse. With a point of sale system in place, at the end of the shift management can run a report that will outline the sales of every employee and how much money is due for the receipts rung up by each server. Another advantage of the POS system is that in most cases only management, or management's designee, can delete something from a bill, lowering the chance of sales going unreported.

AVOIDING THEFT

Another control process that should be implemented in any facility that has cash sales is a series of controls to protect the flow of cash through an operation. Many restaurants have large amounts of cash; without strict controls in place, the possibility of cash disappearing increases greatly. Many operations employ tactics such as self-cashiering, which lessens the chance of money vanishing. This helps by limiting the sum of money that the establishment, or any individual, is responsible for until the end of the shift. This also facilitates the ability to take the money "off the floor" and put it away when the employee checks out at the end of the shift.

Some additional tactics can include the limitation of people having the responsibility or ability to handle cash. This helps because employees know that if money disappears, there are only a few possible candidates that may be involved. Another method that will help ensure proper cash handling is the use of a bonding company to ensure that employees that handle money are background checked and insured against any missing funds. Many establishments make employees responsible for any missing funds; although this is not the most effective way to avoid theft, it will usually limit its presence. Employees who are trusted to handle cash should be given strict guidelines that match management's procedures on how to handle cash and what steps to take to avoid theft.

Theft can occur from employees within an operation and from guests, as well as outside people. Theft can occur in many ways, from product to equipment to cash. There are many ways to secure an operation, but there are also many ways to remove valuables from a restaurant. In addition to those mentioned in Chapter 9, some of the more common methods that management needs to look for in both beverage sales and food sales include the following:

- Employees who under-report the amount of inventory they are counting and then take the product with them
- Employees who under-report the amount of money they are handling and take the excess with them
- Employees who use the cash register and under-ring orders and keep the difference between what is charged to the guest and what is put into the register; a cashier or a server who uses a guest check more than once can do this
- Employees who use the cash register and over-ring menu items, collect the money from the guest, then void out certain charges
- Employees who collect money from a guest, and then make a fake claim that the guest walked out without paying; this has been addressed by many establishments with policies that do not absolve the employee from paying this bill out of his or her own pocket
- Management as well as non-management employees should be observed for unauthorized consumption of goods.
- Employees who either purchase goods or are the end users of items that receive kickbacks from suppliers
- Employees, or guests, who steal products or money from the establishment.

WHY THIS IS IMPORTANT

It is essential to control revenue once it is produced.

■

GUEST PILFERAGE

A predicament common in hospitality operations, and that is statistically on the rise, is the scenario of the guest taking "souvenirs" from restaurants or hotels. This problem can exist on many levels, from the college student taking silverware or salt and pepper from the campus dining commons to guests taking artwork from the walls of a hotel room. Operations handle this situation differently, depending on management's standard operating procedure and upon what item is pilfered. Many operations are aware of the certain particular signature items that are frequently taken by guests, but consider these items as marketing tools and allow them to be taken. If management wants to ensure that small wares or other items are not taken, policies must be established, and training of employees in procedures to protect products given. Management must ensure that employees do not put themselves or others at risk while trying to retrieve any goods (see Figure 14.5).

An additional predicament that can occur in the restaurant industry is "dine and dash" guests: After eating a meal, a guest leaves without paying the bill. Although this cannot be eliminated, through certain procedural steps, the likelihood of this occurring can be minimized. Steps to lessen the risk include giving the guest the bill punctually after they have finished their meal. After giving the check, the server should revisit the table promptly to retrieve the payment. If possible, servers should keep an eye on the table while the guest has the check, and all employees should be educated in behavioral characteristics of someone with the intention of doing this. Additionally, the physical layout of the restaurant can help facilitate the reduction of this crime by placing an employee, a cashier or greeter, near the exit. If theft does occur, management should be informed immediately and if found outside, the guest should be confronted politely. Again, management and employees should not put themselves at risk to retrieve payment for the check.

FIGURE 14.5   Pan Pacific Hotels Have Had Their Share of Pilferage

Singapore, September 2, 1999—Like so many properties throughout the world, several Pan Pacific hotels and resorts have had their share of pilferage . . . some may "alarm" you, others may merely amuse you. Although the Pan Pacific Hotel Kuala Lumpur Airport opened just recently, the hotel is already coming up short on several amenities, as well as guest room furnishings. For example, some of the standard items found walking out of the hotel include alarm clocks, cordless telephones, bathrobes, towels, slippers, glasses, cutlery and the like. In addition, some self-indulgent guests feel entitled to pack up the sumptuous duvet covers, lampshades, irons, and empty fruit baskets.

At the Pan Pacific Yokohama, a frequent guest of the hotel must have taken a "shining" to his guest room's light source, as he took off with one of the floor lamps. In addition, the hotel's much-admired interior design seems to be so popular with guests that sofa cushions from the public lobby are disappearing in droves. After being opened only two years, the Pan Pacific Yokohama has lost over 20 cushions to theft.

The Pan Pacific San Francisco, on the other hand, has not been as lucky. Director of Housekeeping Karyn Rasmussen muses, "If it isn't nailed down, it's been taken!" Examples of the ludicrous items guests feel entitled to include: comforters; bedskirts; umbrellas; silver butler trays; ice buckets; lamps; in-room fax machines; artwork; flowers arrangements and vases; plants; the hotel's signature, on-site fluffed pillows; sofa cushions; the entire bathroom amenity presentation/tray; bath crystal containers; water bottle trays/glassware used for VIP turn-downs; potpourri, which is stowed in each of the dresser drawers; shoe bags, which are delivered with the freshly shined shoes; canvas newspaper parcels; ash trays; and the list goes on.

CASHIER REPORT

One method of checks and balances that can be used for certain items is a physical reconciliation. At the end of every shift, a **cashier's report** is created detailing sales of certain items, or everything that was sold. A physical count is done to compare what was prepared and what was rung up. If this report is computerized, it will have greater validity than if it were calculated by hand. This may not be feasible for every item on the menu, but certain high-ticket items, whether steaks or bottles of wine, can be easily reconciled after a function. In a less busy operation, management might be required to obtain high-ticket items from a locked storage area every time an item is ordered.

POST-SERVICE SALES CHECKLIST

In any sales system it is always a good idea to have a checks and balances system in place to verify that the system is working. One method of doing this in the restaurant industry is to prepare a post-service checklist to ensure that what is missing was either sold or accounted for through another means. The post-service checklist could be part of the production schedule, or it could be a stand-alone document that is created for all food items, only the high-ticket items, or the items that management feels are not being accounted for efficiently. At the end of service, the POS system report or the guest checks can be added up and reconciled with the physical inventory of the remaining product (see Figure 14.6).

CREDIT CARDS

One method of paying bills is with a credit card. Credit cards can increase sales by welcoming a larger clientele than one that uses cash to pay for meals. With competition as heavy as it is in the industry, and the commonality of the use of credit cards, there are very few foodservice and hospitality operations that do not accept credit cards. One of the major factors to be taken into account with the use of credit cards is the percentage of sales that is charged for the ability to use the charge cards, or the need to negotiate for a

FIGURE 14.6 Post service checklist

Item	Issued	Returned	Sold	Discrepancy
6 oz filet mignon				
12 oz filet mignon				
10 oz NY strip				

flat rate for operations that produce a large volume of charges. Management needs to analyze whether or not to accept credit cards, based on the fees the different charge card companies charge. In most operations all of the major credit cards are accepted, but depending on the percentage and if there are any transaction fees, not all of them may be accepted and some brands may be accepted, but the use of them discouraged. Some of the fees charged might be negotiated. Many charge cards also give promotional material to establishments for accepting and promoting the use of their cards. One of the big advantages for restaurants that accept charge cards is the ability to remove cash from the floor and from the server's pockets and responsibility.

In all cases, management must create, implement and practice policies to make sure revenue is received and maintained properly.

WHY THIS IS IMPORTANT

Every operation needs controls in place to ensure employee and guest honesty. Without policies in place, earned revenue can be lost.

■

SUMMARY

- The differences between quantitative and qualitative data are described
- The components of forecasting are described
- Menu analysis is explained
- Sales and revenue control measures are compared

KEY TERMS

Quantitative data	Covers
Historical data	Production schedule
Point of Sales equipment (POS)	Menu analysis
Qualitative data	Bonded
Forecasting	Cashier's report

PROBLEMS

1. Why is forecasting important?
2. What are the six steps to forecasting?
3. What are the differences between qualitative and quantitative data?
4. What is a Point of Sale system?
5. How can a Point of Sale system save money for an operation?

6. How does menu mix help with forecasting?

7. What else can menu mix be used for?

8. Explain any three controls of sales revenue.

9. If an operation does not have an internal forecasting department, what steps and tools can be used to help forecast future customer counts?

10. Why are different timelines of quantitative data needed when forecasting?

11. Why is there a human element in effective forecasting?

12. What is forecasting irrelevancy?

13. What are the pros and cons of accepting credit cards?

14. If a restaurant sells:

Item A	23
Item B	39
Item C	77
Item D	54
Item E	91
Item F	43

what is the menu mix?

15. In the above example, if 48% of the people that order Item C also order dessert, how many desserts will be sold?

16. If a restaurant forecasts 167 covers and usually sells 56 percent of their customers soup or salad:

Menu Mix

Soup A:	13%
Soup B:	31%
Salad C:	22%
Salad D:	18%
Salad E:	16%

how many of each item was sold?

17. In the above example, if management wanted to increase first course sales by 20 percent, how many new customers must order a first course?

15
Maximizing Sales

Chapter Objectives

After finishing this chapter the student will be able to:

Differentiate among menu designs

Calculate menu prices using a variety of methods

Evaluate the importance of a signature dish

Evaluate techniques to improve sales

Implement different suggestive selling techniques and correlate the value of effective suggestive selling

Distinguish the components of a pre-shift meeting

Investigate employee empowerment

Introduction

This chapter will help a business earn an initial profit and remain profitable. Without the information contained in this chapter, a business will have additional challenges in correctly marketing themselves, as well as correctly pricing menu items and selling them. Controlling costs and increased sales will lead to profitability if fixed costs do not change.

PROFITABILITY

Many factors are involved in the creation of a successful business. For an establishment to make money, it must bring in more money than it spends. This is a very basic tenet of any business operation. There are many tools that management and employees can implement that will help enlarge the profit margins of the organization. One such method is the reductions of costs; this was covered extensively in Chapter 7. Another successful method is to maximize sales. Remember that if profits are not being generated, increased sales will only increase losses. As mentioned earlier, as sales increase, fixed costs as a percentage of sales go down.

CLIENTELE

As mentioned many times in this book, the first step to a successful business is understanding the customer. Without an acute awareness of who the client is and what the specific needs and wants of the customer are, how can a restaurant or any business fulfill the expectations of that patron? The objective of most businesses is to maximize profits, and often maximizing sales can accomplish this objective. Specifically, profits will be maximized through sales of higher profit items, but an increase in any sales will usually help increase overall profits, or lower losses.

One of the tools used to market an establishment is the menu. Through effective menu design, management can increase sales and better tool the establishment toward the marketed consumer. If a menu design is effective and geared toward the anticipated customer, sales will increase. Some of the factors involved in the design of the menu include the physical material the menu is made of and the layout of the menu; both of these need to be based on the clientele that is expected in the restaurant.

MENU PRICE DETERMINATION

Sales can be increased dramatically through a successfully designed menu. Menu design was discussed earlier, and how to use it as a marketing tool, but now the discussion will be geared toward increasing sales. The first step toward maximizing sales is to price the menu effectively. If menu price does not produce money toward the contribution margin, it does not matter how many items you sell: Profit cannot be generated. To calculate selling price, an establishment is likely to use one of the four most common formulas, or methods, to calculate menu price.

The first method is to calculate the **selling price first.** This is very common in fast food and other mid-price markets where the selling price is calculated, and then the costs are calculated. This is sometimes referred to as **follow the leader pricing,** in that the selling price is created to be competitive with other establishments that market to the same clientele. In many fast food restaurants there is a 99-cent menu where every item on the particular menu board is priced at 99 cents. After the selling price is established, the costs for the product need to be calculated. These establishments know what the food cost percent should be, leaving enough revenue to cover labor, other expenses, and profit. If the establishment is calculated to run 40 percent food cost and the selling price is 99 cents, the cost of raw goods will be 40 cents. From this figure all of the ingredients costs should be calculated using the standardized recipe and the market value of ingredients. These items can be calculated with figures using up to four numbers past the decimal, as some of the ingredients quantities and prices are very small for that individual item. If after calculations, the costs are over the predetermined amount, 40 cents, the recipe is recalculated with smaller, or different, quantities and qualities of ingredients. If the price of the menu item is significantly cheaper than the pre-determined price, the ingredient quantities may be increased, or additional ingredients added.

Selling Price First Example: Junior hamburger, $0.99

Profit	.08
Labor cost	.27
Overhead cost	.29
Subtotal	**.64**
Ground beef	.19
Bun	.08
Lettuce	.02
Tomato	.03
Condiments	.01
Container	.02
Subtotal	**.35**
Total	.99

In the above example, if the calculations for the costs do not add up to 99 cents they will be recalculated, either raising the cost of the ingredients or lowering the cost. The first three lines generally do not change, as they are established by corporate standards.

This method is commonly used in the fast food industry, but is also used in many other types of establishments. Any restaurant that is marketing to a specific clientele must be aware of the competition's prices as a factor in establishing its own selling price. This concept will cross over all price points in regard to menu items that are similar between like operations.

The second method, the **individual price method** or **differentiated price method,** gives the operation the opportunity to set prices without regard to any other establishment. This is when a restaurant has a signature dish, or through some other method has used differentiated their product or their establishment. This includes establishments that are in unique places or offer something that people will come to as a destination. In these places, the price is less of a determinant of where to eat than other factors; an example is restaurants at airports. Although in recent years, fast food corporations have tried to control over-pricing of menu items in places with a captive audience, when a situation occurs where potential clients are unable to leave, prices can be set at a higher level. Another example of this pricing method is when a restaurant is on the top of a tall building, especially if the restaurant rotates. This type of establishment can set a higher price point than many others due to the uniqueness of the restaurant. An additional example would be of a restaurant that performs tableside cooking. The **perceived value** of this type of establishment will allow the menu prices to be much higher than either the food cost method or the competition's pricing.

Differentiated products will occur in all forms of the hospitality industry, not just food and beverage. Hotel rooms differentiate themselves to allow them to market to a particular niche. Convention centers are established with individual amenities to allow them to market to certain clientele.

Differentiated Products

Wolfgang Puck	Pizza
Cheesecake Factory	Cheesecake
Ian Schrager Hotels	Boutique hotels
Burger King	Whopper
Tony Roma's	Ribs

The third method is the **actual cost method,** when the recipe and ingredient amounts are calculated, and the actual cost is calculated. This method will calculate the projected cost of the ingredients, assuming that the standardized recipe is followed and prices do not change. Once the costs of the ingredients are calculated accurately, a pre-determined food cost percent is used to calculate selling price, cost of food divided by food cost percent. Food cost percent is a figure calculated by management to cover all costs associated with production and service and adding profit. Food cost percents will vary depending on the course as well as the specific item, sales value of the item, area of the restaurant, seasonality of ingredients, and many other factors. This is the most common method used to develop menu prices.

Actual Cost Method

Ingredient	Unit Measure	Unit Price	Amount Used	Ingredient Cost
Broccoli	Pound	0.79	2.00	1.58
Onion	Pound	0.59	0.50	0.295
Chicken stock	Gallon	1.19	1.00	1.19
Roux	Pound	2	1.00	2
Cream	Quart	2.99	0.75	2.2425
Total product cost				7.3075
Garnish cost	Each	0.01	1	0.01
Supplementary cost	Each	0.1	1	0.1
Total cost				7.4175
Yield	1 gallon			
Portion size	6 oz			
Yield in portions	20			
Cost/portion	0.3532			

Using the costing sheet, with a food cost calculation of 35 cents and a management designated food cost percent of 20, the selling price is calculated as follows:

$$\frac{.35}{.20} = \$1.75$$

The method used least commonly to calculate selling price is the **contribution margin method.** In this method, a management's pre-determined contribution margin is added to the cost of each dish. Using this method, management would calculate that given the forecasted covers for the future period, the contribution margin of each dish sold would have to be a certain amount of dollars. That amount would then be added to the variable costs of each menu item. If sales forecasts were met, the contribution margin would cover the fixed costs and create the profits anticipated within that timeframe.

EXAMPLE PROBLEM

In the contribution method, the recipe cost would be calculated as in the above example. Once the costs are calculated a pre-determined contribution margin will be added to the costs of each dish. The amount is usually a dollar figure, but can be a percent of cost, and it may vary for the course or menu category. In the above example, $1.00 may be added to the soup, generating a selling price of $1.35, whereas $5.00 might be the contribution margin added to entrées.

WHY THIS IS IMPORTANT

Pricing menu items correctly will allow sales dollars to cover variable costs and create a contribution margin that will cover fixed costs and create profit.

■

MENU ANALYSIS

To help maximize sales and profits, an analysis of the menu prices and sales quantities must be established. If profit expectations are not met, management needs to adjust one component in the formulas used to calculate costs or selling price. The two responses that management can make are either to raise menu price or lower costs. If menu prices are raised, there is potential for customers not to return to an establishment, and this needs to be kept in mind when raising prices. The second way to increase the contribution margin is to lower costs associated with sales. In the back of the house, this may include either lower quality ingredients, or a lower quantity of ingredients. In the front of the house, this may also include a lower quality of service, created by hiring a serving staff of less experienced people, or by increasing the quantity standards of the present employees. In either method, customers may notice a difference in service or quality, and this may prevent them from returning to the establishment. There is a fine line in savings that can be made without the customer's noticing. If customers notice the changes it may not affect whether they return or not, but if the changes affect sales, a cost-benefit analysis of the value of the price increase or service decrease should be performed.

MENU DESIGN

Another way to increase sales is through correct design and layout of the menu. There are many approaches to menu design, as discussed in Chapter 13. In most cases the design ideas will be based on promotion of items that have a large contribution margin. When creating a menu, the placement of an individual item within the category will help create salability of the item, as well as hinder the quantity of items sold. The items should not be listed in order of selling price on the menu, neither lowest to highest or highest to lowest. When menus are created using this method, patrons, whether knowingly or not, will stop looking at the list of items when they reach the predecided spending limit for that meal. If the menu items are non-systematically laid out in the list, patrons will need to look at the entire list of items before deciding what to purchase. By looking at the entire list, they may find a dish that has a higher contribution margin than they originally decided to spend, or they may be enticed by a dish that is more costly, for a future visit.

Menus also should be created using various tools that highlight or emphasize certain items that management wants to sell. These items usually contribute a higher amount to the contribution margin, but in menus that are created daily, or on a frequent basis, these items also could include special purchase items or items that might lose value if not used promptly.

IMPROVE SALES VOLUME

There are many ways in which to improve sales volume in the hospitality industry. Due to the nature of the industry, high and low service times, management may need to implement strategies to improve customer counts or increase sales volume per customer. One way to improve customer counts is to broaden the characteristics of the clientele that the facility markets to. This is seen very often in the industry where management opens the facility at a different time to attract a different crowd than would be expected during normal working hours.

DIVERSIFY CLIENTELE

An example of this type of expansion is when a restaurant may open the doors early and offer an early bird special. The customer who comes into the restaurant to take advantage of this type of special is not necessarily the targeted clientele that the restaurant owner had envisioned. This early bird special is usually a smaller portion of food that is served during a time that is traditionally slow in the foodservice industry. Early bird specials end prior to the time a restaurant is starting to generate the clientele that it was created to serve. The early bird will fill the seats in the facility at a time when employees are already on property to prepare for the traditional service. The power and gas are already being used to prepare the facility for the targeted customers. If the additional costs were less than the additional contribution margin, it would prove profitable to open early to serve additional guests, as shown in Chapter 7. The negative to early bird specials might be that they may take away customers that would have spent the full amount of money for a meal during traditional dinner hours. This is one danger of any advertising or marketing plan. Before offering 2 for 1s, make sure that they bring in additional customers, not just give your current customer a free meal.

Similarly, when an establishment opens the facility in the evening for a nightclub, it may attract new customers. The facility would normally be closed, but to increase sales and market to a different audience, management might create a different marketing plan and bring in clientele that would not normally be attracted to the facility. This will improve sales during the time the place is usually closed, and may attract additional guests to normal working hours, after having been made aware of the restaurant.

One of the most effective ways to increase sales, especially without increasing customers, is the promotion of additional sales to the existing customer. An increased per person check average will usually increase the contribution margin of that check much more than increasing the variable costs associated with the check. Once the customer is in the establishment, the fixed costs associated with the guest are already being applied, and the variable costs will be the only additions to increase per person checks, leaving the remainder to add to the profit column.

SUGGESTIVE SELLING

A pivotal technique in profit is **suggestive selling.** Suggestive selling is a method that employees use to increase check averages, profit margins and customer satisfaction. There are many methods of suggestive selling that employees can use and although they are meant to bring about the same end result—higher check averages—they go through different means to that end. If suggestive selling is implemented correctly, it can create win, win, and win situations for the guest, the server, and the owner.

One method of suggestive selling is to sell an additional course. This happens very frequently in foodservice establishments with lines such as, Would you like a drink while you are looking at the menu? Would you like dessert? Would you like fries with that? When being asked these questions the server is trying to increase the check average by having you purchase something you had not intended to buy. One would hope that through this process the customer is getting something that they enjoy or might actually want, but the main objective of the question is to increase sales.

A second method of suggestive selling is to try to promote something that has a higher contribution margin, not always the higher menu price item. This would include a server promoting one item over another and can be done effectively through effective menu design. An example of this is: Would you like a bowl of soup? Would you like to "supersize" that? Or in menu design by having a king and queen cut prime rib.

When an item is supersized, the costs associated with the larger portion are negligible compared to the increased sales dollars. Considering that most fast food restaurants give you unlimited soda, the increased costs for the additional French fries gives the supersize one of the best food cost percents in the industry. The addition of the sale dollar associated with the supersize of an item is not very high, but the contribution margin associated with that increase in sales is astronomical. When servers are asked for a suggestion for a meal, management should have them trained to answer the high profit item, not the highest menu price or the one that they like best, assuming all menu items are of the same quality.

With an effective suggestive selling system in place, an objective of satisfaction for all parties interested can be met. For a manager/owner, increased sales, only if profits are being generated, will mean an increase in profits. This is usually the main objective of any establishment. For the patron, suggestive selling should create a more memorable meal if it is done with the interests of the customer in mind. If suggestive selling is used only to increase check averages, and not for the fulfilling experience for the guest, this may not be successful. A server should promote items that will enhance the customer's experience, while increasing the check and the profitability of the restaurant. For the server, suggestive selling can increase an average check, and since tips are generally based on the size of the check, this should increase income for the server.

There are different methods of suggestive selling for alcohol. For the safety of the customer, and in respect for the dramshop laws, it is not wise to suggestively sell more drinks or larger drinks to clients. For alcoholic beverages, suggestive selling needs to be for increased contribution margin items, not for a larger quantity of drinks sold. Drinks that have higher contribution margins will vary, depending on the establishment, and it is management's job to inform a server which drinks these include. One assumption that can be made is that beer on tap will have a higher contribution margin than beer served in bottles and cans. Keeping this in mind, if a guest asks for a beer, the first promotion of the item should be to what is on tap, rather than the other options available. In regard to liquors, usually the sale of a call brand of alcohol will contribute a higher contribution margin than the sale of a generic or well brand of liquor. As with food, through a server's suggestive selling and sales technique, the promotion of higher profit items can help establish a more profitable operation.

WHY THIS IS IMPORTANT

Increased sales per guest, and increased guest count, will increase sales without increasing fixed costs. This will create more opportunity for profit.

■

PRE-SHIFT MEETING

The **pre-shift meeting,** when staff can get together and discuss the coming days events or events of the previous shift, is an effective way to ensure that all staff is looking at the operation on the same page. With staff included in the meetings about upcoming events, larger parties, or special guests, the flow of the operation will run more smoothly and successfully. By having pre-shift meetings, you allow staff the opportunity to discuss successful sales techniques, including the up-selling of certain items. If staff members have success with selling more appetizers or any other course, allow them the opportunity to share their methods with co-workers to help increase sales as well. Non-management staff might run pre-shift meetings, allowing them comfort in expressing their feelings. Remember: Serving staff are the employees who have direct contact with guests.

Another positive result that will come from an open pre-shift meeting is that employees will feel more open in discussing issues that they are aware of to which other employees might not be alert. Management may interact with some of the guests, but depending on the operation, might not be personally involved with guests unless there is something wrong, or possibly as guests leave the restaurant. Servers, with direct contact with guests, see what the customer enjoys and what plates are returned uneaten. They also see the reaction when a plate is served—whether it has eye appeal or not. Another point that a server may be more aware of than other employees is whether patrons like the physical layout and design of the restaurant. If management wants to hear from these employees to better the establishment, this meeting will facilitate such a dialog.

An additional point is that the pre-shift meeting allows the servers to try the specials that the kitchen has prepared for the shift. The tasting of the items will facilitate sales of the item; the server is better able to market the items after experiencing them, not reading what the kitchen has written to describe them. Customers appreciate it when employees can tell them about the product from having experienced it rather than by serving it to others. It is usually apparent when the server has tasted and enjoyed a menu item. For the same reason it is wise to allow the staff to try a rotation of menu items so that when the customer asks What is good? How does this taste?, all employees can answer those questions.

In many cases specials are created. Specials can be created to use older product that needs to be sold quickly. In this case if the product goes bad, the cost of the raw product will come directly off the bottom line of the restaurant and become very costly. Another reason for creating a special is that the item will contribute a larger share of money into the contribution margin; and this helps add to the bottom line of the restaurant. In either case, increased sales will help the establishment create a higher profit margin.

EMPLOYEE EMPOWERMENT

One of the most effective tools that can be used in the restaurant industry is **employee empowerment.** Empowering employees who have direct interaction with the customer will raise the level of customer service. Employee empowerment is an integral component of the very popular **Total Quality Management (TQM)** philosophy of leadership. Empowerment is based on the principle that if employees feel they are needed by the organization as much as they need the organization and the leaders understand that employees are the most valuable assets in the firm, then employees will work to their fullest ability. Participative management has increased greatly as managers realize there is a direct connection between participation and employee satisfaction, and between motivation and employee performance.

Middle management personnel usually is the least open to these concepts, as they may feel their jobs can be threatened, but in reality TQM can improve working conditions for all employees. Managers not accepting of these ideas may feel that by losing authority, they may ultimately lose their position, but this does not happen often in businesses that employ strong empowerment plans. More frequently, upper management sees the success that empowerment brings and rewards employees. Management needs to realize that employees who are not treated well cannot be expected to treat customers any differently.

One of the most effective tools of advertising is the positive word of mouth given by customers to people they know. This also will negatively effect an establishment if the word of mouth is negative. An effective way to ensure positive feedback and word of mouth is to ensure that the customer has an enjoyable experience in the establishment. This can be greatly enhanced by employees given a little authority to make the experience as positive as possible. In the hospitality industry there are many variables that can affect whether a guest has a positive or negative experience. Some of these variables are controllable in house, and they need to be dealt with to assure that the problems do not repeat. But many problems are not controllable. When these situations occur, front line employees should be allowed to solve the problem, within reason. With employee empowerment, certain level employees may only be allowed to "comp" a dessert or appetizer, while other employees may be able to buy a bottle of wine for the table, or pick up an entire dinner tab.

By allowing the employee the resources to placate the dissatisfied guest immediately, the establishment has a way to solve the problem quickly, which will stop the situation from escalating. Other positives of this policy are that the guest and server do not need to retell the story to management and create a chance for the story to change, and the guest will feel better immediately and enjoy the rest of the experience. Many establishments, including McDonald's, allow their cashiers to solve the customer's complaint immediately and then try to figure out the cause of the problem. One issue that needs to be addressed is the abuse of this empowerment, by an employee who wants to give free food or services to the guest, and by the consumer who knows the policy and abuses it to get free product.

At certain times, higher levels of management might be needed to please the guest, but if the first employee who deals with the guests takes the correct steps, guest satisfaction is sure to increase. After any employee empowerment situation, management needs to investigate the cause of the guest dissatisfaction, if it is controllable, and take steps to prevent this problem in the future.

WHY THIS IS IMPORTANT

Employee knowledge and empowerment create greater employee job satisfaction and a high standard of work ethics. This will lead to less turnover and greater guest satisfaction.

SUMMARY

- Menu design principles are discussed
- Menu price determination methods are discussed
- The importance of suggestive selling is discussed
- The methods of suggestive selling is discussed
- The importance of the pre-shift meeting is discussed
- The value of employee empowerment is investigated

KEY TERMS

Selling price first
Follow the leader pricing
Individual price method
Differentiated price method
Perceived value
Actual cost method

Contribution margin method
Suggestive selling
Pre-shift meeting
Employee empowerment
Total Quality Management (TQM)

PROBLEMS

1. What are five items that should be discussed at a pre-shift meeting?
2. Why is employee empowerment an important part of the hospitality industry?
3. Give an example of employee empowerment in five segments of the hospitality industry.

4. What are the types of suggestive selling?

5. Who wins with effective suggestive selling? How?

6. What items should be marketed through suggestive selling?

7. List four menu design principles and how they can affect sales.

8. List and describe the four methods of determining selling price.

9. What are the values of having a signature dish?

10. Determine the selling price for one portion of a recipe yielding 18 portions when the standard recipe cost and desired cost-to-sales ratio are recipe cost: $52.65, cost percent 28.65%.

11. List four signature dishes in the hospitality industry not mentioned in this book.

12. Calculate food cost and selling price given the following:

    Ingredient list/prices

    Butter @ 2.49 per lb
    Carrots @ .29 per lb
    Onion @ .49 per lb
    Chicken stock @ 1.20 per gal
    Potatoes @ .39 per lb
    Salt and pepper .05

    Recipe: Puree of carrot soup (yield 24 servings)

    4 oz butter
    4 lb carrots
    1 lb onion
    5 qt chicken stock
    1 lb potatoes
    Salt and pepper to taste.
    Food cost is 21%.

Glossary

À la carte menu—A menu that prices every item individually.

Actual costs—The true costs associated with the preparation and distribution of the food product, whether standards have been followed or not.

Actual cost method—The actual cost calculation for preparing a dish.

Actual price method—An inventory valuing method that can be calculated only by using the price paid for each item left in the storeroom.

As purchased (AP)—The amount of product or the price of the product before trimming.

Automated beverage-dispensing machine—A machine that measures exact quantities of ingredients in drinks.

Average costs—Costs that are calculated by taking the total cost of a menu category and dividing by the quantity produced.

Average inventory—A calculation used to estimate inventory at any time. The calculation is opening inventory plus closing inventory divided by two.

Average sale—Calculation of the total sales divided by the number of items sold.

Average sale per check—Calculation of the total sales divided by the number of checks.

Average sale per customer—Calculation of the total sales divided by the number of customers.

Beverage differential—The difference in sales that is generated by selling a mixed drink, as compared to an ounce measure of the liquor.

Bin card—Card that is attached at the inventory location, which allows the warehouse receivers and issuers to write down transactions.

Bonded—Designation for a person showing that a company has investigated them and insures them while carrying money.

Break-even point—Formula used to calculate either dollar sales or unit sales needed to break even in business.

Butcher's yield test—A tool utilized by the industry to find out the actual costs associated with buying larger cuts of meat and butchering (fabricating) it into smaller ready to use cuts.

Call brands—Alcohol brands used for ordered drinks that are specified or requested by the guest.

Cashier's report—Detailed sales report of certain items or everything that was sold at the end of a shift.

Centralized purchasing—Done with multiple properties and franchises, where the corporate office develops the product specifications and the purchasing contracts. The local establishments and buyers contact the suppliers or company distribution centers to obtain the product.

Checkpoint—Place to check inventory before leaving storage.

Compensation—Expenses of an establishment indicated for the purpose of paying employees for their completed jobs.

Contract—A written guarantee, usually for a set period of time, for the price and product availability to the buyer.

Contribution margin—The fixed cost and the profit generated by sales.

Contribution margin method—Sales price calculation where management pre-determines the contribution margin and adds it to the cost of each dish.

Contribution rate—The percentage of sales that goes toward paying for the fixed costs and generating profit.

Control state—States where alcohol sales are strictly controlled through state run distribution centers.

Controllable costs—The expenses that can be raised or lowered in the short term; these are usually the variable costs.

Cooking loss test—A test used to calculate how much the meat costs by incorporating the loss of weight through cooking.

Co-operative (co-op)—An approach to purchasing where small buyers combine their needs with others in the co-op in order to strengthen purchasing power and receive a volume discount.

Cost approach—A method where a monthly inventory is taken to determine the value of the inventory. This is subtracted from available inventory.

Cost-benefit analysis—A method used to calculate the costs associated with performing a task; this may include benefits, insurance, supplies, and other expenses associated with completing the task.

Cost plus—A common buying plan used in the industry in which the buyer and the supplier agree upon a set mark-up for the product.

Covers—Number of checks in a given period.

Current compensation—Payments to employees that are paid within a short period of time for the performance of the employees' duties.

Cycle menu—Menu that repeats itself when the timeframe of the menu is complete; usually designed on a weekly, bi-weekly, or monthly basis.

Data mining—An information extraction process used to discover hidden facts contained in databases that give operators information about consumers.

Deferred compensation—Labor expenses which do not come until the future, usually after separation from employment; examples are stock options and pension.

Depreciation—The deduction or allowance given to owners of commercial buildings for their equipment as it gets older; an important concept in the accounting aspect of a business.

Differentiated price method—Pricing products, and purchasing products, differently because of their uniqueness.

Differentiated product—A unique menu item.

Direct compensation—Money given to an employee in a paycheck.

Directs—Products that go directly to the department that uses them, bypassing the storeroom both physically and for accounting purposes.

Dramshop laws—Laws that pertain to third person liability. If a server or bartender serves a patron who then hurts someone due to intoxication, the server and the establishment can be held responsible for the liability due to the accident.

Edible portion (EP)—The amount of product available after trimming.

Emphasize—Highlighting an item on a menu through means such as changing the font size or color of the letters.

Employee empowerment—Principle in which employees feel they need the organization as much as the organization needs them; proven to improve employee work ethics.

FIFO method—Inventory value method which values the inventory based on time of purchase. Also, inventory rotation system.

Fixed costs—Costs that do not fluctuate with the rise and fall in business volume.

Focal point—The place on the menu that the eyes of the reader automatically go to first.

Follow the leader pricing—A pricing method used by creating a selling price that is competitive with the other establishments that market to the same clientele.

Food cost—The actual cost of food issued.

Food cost to date—A process that allows for purchases that are made on one day and issued over many days to not skew food cost calculations.

Forecast costs—Costs that are pre-determined, expected, and planned for by management.

Franchise state—Procedures that allow only one distributor to sell a certain brand of product within a particular state.

Franchisee—An owner who operates a business as a representative of a chained company; a percentage of business sales are returned to the franchisor for the right to sell its product.

Franchisor—The developer of a business franchise, or a chained company.

Free pour—A method of pouring drinks without using any measuring devices; maintains the least amount of managerial control and may be easily abused by employees.

Historical data—Information amassed during the history of the establishment.

Hourly employees—Variable and controllable wage employees who are paid strictly on an hourly basis.

Indirect compensation—Compensation that includes everything the employee is given except for the actual paycheck; an example may be offered benefits.

Individual pricing method—See differentiated product.

Inventory turnover—The average number of times that the value of inventory is replaced in the storeroom.

Inventory valuation—The process of counting inventory and calculating its value.

Jigger—A two-sided alcohol measurer that has a handle and two cups, one at each end.

Job description—Written performance criteria for employees.

Job specification—The specifics needed for each job.

Last price method—Inventory method that uses the last price paid for an item as the value for every similar product in inventory.

Licensed state—States that must issue a license to a distributor that allows them to sell its products.

Lifetime costs—Costs incurred during the life of a product, including operating expenses, trade-in value, and labor savings or expenses.

LIFO method—Inventory valuing method that uses the values of the latest purchased items to calculate inventory values.

Liquid measure approach—Known as the ounce control method; a daily physical inventory of each bottle is completed with which the actual usage in ounces is compared to the ounces sold.

Make or buy analysis—Method used to decide whether it is cost effective to make something yourself or use a convenient pre-prepared product.

Menu analysis—A tool used by management to calculate the whether an item is popular and whether it is profitable.

Menu mix—Also known as a sales mix; is considered the percentage of sales for any item within a certain category.

Mise en place—Means "to put into place." An organizational process for kitchen/dining room production.

Multiplier—Calculation of an increased or decreased ratio used for butcher's yield calculations.

Mystery shopper—Trained individual who uses the services of a company and monitors the success or failure of an operation; used for monitoring productivity of a company.

Non-controllable costs—Costs that are associated with the fixed costs and are unchangeable in the short term.

One-stop shopping—Method of purchasing where the buyer purchases everything from one company that can supply all of their needs. Examples are U.S. Foodservices and Sysco.

On-line purchasing—Method of purchasing which allows the buyer to send out the specification to anyone who is connected to the system; they can bid on the items in real time and within the parameters set by the buyer.

On-the-job training—Employees either entering the workforce completely, or following another employee for a pre-determined or undetermined timeframe in order to train for a job position.

Open bid—One of the most common buying methods used; an establishment sends out its specification to a variety of companies that supply the items needed. Any one of the companies can put a bid on the items and send this bid back to the buyer.

Operating budget—Forecast breakdown of income and expenses.

Ordering point—The amount of inventory needed to cover the usage of the product from the moment that the order is created to the time the order is delivered.

Organizational chart—A chart that includes all the positions and jobs for the property, including management, front of the house, back of the house, and support positions.

Outsource—To hire an outside company to perform certain task, as opposed to the establishment's doing it itself.

Overall labor costs—A calculation done by dividing the total cost of labor by the total sales amount.

Overhead costs—Costs associated with the operation of the business such as rent, franchise fees, landscaping, etc.

Par stock/par level—Inventory minimum or maximum level.

Payroll budget—The amount of capitol allotted for payroll for a given period.

Perceived value—A method that allows menu prices to be higher than either the food cost method or the competitive pricing due to the uniqueness of a product or service.

Periodic order method—Method where the order dates are set at consistent intervals, and order quantities change according to the amount needed at the pre-set order time.

Perpetual inventory method—Inventory method where the product is counted as an on-going, theoretical count of what should be in inventory.

Perpetual ordering method—Method where the quantity of a product that can be ordered remains the same and the order dates change, fluctuating around the needs of buyers.

Physical inventory method—Method by which all products are physically counted and valued; this should be conducted on a periodic basis.

Planned portion cost—The established standard that every dish that leaves the restaurant should cost.

Point of sale—Computer-based sales control and data mining machine.

Popularity index—The menu mix percentage of each individual item and its popularity.

Pre-shift meeting—A meeting where the staff can get together and discuss the coming day's events or events of the previous day, larger parties, or special guests.

Price/cost standard—The costs established by management for the preparation of a dish.

Product specification—A listing of all the criteria about ingredients and supplies used to order a product.

Production schedule—Chart that allows the kitchen to prepare products that will allow for speed and accuracy in the service of food, as compared to over-production that can lead to waste.

Productivity—Quality or state of being productive or yielding results.

Profit and loss statement—Document with actual food and beverage costs, sales, and other operating expenses.

Purchase specification—Form that includes all information about receiving the product into the establishment; this includes delivery instructions, compatibility requirements, credit terms, etc.

Qualitative data—Data that is not concrete, such as weather and construction.

Quality standard—A standard that needs to be established by management to meet the guests needs.

Quantitative data—Historical data from previous periods.

Quantity standard—A standard that needs to be established by management to meet the guest's needs.

Real portion cost—The actual cost of preparing a dish.

Receiving sheet—A list of all the delivery invoices for a given day.

Recipe costing sheet—Used when a standardized recipe is followed; it details the cost out of all the ingredients in the recipe.

Safety stock—An additional amount of inventory used to cover any emergency situation, such as unexpected increased sales or a delivery delay for the following week.

Salaried employees—Employees who are paid a certain amount or salary, no matter how many hours are worked; these are also considered fixed and non-controllable expenses.

Sales by category—Figures that are an expression of total numbers of sales within whatever category is being assessed.

Sales mix—Also known as menu mix; is considered the percentage of sales for any item within a certain category.

Sales value approach—Method in which management calculates how much in sales each individual bottle should generate.

Sealed bid—Process where a specification is sent out to suppliers and they sent back a bid that no one else is aware of.

Selling price first—Pricing method where the selling price is created first and then the costs are calculated.

Semi-variable costs—Costs category that includes both fixed and variable costs.

Service gun—Beverage service technique where the liquor is controlled from a beverage storage area and is pumped through plastic tubing to a gun in the bar.

Shot glass—Glass device used to measure liquor.

Signature dish—Any product unique to an establishment, which cannot be re-created elsewhere.

Smart cards—Card that contains an integrated circuit allowing guests to access their hotel rooms or other services in the hotel.

Standard costs—Forecast costs, if all standards are met.

Standard operating procedures—Rules created by management for everyone to follow.

Standard portion cost—The price set for a standard portion size of a product.

Standard portion size—The amount of product to be served to the customer.

Standardized recipe—A recipe that is created specifically for an establishment and is written in a form that should be readable by anyone preparing the dish.

Standing/standard order—Form of purchasing used when a restaurant has an order with the distributor that is the same for every delivery period.

Steward's Market Quotation Sheet—Inventory sheet used to keep track of bid from more than one company.

Stores—Products that get put into the warehouse and then distributed, and charged, as needed.

Suggestive selling—A method that employees use to increase check average, profit margin, and customer satisfaction by suggesting other items that the guest might want.

Supply chain management—The overseeing of supplies, information and monies as they move from the supplier to manufacturer to wholesaler to restaurant. The ultimate goal of any supply chain management system is to reduce inventory, and the investment of money, due to the premise that the product will be available when needed.

Table d'hôte—A menu where dinners are priced combining multiple courses and including starch and vegetables with every entrée.

Task analysis—A series of questions related to what needs to be done, when it needs to be done, and how it needs to be done.

Total Quality Management (TQM)—Philosophy of leadership including employee empowerment.

Total sales—All sales which pertain to a particular category.

Transfer-in/transfer-out—Costs of products that are added to food cost if they are transferred in, and deleted from food cost if they are transferred out.

Turnover rate—The percentage of employees that leave an establishment compared to the total number of employees for the establishment; usually runs around 100 percent for the hospitality industry.

Unemployment insurance—A percentage charged on the wages of all employees of an establishment; the higher the turnover rate, the higher the insurance rate.

Variable costs—Costs that change with an increase or decrease in the volume of business.

Variable rate—The percentage of sales that goes towards the variable cost.

Warehouse buying—Form of purchasing used usually by smaller operations; purchasing usually includes the need to shop and carry the products yourself from the warehouse.

Warehouse requisition form—Form used to pull the inventory and to then charge the appropriate department for the materials taken out of storage.

Weighted average price method—Inventory valuation method that takes the varying costs for all the cases purchased and divides it by the number of cases purchased.

Well brand—A brand of alcohol that is used when a patron asks for a drink without specifying a brand name; generally, well brands are cheaper than call brands.

Yield percent—The amount of product left after trimming.

Index